At Home in the Heart of Alaska

Modern Day Pioneers

Pat Kerfoot Shoffner

Foreword by Justine Kerfoot

Women's Times Publishing
Grand Marais, Minnesota

Cover Design: James Ringquist
Back Cover Photo: Dr. C. C. Shoffner
Front Cover Photo: Pat Kerfoot Shoffner
Author Photo: Charlotte Merrick
All Map Production: Betsy Bowen
Editor: Jane Lind

Distributed by Adventure Publications
Box 269, Cambridge, MN 55008

First Printing: May 1990.

Library of Congress Cataloging in Publication Data

Shoffner, Pat Kerfoot, 1942-
    At home in the heart of Alaska : modern day pioneers / Pat Kerfoot
    Shoffner : foreword by Justine Kerfoot.
        p.   cm.
    ISBN 0-910259-07-0
    1. Frontier and pioneer life--Alaska--McKinley, Mount. Region.
2. Shoffner, Pat Kerfoot, 1942-   --Family. 3. Shoffner family.
4. Pioneers--Alaska--McKinley, Mount, Region--Biography.
5. McKinley, Mount, Region (Alaska)--Biography. 6. McKinley, Mount,
Region (Alaska)--Social life and customs.   I. Title.
F912.M2S56   1990
979.8'3--dc20
[B]   90-70188
                                                    CIP

TO
   my family with all my love

   James
   Trish
   Justin
   Mom

CONTENTS

ILLUSTRATIONS

FOREWORD

by Justine Kerfoot

Pat arrived at Gunflint Lodge on Gunflint Lake in northeastern Minnesota on a mid-June day. It was the time of year when the earth renews itself with new life. The moose, deer and bear are presenting their young. The beaver, mink, fox, wolves, pine marten, otter and a myriad of other animals are teaching their young the art of survival.

This country of forests and lakes abounds in flowering plants of every size and color. The mosses, in places, cling to overhanging rocks and in swamps are lush and thick. This is the land where Pat was born, raised and established her values.

As a tiny tot she was carried in a Tickanoggin (Indian cradle board) on her mother's back. She rode over portages and in canoes. She was propped against a tree while blueberries were gathered. She rode on winter snowshoe hikes or was secured to a sled and whisked across snow-covered lakes by dog team. Her neighbors were ever-watchful Chippewa Indians.

She had no fear of animals. Once we rescued a young deer from the lake on a windy day. We kept it in a storage room for protection, while it regained its strength. One day while I was checking available food for the deer, I placed Pat on the floor inside the door.

She crawled to the deer and sat down at its folded front feet. They looked at each other. Pat stuck her finger in the deer's mouth and wiggled its lips. She stuck her fingers into the sensitive nostrils and swished them back and forth. The deer remained motionless.

I slowly offered the deer food from my hand. It rose, jumped over Pat and dashed to the other end of the room. The deer never accepted me.

As Pat became older she learned to water ski by riding a toboggan behind a motor boat. She slowly graduated to two skis and finally to one, as she weaved back and forth behind the speeding boat. As time went on she learned to paddle a canoe, take canoe trips, and run an outboard motor. She learned to ski the slopes at a winter resort on the North Shore of Lake Superior.

She was taught school at home for several years when school buses were unknown in this remote area. Finally, as was the custom at that time, she was boarded out during the week for the school year to a family in Grand Marais — the nearest town.

With the passing of time she became a waitress at the Lodge in the summers, with the exception of one summer when she took a bicycle trip through England, France, Austria and Italy. She attended a college at LaCrosse, Wisconsin and taught school in Washington state, where she met her future husband, also a teacher, Jim Shoffner. Jim had a small plane and loved to fly. It was not long before Pat also got her private flying license.

They decided to take a teaching position in Kodiak, Alaska and eventually to build a fly-in resort on a lake where they could see the Alaska range and Mt. McKinley on clear mornings and evenings.

It was from this resort that Charlotte Merrick, a friend of mine from St. Paul, and I flew to the Nowitna River and took a week's canoe trip with the Shoffner family. A never-to-be-forgotten experience.

Pat's background and love of the wilderness made it possible for her to meet the challenges she relates in her book.

J.K.

At Home
in the
Heart of Alaska

Modern Day Pioneers

THE BROOKS RANGE

YUKON RIVER

THE ALASKA RANGE

THIS AREA ENLARGED AT RIGHT

The Heart
of Alaska

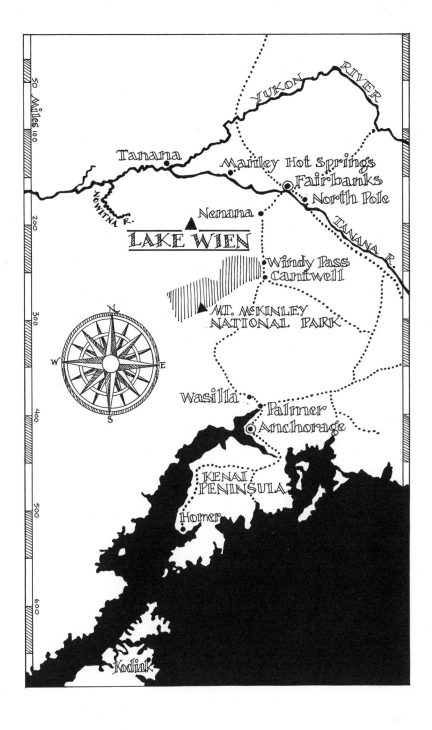

INTRODUCTION

UP TO ALASKA

Last night's freshly fallen snow crunches under my feet as I walk along the lakeshore. It is 20 degrees below zero, and the sun is shining brightly from a blue sky with a spattering of fluffy, cotton-like clouds. With the ice on Wien Lake now three and a half feet thick, walking is quite safe.

The new snow on the trees glistens in the sun like crystals on a glass. A snowshoe rabbit, bundled in his winter white coat, bounds from shore to a spot about 100 feet ahead of me. I slow my stride and finally stop to watch as he twitches his pink nose questioningly. He does not appear afraid, and we have a staring match from afar. He starts to hop away and I whistle. He stops again for a few seconds, but then he quickly and easily hops back into the woods.

A few minutes later I hear my dog yipping on the ridge when he comes upon the scent and takes chase. Never have I known Rusty to catch a rabbit, but he is forever enjoying the game.

As I meander along the lakeshore, I see the majestic mountains of the Alaska Ridge in the distance, with the "Big One," or Mt. McKinley, looming high above the others.

This is the very heart of Alaska — known as the central interior. It is now the dead of winter — so peaceful it makes me feel guilty for enjoying life so much. The "Big One," the highest of all mountains in North America, stands in all her mighty beauty. Today the whipping wind has blown a white cap to an

3

angle on her head. Reminds me of a soft ice cream cone with the top tilted.

I am almost at the far end of our five-mile lake, and I must turn back. A trapper has set out a series of traps beyond this point. Rusty could get caught again, as he did last week. Then I had my two children with me. With them crying and the dog yelping, it was very difficult to free him. Rusty is fine today, but I turn around and head back home.

Now the 10-knot wind is blowing in my face. The sun is already beginning to set. My steps quicken for more warmth. My shadow bounces along in front of me and reaches our log home just before I do. It is warm inside. I stand by our wood-burning stove.

Today has put me in a reflective mood. I know this will be my last winter "in the bush" for quite a while, and I am remembering. Remembering how it all began. Remembering what has transpired these past eight years since we started our homestead, but mainly these past four years, living in the bush year round.

My memories are of hard work, many dreams, some disappointments, but mainly of the dream that came true for my family and me. Next year we will return to civilization. One part of me is a little afraid of the move, and the other part is looking forward to it. But first, I will put down and remember this part of our lives.

*　　　*　　　*

My story really begins in Washington state in late 1970. My husband Jim and I had been married five years. We had a daughter, Trish, age two. We were both enjoying our teaching experiences in Washington, but teaching, as a profession, does offer relocating if one desires.

Both Jim and I had an itch to see what Alaska was all about. Referring to a map of Alaska, I wrote to schools in about 50 cities, inquiring for positions in either of our fields, (Jim's -

biology; mine - physical education and math). I knew nothing about Alaska. I just chose cities which were large enough to be on the map.

I received many typical responses, "No openings available this year; try again next year." Then one day a letter came from Kodiak. There was an opening in my field, but none for Jim. I was being offered the job. Did I want it? Of course I wanted it, but a discussion was in order.

In Washington we were both teaching, and together we had a satisfying income. We had just learned I was pregnant again. This meant if I took the job, I would quit in February; the baby was due in March. Did we dare make such a move with no job in sight for Jim? We decided we'd do it. (My mother thought we were out of our minds!)

We didn't even know where Kodiak was. We soon learned it was an island south of Anchorage, accessible by a 45-minute flight from Anchorage or a 12-hour ferry ride from the city of Homer on the Kenai peninsula. We sold our trailer, our land, our truck, and we shipped our worldly goods on Sea-Land, a barge service running between Seattle and Kodiak.

At that time we owned a small two-seater 65-hp Champ aeroplane. I called her Jim's Mistress, for all the time and affection he lavished on her. Thus, he and The Mistress headed north along the Alaskan Highway, and I was left to gather the remaining pieces. Ten days later Jim called from Anchorage. In the morning he would fly to the island of Kodiak. Would I please hop the next commercial flight up and he would meet me.

As I boarded the Wien flight to Anchorage that summer day in 1971, I was more than a little apprehensive. I had two crates — one for each of our two dogs. At the last minute I threw our cat in with one of them, slammed the door and was on my way. They were checked through, our luggage was checked through, my tickets were in my hand, and Trish and I rushed for the plane. Exhausted, I slumped in my seat with my

5

daughter on my lap and a prayer on my lips. "Go to sleep daughter, please." She complied instantly.

We arrived in Anchorage, the largest of all Alaskan cities. It looked much like any large city and much like Seattle — situated close to mountains and ocean. We disembarked, changed planes and were immediately on our way to Kodiak.

I was fearful. My entire security lay in Jim's being there to meet me. I didn't know one person in the whole state of Alaska, much less on Kodiak Island.

Our plane came in over the ocean; it looked to me just like we would land in the sea. Then we touched down on the paved runway that begins right at the edge of the ocean — as many Alaskan airstrips do.

This was a beautiful day with an extremely blue sky and a smiling sun reflecting off the majestic mountains. Fishing boats filled the harbor, and the hillside was colored a lush green. The plane taxied to the terminal. There was Jim with a smile a mile wide and his arms open in welcome.

Kodiak is a very special place, where the people are real — as we learned within an hour of our arrival. We needed to transport all our luggage, our pets and ourselves to town and find a place to stay. A man in a truck in front of the terminal hailed us. If ever there were someone sent at the right time, it was he. We probably looked to him like a family of *Cheechakos* (newcomers to the state) — and he took heart. Within 10 minutes all our "valuables" were thrown in his old pickup, and we were heading for town.

The road to Kodiak is built as close as possible to shore, offering breathtaking views of the ocean. Topping the last knoll to descend into town, we passed two canneries indicative of the main industry: fishing. Smells of the ocean and fish were prevalent.

The weather on Kodiak Island is influenced by the Japanese ocean currents: very wet, but with year round mild temperatures.

We would experience a period of six months when the rain was evident every day. When the sun finally did shine through, it was a Friday. School was dismissed at noon because of the nice weather (as other schools might be dismissed because of severe temperatures or heavy snowfall).

This was 1971, and the city of Kodiak was new, modern, and quite clean. It was rebuilt after being completely destroyed in 1964 by a tidal wave resulting from an earthquake.

Our friend agreed to take care of our "critters" until we could find housing. In three days we found a house to rent. It took another two weeks to clean it up to be livable, but it was a start. In another week I began teaching, and Jim was looking for anything to help us get by.

In December the high school biology teacher died from a heart attack. It was very sad. He was a good teacher and was loved by the students. Jim replaced him, and so our teaching jobs overlapped by about two months. I quit teaching in February. Our son Justin was born in March, and I remained out of school the rest of that year. The following fall Jim and I were both on the staff full time, where we would stay another six years in the Kodiak School System.

CHAPTER 1

STARTING THE HOMESTEAD

Jim's first love is flying. During our first two summers in Kodiak, Jim worked as a pilot flying tourists around Mt. McKinley National Park in the mystifying interior. He came to know the region very well. I enjoyed the summers with our two children keeping me quite busy. In 1973, during our second summer in Alaska, the Homestead Act was reinstated. We investigated areas open for homesteading by checking available maps. Jim learned about one area relatively near Mt. McKinley, where he had one particular lake in mind.

Lake Wien is located about 100 air miles southwest of Fairbanks, or 60 miles west of the smaller city of Nenana, and can only be reached by air. Lands accessible by road were considered too valuable to open for homesteading. Lake Wien was named for Noel Wien of Wien Airlines, who was well-known for fishing in the area.

There were four choices under the Homestead Act. The first, a Homesite of five acres — the applicant must build a habitable dwelling and live in it year round for at least three of the next five years. The government would pay for the survey at the end of five years, if rules had been complied with.

The second choice, a Homestead — the applicant must cultivate a crop on a certain percentage of the land. If all requirements were met, the survey cost would be picked up by the government as with the Homesite.

The third choice was a Headquarters Site, a five-acre plot — the applicant must show it as a headquarters for some business. This was usually taken out by game guides, who had a hunting area, or trappers, who had a trapping area, and the five acres was their home base.

The fourth choice was a Trade and Manufacturing Site. The applicant, utilizing the land, built some form of business on it. If these regulations were complied with and could be proven, the applicant was granted the land, but he would bear the cost of the survey.

We decided on the fourth option. We planned to build up a small American Plan Resort and run it during the summers, still teaching through the winter months. The Bureau of Land Management (BLM) informed us the survey would cost $1500, and that we had five years to develop our business. We felt, naively enough, that it would be easy and not too expensive. We were to be rudely awakened.

Any homesteading venture begins with a roughing-it stage; this did not deter our enthusiasm. I was raised in northern Minnesota, working at a fine resort, Gunflint Lodge, which my mother started in 1928. During my time there, I did extensive camping. The outdoors had become a part of my very soul — a part that teaching, even though I loved it, could never replace.

Resort life was not new to me, and Jim had expertise in flying with his commercial, instrument, float and instructor's ratings. I held my private license only.

That then became our goal for a business venture during the summers — a small, fly-in American Plan Resort. We filed on 50 acres on Lake Wien, a beautiful clear water lake five miles long by one mile across.

Although we owned a small two-seater plane, it did not have floats. So for that first summer, we chartered in from Fairbanks. With camping gear, food, two children, one dog, one cat, one canoe, and Jim and me to fly into Wien Lake, the chartered plane made two trips. Finally we were standing on the shoreline, watching the plane retreat into the distance.

The pilot would pick us up in three weeks — all the summer remaining until we returned to Kodiak for teaching. At that moment, teaching was far from our minds though, and we began to set up our camp. We would have liked to enjoy our surroundings first, but we went right to work on settling our family. We cleared brush for our tent-site, set the tent up and put all things in their proper places. Jim and I had two sleeping bags zipped together on the far end of the tent. The kids' sleeping bags ran each along one side. Enough room was left in the center to change clothes.

Jim cleared more land and I laid a canvas on the ground, on top of which I spread out a blanket, on top of which I laid down Justin for his first nap on Lake Wien. Keeping one eye on him as he napped, I set up a cooking area and made ready for a tasty steak dinner. Jim made a rough table and bench that would be our "dining room" for the next three weeks.

We were tired when we sat down to our dinner. We particularly enjoyed the sizzling tender steaks. In the future we would depend on the fish in the lake and the canned goods flown in. Our campsite was on a level plateau about 30 feet wide, close to the lake. At the edge of this plateau was a 30-foot-high bluff which we had already chosen as our home site.

Thus we sat facing the lake with the bluff behind us. We relaxed after dinner and were content, watching the still blue lake with its clean drinkable water. To the south we saw the rugged Alaska Range, with Mt. McKinley proudly standing displaying her towering might.

We heard a rustle on the bluff behind us. Jim listened carefully, then he asked what I thought it was. "Just the darn cat," I replied with confidence. When we turned, we looked up into the eyes of a black bear. He was looking down from the bluff surveying the remains of our dinner. Jim told me to get the gun from inside the nearby tent. He stayed with only a knife for defense, while I grabbed the kids and threw them in the tent. I returned with the gun, and the bear was walking down the bank toward our table. By the time Jim had the gun, the bear was about 15 feet away. Jim fired and the bear collapsed.

In our experiences, we have always found the black bear unafraid of us, and they have never attacked. We have yelled at them, banged pots, and shot them with birdshot in the rear. Because they are so inquisitive, we have always had to kill them for the children's safety.

We did not keep that first bear, but later when relating this story to a *sourdough* (someone who has lived in the state quite some time) we were hissed on for wasting good meat.

That first summer we made plans for our home, which had first priority. The lodge and cabins would wait. After due consideration, we decided on an L-shaped structure. The long leg for our living room and bedroom would be 16x20, and the small leg, the kitchen/dining room, 16x12. On paper we figured and calculated that we would need 100 logs for such a structure. Our goal for this first summer was to prepare those 100 logs.

We would take one day to explore the lake and start cutting logs the following day. In the morning we cooked a hearty breakfast over our campfire, packed a lunch and cleaned up camp. Then we all jumped in our canoe to glide over the mirrored waters. The kids were wearing life jackets. Trish had been in a canoe often. She was five, and Jim and I had canoed in Washington. Justin was only two, and this was his first trip. Trish was in the center; Justin was by my feet in the bow so I could keep an eye on him.

We skimmed along the shoreline dipping our paddles in unison quietly and rhythmically. Passing around one bend we came upon a family of ducks of mom and eight youngsters. Our kids got very excited, and Justin kept wanting to stand up in the canoe. This is a no-no rule we establish from the start. I did lift him up to see the ducks and then set him back down on the bottom. He stood after being told not to, and I quickly put him back in his place. He whimpered only a short time, as a loon's call caught his attention.

11

Loons have a special meaning for me. They were always present in Minnesota. Some think their distinct call lonely, but for me it expresses the freedom of the wilderness.

We paddled to the north end of the lake, where a forest fire burned two years before. The fire started from lightning and was put out by firefighters. This north end was a blackened, dirty area, with naked trees pointing to the sky.

At that time there was one old trapper living there. We saw moose racks and caribou horns, so we knew he had lived well during the winter. The fire destroyed his home and chased him out into the lake, where firefighters rescued him. The ordeal was too much, and he was hospitalized. Now we were the sole residents on the lake.

We stopped at this beautiful north end, which had the only gravel beach and a view of the lake's entire length. This had been an enchanting spot before the fire. We could have chosen this site for our resort. We knew the forest would grow up again over time. However, we didn't want to make our start in a burned, sooty, depressing area. We were still content with our selection on the west side, with our view of the Alaska Range and Mt. McKinley.

We saw fish swimming leisurely in the clean water and tried our luck. Within two casts I felt the familiar tug and landed a fighting six-pound northern. This was plenty for a dinner, so the pole was set aside for another time.

After lunch we paddled to the south end of the lake and found a sand beach adjacent to an area of thick reeds. The reedy swamp area had a beauty all its own. We found it full of nesting Arctic terns, different species of ducks, and other species of smaller birds. Then we returned home. I quickly cleaned the fish to have two fillets and cooked dinner. Jim had already started the fire.

Northern pike is a very tasty fish, but some people shy away from eating it. There is an extra row of Y-shaped bones, which are a horrible nuisance. I spent some time flaking the meat apart, to remove all possibilities of bones, so I could feed it to the kids. I vowed to find a different way to clean northern pike.

After a year of practice I could clean this fish, eliminating the extra row of bones. Our resort guests were pleased with the northern's taste and impressed with the guarantee of never finding a bone.

We began work in earnest the following morning. Jim left for the dense woods, and I cleaned up the camping area. I heated water in a large washtub over our campfire and began my first session of washing clothes by hand and hanging them up on a rope strung between two trees. This was much more time-consuming than throwing dirty clothes in a washer, pushing a button, and walking away. On the other hand, the fresh smell of clothing blown dry in a breeze is incomparable.

By noon Jim returned for lunch. He had located some good-sized trees and would begin cutting and trimming logs for our home right after lunch. He would float them to our camp where I would peel them. We had already agreed I'd do the peeling, as I had the kids to watch.

That afternoon I enjoyed being lazy as Jim headed back into the woods. The mosquitoes were like a smothering blanket in the forest, and he had to wear a head net. In our clearing by the lake, and with a small breeze, the bugs were no problem to the children and me. I took a bath in the lake with Trish happily splashing along the shore and Justin contentedly taking his nap.

Jim brought in his first raft of logs. He dragged them to the water and then walked along the shore pulling them home, like a mule pulling a load along a canal. The next day was the beginning of some heavy work for me.

Although I had never held a draw knife before, I figured I was just as capable as the next person to learn. The knife is a large blade with a handle on each end. A person sets the blade into the bark and pulls, or "draws" with it. The bark is easily removed from the wood. It took me a little time to get the angle just right. If the blade is slanted too sharply, it is harder to draw, and some wood is peeled off. If not slanted enough, only half the bark is peeled, and an extra draw is required.

Of course I started by peeling the log while it rested on the ground. That was definitely not the way to do it. Before long, my back was so stiff from bending over that I had a rigid right angle posture.

Next time back to camp, Jim built a large sawhorse with V-shaped supports on each end to hold the log up off the ground. Then I could peel logs standing up.

I contended with knots in the logs and fought the ever-present pitch. I rolled the log over and peeled the underside. Soon I got the technique down and tried to make a game of the job. Could I actually peel a piece the full length of the log? I had a contest to peel a log in five minutes or less. Or better yet, could I cleanly bark two logs before one of the kids demanded something? The first day I was proud to see six peeled logs stacked to one side of my horse. Their shiny yellow color smiled at me. Never mind the much larger pile of unpeeled logs on the other side of the horse. After all, that only left 94 to go.

That first summer on Lake Wien, only three weeks, continued at the same pace. Jim cut the logs and got them to camp. I kept house, washed clothes the old-fashioned way, caught a fish for dinner and peeled more logs. The number of logs I peeled in a day increased as I gained experience.

When our time was up, we had our 100 logs — all peeled and stacked to dry over the winter. We had cleared a spot on top of the bluff and knew where we would build our home next summer. For sure, in one summer, we'd be able to finish our house.

We couldn't wait to return and begin the next step in our dreams. We put our canoe away and packed away our tent and gear. The chartered plane arrived, right on schedule.

That school year passed more slowly than usual, but eventually it was summer again. We still had not saved enough to buy floats for our own plane and so once again had to charter in. This summer, 1975, we would stay six weeks.

CHAPTER 2

BUILDING OUR LOG HOME

During the school year we kept our ears and eyes open and found both an apartment-sized propane stove and a wringer washing machine. We bought a small generator to run the washing machine and electric tools. After these were flown in, it seemed like a summer of luxury lay ahead for me: no more tending an open fire for cooking and no more doing laundry by hand.

We also met a young couple who would help us build our home for the price of their food and chartering in. Already this was costing more than we anticipated. But surely the next year would be cheaper.

First Linda and Dave were chartered in, then the kids and I went on the second trip. Jim was in Fairbanks, hurriedly getting together the rest of the supplies. It was the middle of June. Earlier than our stay of the summer before.

I was shocked to find that there were many people on the lake. The Homestead Act was still open, and it would not close until summer's end. Linda and Dave, after enjoying the summer so much, filed their own claim on Lake Wien that fall. In all, there were 12 claims on the lake where there was only ours the summer before. Our solitude was interrupted.

We set up our tents once again — a tent for our family, a tent for the other couple, and a new screen tent to be our kitchen. The propane stove was placed in the screen tent and groceries stashed and put away. The washer stood outside with a canvas for protection from rain. At the first chance, I took the canoe out and paddled toward the lake's south end to check on the bird population.

Ducks and their families were more prevalent this year. To my great delight, I found the reedy swamp full of nesting Arctic terns. Since I had seen them for the first time the summer before, I did some research during the winter. I was astounded to learn that these birds winter in the Antarctic Ocean and summer as far north as the Arctic Ocean — making a round trip yearly migration of up to 22,000 miles! They see more daylight than any other living creature, since they are in both the Arctic and Antarctic during the periods of longest days.

Like other terns, the Arctic tern will defend her nesting area by making painful diving attacks on the heads of intruders (animal or human). While I explored their area, I found as I approached their nests, they did indeed dive bomb me. They came straight down like kamikazie pilots and pulled up at the last moment — about two inches from my head. I took some pictures and then left them in peace.

On my way back to camp I reflected that a short week before I was frantically making out final grades for the 150 junior high students attending my Physical Education and Health classes. With a grade for each subject, rather than an average for the two, there were 300 grades to be recorded twice, first on grade cards then on permanent records in the main office. This was a hectic time of year for all teachers. Yet, here I was, slowly paddling home, feeling so absolutely contented and one with nature.

Jim was not due for another day. That evening after we retired, I heard a noise outside. I crawled out of my warm and cozy sleeping bag and opened the tent flap to peek. A black bear was climbing over a pile of my peeled logs between the screen tent and our sleeping tents. The gun was in the other tent. I thought it unwise to walk over there to "knock," so I screamed to call for Dave. "Wake up, there's a bear in camp!"

Dave stepped out of their tent clad only in shorts, took careful aim and shot. He leisurely walked over to the bear and claimed it was dead; it could be cleaned in the morning. He went back in his tent and back to sleep.

Next day we found the screen tent slashed by the bear's sharp claws; he must have investigated the kitchen before approaching our sleeping tents. Linda sewed up the tent, I cooked breakfast, and Dave began butchering the bear.

Jim arrived by charter with the remainder of our supplies. We confirmed our scheduled pick-up date for August 5, and the pilot headed back to Fairbanks. Jim dug right in and helped Dave finish cleaning the bear. The quarters were hung and well-peppered to repel flies.

This time we did taste the meat and found this bear delicious. The bears in Minnesota are "dump" bears, and the bears on Kodiak thrive on dead salmon — their meats reflect those flavors. But in this area the bears live on berries and are excellent for eating. We ate only bear meat for the next few days, and like the natives who wasted nothing, we kept it and used it all.

The guys built a large table for the cook tent for eating, making bread, rolling out pie crusts (this year I had an oven) and for playing cards in the evening after work.

In Alaska June has long daylight hours. By the 21st, we peaked out at 20½ hours of daylight and 3½ hours of no sun. It was never dark, only dusk or dawn. Some people find it hard to sleep at night, but we found sleep came easily after our hard day's work.

Jim and Dave started on the foundation by digging holes 10 feet deep for the pilings. Some were shallower because they reached permafrost. With the pilings in and the floor joists in place, the actual building could begin. The peeled logs were now dry and much lighter to handle. Still, it seemed that bluff became higher and steeper with each log carried up. The first day of actual raising the walls, was only two logs' worth, but we were thrilled to see the beginning. As the men added more logs each day, Linda and I made lots of bread, pies, fresh doughnuts and cookies for extras.

The kids had a swing set made from trees that summer. Trish thought it was a super toy. But Justin, just three, was still too short to touch the ground. He kicked madly and got no-where. Then he got very upset and began to scream. Linda and I spent lots of time pushing that boy on the swing all summer.

Each afternoon, after the kids had their naps, Linda and I took them out in the canoe to catch a fish for dinner. We were never disappointed, and we caught only what we needed for dinner that day. Returning to camp, I cleaned the fish (removing all bones), while Linda started the potatoes or vegetables. Our dinners were large, as the guys needed it in their physical labor.

After one week of work, the walls were only about three and a half feet high — and all 100 logs had been used! This was discouraging to all of us.

About that time a plane circled above and skimmed in for the landing. The pilot came in to shore, and we offered him some pie and coffee. During his short stay he, of course, took a look at our progress. He saw that the walls were up a little over halfway and that we were out of peeled logs. He said he'd seen a lot of houses in the bush built just this high and then never finished. He also thought that, like many others, we probably would quit at this time too. He said, "Besides, putting your cabin on the bluff was a damn fool thing to do in the first place, 'cause it's too damn much work hauling all those logs up the hill."

Soon after that he left.

It is strange how people passing you in your journey of life and making some comment can affect you one way one day and maybe the opposite on the next. We may have looked disap-pointed, but we sure weren't down yet!

The following morning Jim and Dave started cutting more trees, hauling them to the lake, and dragging the log-raft to camp. Linda and I started peeling. With two of us the peeling went a lot faster, and we made it as much fun as possible. We worked well together.

Within another week we thought we had enough cut logs to finish our home. Linda and I continued peeling. The guys again raised the walls — more difficult than before. Green logs are heavier, and these logs had to be lifted higher as the walls went up. The bluff (high enough in reality) became a huge mountain. Each log must be lugged to the summit. Finally the walls were completed.

Larger logs were now needed for the ridgepole and stringers. These were found only on the opposite side of the lake. One trip across produced the four large logs needed. They were slowly towed back behind the canoe and peeled. Hoisting these up entailed crucial leverage to place them in correct position. Then everyone stood back for a look.

Even without the roof and floor, the building appeared as that house on the bluff overlooking the lake — seen so often in our dreams.

We hadn't enough money left to buy plywood for the floor, nor decking for the roof. We would have to leave it open for the winter. All things considered, this was probably best (although we didn't think so at the time). The top green logs had a year to dry in the open.

Until then, we were working too hard to observe what was going on around the lake. We did note a good deal of activity. So now we took time off to enjoy ourselves.

On our left about a mile away, there was a family living in tents with two children still in diapers. This was their first summer at the lake. The father, by himself, was trying to cut, drag, peel, and stack logs for their home. He planned to build the home by himself and then use a pole roof, covered with sod, like the old timers used to do. He was trying to accomplish all this before the first snow arrived, as they had every intention of spending the winter in this interior. Their claim was a Homestead Site, and their plan was to plant some crop the following spring — after clearing land for such an endeavor.

They were really nice people. But with no experience in camping, canoeing, fishing or roughing it, they were to find it harder than they bargained for.

Continuing north along our west shore of the lake, the next claim was made by a man living by himself. He also planned to put his land under cultivation. He had not started his cabin, because he had no intention of staying in that winter. He wanted to just get the *feel* of the land first.

Next came three claims where a man and his family had ideas of building a large resort and making millions. Four more claims were for Homesites — just five-acre plots. Linda and Dave found an area that they particularly liked and staked out their claim. That fall the land was closed.

We still had a little time before our plane arrived to take us out. We built a small 8x10' tool shed as an experiment in vertical log construction. The building went up much faster, but it was almost impossible to make tight. Linda and I chinked that tool shed with moss between the vertical logs as tightly as we could. In contrast, using the horizontal log method, the weight of the logs upon each other, with insulation between, makes a tighter fit.

Our plane was due to take us out, and the summer was over for us. We had not accomplished all we hoped to, but we did make progress. My estimate of food came out about right, and we would leave very little. We put all the tools away in our new tool shed and tucked the washer in out of the weather. On August 4 we sat down to our last dinner. The next day we would be flown out.

We awoke to a bright sunny day. A great day for flying, so we were confident our chartered plane would arrive as expected. We ate a leisurely breakfast. Then we took down the tents and stored them away. We put the canoe up and sat down to wait. And wait and wait and wait. Our expected plane did not arrive.

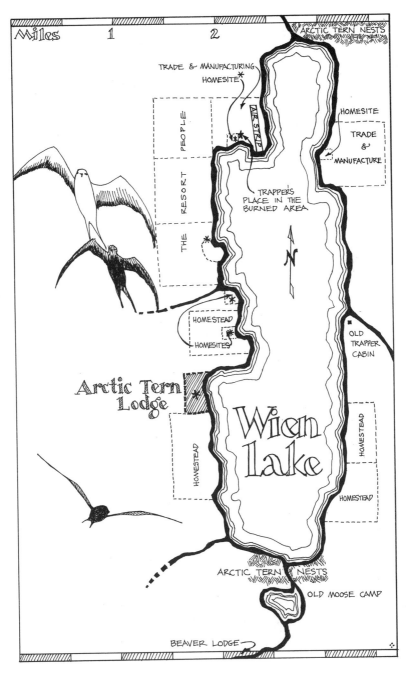

Miles 1 2

ARCTIC TERN NESTS

TRADE & MANUFACTURING
HOMESITE*

THE RESORT PEOPLE

AIR STRIP

HOMESITE

TRADE
&
MANUFACTURE

TRAPPER'S
PLACE IN THE
BURNED AREA

N

HOMESTEAD

HOMESITES

OLD
TRAPPER
CABIN

Arctic Tern
Lodge

Wien
Lake

HOMESTEAD

HOMESTEAD

HOMESTEAD

HOMESTEAD

ARCTIC TERN NESTS

OLD MOOSE CAMP

BEAVER LODGE

*Final claims granted.

Out came the tents! We were optimistic that the plane would arrive the following day, so we had no great concern over the matter. Looking over our remaining food, I decided on dehydrated soup, thickened with potato buds. It was filling.

Five days later we knew there was a definite problem. We had no means of communication. No one else on the lake had a plane. The family around the corner closest to us was in for the winter. The only other people on the lake this late were the "going-to-build-a-huge-resort" people. Their charter pick-up was scheduled for the end of August — about three more weeks!

We didn't panic, as that wouldn't help the situation. But we did discuss what we'd do to the pilot who forgot to pick us up (when we finally got to town)!

As it happened, a week later (and after many meals of dehydrated soup) an unexpected plane flew in to the resort people. Dave and Linda flew back to Fairbanks then and arranged for a different charter to pick us up the following day.

Our experience that summer left us with two serious concerns. Another resort operating on this one lake could present problems for us. It looked as if these other resort owners were well-financed. Secondly, as a matter of survival, we would have to have a float plane of our own if we chose to continue with this venture. Depending on charters could have serious consequences.

Once again we started the school year in Kodiak. This time with important decisions to make before we returned again to Lake Wien.

*   *   *

We decided to return and keep working toward our goal. If we couldn't prove up on our Trade and Manufacturing Site, then we would change it to a five acre Homesite. We could easily qualify, as we had lived there each summer. But, we weren't throwing in the towel yet.

We sold our Champ and bought a new Citabria on floats — a beautiful plane, with hefty payments. With confidence we flew it into the lake that summer. Jim was in seventh heaven with his new Mistress. Circling before landing, we saw how the other resort was developing. But our thoughts returned to our own situation, as we taxied up to our home. We took out our gear and were established quickly. After all, we were getting pretty experienced. Jim spent the next few days flying in our summer's supplies and also materials for the roof, floor and windows.

We soon found out more about the lake's other inhabitants. The family of four right around the corner had a very difficult winter. They did not get a moose in the fall for their winter's meat. Also they found it impossible to cut through the lake's ice, four feet thick, for their water. They melted snow for water, which takes tons, it seems, to make much liquid. The mother was washing diapers by hand each day. (I will tough it in most ways, but when Justin was still in diapers I used disposables.) Due to these experiences, this family was fed up with their dream expectations. They had already left the lake by the time we arrived. Later they sold their log home and their five acres. The new owners came up from Anchorage for about two weeks every year, otherwise the place remained uninhabited.

The single man was in again and starting his log cabin this summer. The resort people had started early in the season, flying in materials and a crew, landing on the ice. Now there was a completed, furnished lodge building and 10 cabins along their shoreline! This developer seemed to be out of our league, but over the summer we learned from businesses all over Fairbanks that he owed them money — lots of it. He had formed three different corporations that we knew of, and he hadn't invested any money of his own. Businesses were demanding their payments and were closing in. No guests were in that summer; the buildings and lodge just sat there.

My mother and a good friend of hers, Charlotte, drove a camper all the way from Minnesota. They wanted to see Alaska this way. They also wished to see how we were doing, what I had been writing about in my recent letters home. Jim flew them in. He offered to set up a tent for the two of them, but they suggested sleeping on the floor of our tool shed. Thus we bestowed the name, "Waldorf," on that building.

Although we still weren't moved into our cabin, they could see what it would be like when finished. Avid canoeists and anglers, they enjoyed fishing every day and exploring the lake. They were as excited about observing the nesting terns as I was the previous spring. One night, while sitting around the campfire, we discussed prospective names for our resort. We settled on "Arctic Tern Lodge," depicting the much flying that goes into caring for our guests while they vacation with us.

Jim flew the two women out after their visit of a few days. He would return the following day. Of course that evening we were visited by a bear, the first of that year. He came down the path on the bluff and I, at first, tried scaring him off by banging pots and pans. I turned to get the gun, and looking back I saw the bear ambling off toward our tent. By the time I climbed the bluff, the bear was halfway inside our tent. I yelled an obscene remark, and he slowly backed out. Then I shot him. I can be a deadly shot when the occasion calls for it, and this was one of those times.

I never had butchered a bear by myself, so I went down to get Linda and Dave. They were working on their own cabin that summer. They came up and Dave took care of the bear in no time. When Jim returned, I told him about the bear. He just smiled and said he knew I could take care of things while he was gone.

We made progress on our cabin. The floor was put in; openings for windows and a door were cut. On went the roofing. Then, for the first time since we started three summers before, we actually slept in a cabin . . . and thought about the poor people still in tents. (We also built a cozy outhouse, which was badly needed, but was second to finishing the cabin.)

By August we were working hard at brushing. This involves clearing underbrush out and hauling the debris to piles, which we burned on rainy days. In early August two friends from Kodiak dropped in. Claudia and Stosh flew their own plane in. Having been hard at work for so long, we talked ourselves into taking one day off. We packed a lunch for a day's trip over to Manley Hot Springs — a little town about 20 minutes north. We took off, looking forward to a relaxing time together.

Claudia and Stosh's plane was ahead of us. About halfway to our destination, we flew over a small lake. Jim caught sight of a man frantically waving at us. His other arm rested in a homemade sling. We wagged our wings to let him know we'd seen him, then flew ahead to catch up with our friends. They had no plane radio, so we signalled to them to turn around. They turned without question and followed our lead.

We both circled the small lake once, and then touched down. The pontoons touched bottom 20 feet out from shore. Jim made several trips carrying the kids and me in to shore on his back. We were met by a man and his two boys who related their story.

They had staked out 80 acres and planned to cultivate a percentage of it to prove up on their land. They were dropped off the first of June and were not to be checked on again until the 4th of September! In June they had to shoot a bear. They ate some of it, but then as it started to spoil, they buried what remained. (They didn't know you could pepper it to keep it for a long time.)

Evidently they had calculated very closely the amount of food they flew in for the summer. Also they did not take into account how much their appetites would increase when they worked outdoors every day. Early in their stay, they realized that their calculations were very far off. Rather than start rationing out what remained, they just ate as much as they pleased every day.

By the middle of July, with about six weeks left, they were out of food. They had no fishing gear. They did not think a person could eat the blueberries, half-ripe cranberries and rosehips so abundant in the woods. In desperation, they dug up the long-since buried bear meat and had been eating that. I saw some in the kettle and almost swore off eating ever again.

We gave them our survival gear. Jim and Stosh would return from Manley Hot Springs to rescue them after dropping off Claudia, the kids and me (to make room).

We approached the village from the south. First we crossed over the Tanana River, which dumps into the mighty Yukon about 30 miles west. We planned to land on the Manley Slough. From the air, this smaller river nestled in between tall trees looked dangerous for landing.

Landing on any river can be dangerous. A pilot must approach slowly and carefully, constantly watching for boats or deadheads.

I took one look at that small river below me and the bridge on the north end, and I was certain Jim could not land our float plane there. Jim knew better and easily glided the Citabria to a smooth landing, then taxied to a small park along the river. We disembarked, and Jim and Stosh flew back to make the rescue. They completed the rescue without a hitch.

We found Manley Hot Springs a joy for the rest of our day off. It once was a busy gold mining town, but after mining gave out, only a very small community remained. A trading post was still active, selling groceries to many of the Indians living along the Yukon and Tanana Rivers. There was an old Road House, in use since the beginning of the century. The tall, narrow building had rooms for rent upstairs and, on the first floor, a lounge complete with double pot bellied stove in the dining area and a bar toward the rear. Artifacts on display from the mining era included an almost complete mastadon tusk hanging horizontally across the lounge. Wall calendars dated back to the 1920s.

We played at the playground near the Road House which had well-constructed swings and a large teeter-totter. This small community was so exceptionally clean it appeared like a fairyland. Flowers bloomed in almost every yard, and there was no litter. Not even a can pull-tab could be found.

We walked along the dusty road, over the one bridge, following directions to the local bath house. Sure enough, after we followed the road along and up a small hill, we found it. For a small fee, we were treated to a hot bath. The owners of this property took full advantage of the hot springs; they also had a large greenhouse. They graciously showed us their produce — tomatoes, cucumbers, lettuce, cantaloupe and more. We were even able to purchase some tomatoes from them. What a delicacy!

Soon our day ended. We all loaded into the two planes, and taxiing along the river, took off to head home. Two days later Stosh and Claudia left.

About that time we had a scary encounter with a bear, although it did have a humorous side. The weather had been hot for a couple of weeks, so we had replaced a kitchen window with a scrap of screen, to get some circulation through the snug log cabin.

We were all bedded down for the night. The kids were on their army cots. Jim and I were on a mattress on the floor. We had not flown in a bed frame yet. Jim, like a lot of fathers during the raising of babies, did not awaken to their whimpers or cries during the night that I, their mother, always heard. But this night it was he who awoke, and I who slept soundly.

Jim awakened to a sound in the kitchen. He rolled over to look. Because we were on the floor of the living room, he was looking sideways and upward at — half a bear hanging in the window!

He yelled and jumped up and out of bed. I awoke in time to see . . . nothing. The bear had quickly retreated, on all fours, but then stood just outside the window. Jim picked up the first thing he could grab from the table and threw it at the bear. It was a bottle of syrup, which bounced off the bear's head at such close range, but it did chase him away.

Two days later the bear returned. We did not kill him, because we were scheduled to leave in just a few days. To be more effective this time, we shot guns simultaneously. On the count of three I shot the bear's rump with a 4-10 shotgun, and Jim shot over its head with a 30-06 for noise. The bear retreated more rapidly than I thought possible.

We continued brushing our land and stacking the brush into huge piles for burning. I have always hated that job. We did so much, and there was always more to do. While a big piece of equipment in town clears an area in no time, in the interior we had to do everything by hand.

Summer ended for us, and we returned once again to teaching.

CHAPTER 3

THE YEAR OF DECISION

Both Jim and I were becoming less enchanted with teaching school as the years went by. At first I loved teaching more than anything in the world. I was willing to put in extra hours before and after school and on weekends. I felt the students needed it. And they were appreciative of my efforts.

Then when I went to Kodiak, I was team teaching for half the year. I never adjusted to team teaching, as it just couldn't work out with a "partner" on an equal basis.

We were in that period in our educational history when teachers were not allowed to touch a student. Later, the Supreme Court would overrule this, but at the time, teaching in a junior high was very difficult. It is human nature for children, growing and learning, to challenge authority. I feel it is our job, both as parents and as teachers, to teach and guide them the best we know how — which sometimes calls for a little swat or shake to let them know we mean business.

Also drugs were becoming more prevalent in public schools. Teachers needed strong backing by the administration and the school board, when they reported on deals they observed or situations they happened upon. When no consequences were imposed on the students, the reporting teachers became objects of student ridicule. Then the teachers stopped reporting.

The school situation became a jungle. And, although Jim and I had always loved teaching and loved kids, we began to wonder if we could stay in a profession that was seemingly deteriorating before our very eyes.

29

That year we teachers worked the first few months without a contract. Feelings on both sides were getting out of control. We came within an hour of going on strike, and many people carried bad feelings for the remainder of the year. We left school in June with no next year's contracts issued, although we were promised they would be forthcoming.

When we arrived at the lake that spring, Jim and I were drained — physically and mentally. We took the first two weeks for vacation to replenish body and soul. We did fly in one new item, a Franklin fireplace for our log home.

We usually slept late, had a leisurely breakfast, and then took the canoe out. We'd catch a fish for dinner, breathe fresh air, go skinny dipping at the sand beach (there were no people except a bachelor at the other end of the lake) and drink in the beauty of the lake.

We watched the ducks with their families, the eagles soaring gracefully to their nests, the moose trotting along the lakeshore, the Arctic tern protecting her young. And we absorbed the peace that comes while watching the last glow of sunset reflect off Mt. McKinley. After two weeks we were pretty much healed, but we were deep in thought about our future.

Tracy Shawn, the daughter of friends in Washington, wanted to stay with us for the summer. She didn't want pay, she just wanted to help us out and enjoy our surroundings as we did. She had just graduated from high school and would start college in the fall. I said yes, and as it turned out, it was the right decision.

Although she may not have known it at the time, Tracy Shawn also helped to heal my soul that summer. She was one heck of a worker — not afraid to do anything. I admired her backbone. Jim was busy digging out our walk-in cooler (which was in permafrost), building a small smokehouse and new fish-cleaning table. Tracy and I spent our time in other ways. Of course our main job was keeping the kids busy and involved with what we were doing.

Justin with the catch in front of the cooler.

With the children now aged five and eight, they showed more than a passing interest in the art of fishing. From my childhood, I remembered only the frustration of learning to cast: retrieved hooks from trees, snags, rocks — even my own finger a time or two. Surely there was a safer approach.

Jim removed only the hook portion of the kids' lures. This worked marvelously. After some practice sessions, the kids were actually casting into the lake and not around people's heads.

One day I noticed a fish followed the lure to the shore time and again. Both kids wanted to know why they couldn't hook the fish. On went the hooks, and in came the fish!

31

Tracy, both kids, and I spent many hours fishing together, as fish was our main dinner fare. Usually we loaded up the canoe right after breakfast. We paddled down to the other end of the lake, where the raspberries were ripening. We picked berries for an hour and returned in time to make lunch for all of us. After lunch we washed our berries, made jam and canned it. Then we paddled out to catch a fish.

One day drifted into another. Some days we picked raspberries for jam, and other days blueberries. By keeping to only an hour a day, we did not tire of the picking. Soon we had two cases of quart raspberry jam and one case of quart blueberry jam for winter use.

Jim and I continued to discuss our future. The so-called resort at the end of the lake — with very nice lodge building and comfortable cabins — had been repossessed. The man who had it built had "forgotten" to pay his debts.

Jim and I were reflecting on where we were in our lives. Did we really want to return to teaching in the fall? Or did we really want to commit ourselves to building a resort? With all the work, effort, and money that a resort would entail, it was still a gamble that we could survive. If we returned to teaching, we could depend on a good income next year and every year in our future.

If we chose this bush life full time, would it be fair and right for our children? Was I competent to teach them in all subjects myself? Would we deprive them socially? Or, might we give them an experience with more positive effects than negative? Thoughts, thoughts, and more thoughts. Talk, talk, and sleepless nights.

We received our contracts in the mail on July 31, 1977. We returned the contracts on August 1 — unsigned — with our letter of appreciation for working for them for the past six years. After that we did not hear a word. So our course was set. Right or wrong, good or bad — the decision was made. We marched shakily into the future.

Summer use of our cabin, and now winter use, were two entirely different things. Tracy Shawn and I rechinked all the logs tighter than ever. We bought storm windows for some windows and plastic for others.

While Jim was away for two weeks in August, we started on the basement. Our bedrooms would be moved into a new basement, giving us more living space upstairs for the long winter. First Tracy Shawn and I started digging under to make the room. We dug out about half easily, as there were no rocks. Then in the back corner we hit permafrost. No more digging. Twice a day we scraped off what soil thawed during that time. It was back breaking work.

Rocks were needed to build the foundation. As the lake's north end is the only place with rocks, we hauled rock by the canoeload each day. By the time Jim returned, the basement was completely dug out, and a very large pile of rocks awaited.

One early evening in August, I saw a cow moose walking in the water close to our shore. I grabbed my movie camera and ran outside. I started taking pictures from the bluff. She walked a few steps in the water, then stopped and lowered her massive head to munch weeds. I took a few steps closer. She looked up and lay her ears back, like a horse does when it's upset. I waited, and her ears came forward again curiously.

I yelled for Tracy Shawn to come see this moose close up. She heard me and came out running. But so did Jim, and he was getting angry. He brought his gun and came up behind me. He warned me to stay back. I took a few more steps forward to get better close-ups. When I did, the moose snorted and turned a circle in the water. Jim was yelling at me. My camera was rolling. Finally I ran out of film and retreated. The moose walked away, slowly down the shoreline.

My film later revealed the close-up threat. Jim didn't forgive me for being so brash; he knew how dangerous a moose could be. A friend of his was taking pictures of a moose in

McKinley Park one spring, when that moose turned around, and literally walked right over him, breaking several ribs.

Tracy Shawn left in late August after many tears. She had been a tremendous help to me personally, and we had become very close friends. Our relationship still continues through correspondence, although our paths have not crossed for many years.

*   *   *

I checked with the school district office in Nenana regarding teaching Trish and Justin through correspondence. We could take the courses set up by the State Department of Education, or we could take the Calvert School courses. Either way, we would be responsible only to the district office in Nenana. We chose the Calvert School — the system I was taught under for a couple of my early years.

When the materials arrived, I checked them over quite thoroughly. One box, about one foot square, came for each child. I thought this surely wasn't much for an entire year of a child's education. Upon further investigation I found the necessary texts for each grade, plenty of tablets and pencils, erasers, workbooks, drawing paper, and a manual for the home instructor. The manual contained lesson plans for the entire year. It was set up with 160 lessons per grade, to be completed with good grades, before the pupil was promoted to the next level.

We soon discovered that pupils could work at their own rates. The students had the option of doing more each day, or doing more work in a subject where they had trouble. I felt this was optimum education. Yet it was almost impossible in a class of 35 to 55 students, as I taught in Kodiak. The idea of teaching only two students was exciting to me.

We experimented as to what Trish and Justin could handle best. I began school at eight sharp. I think routine is good, especially for grade school children. At first we took breaks outside like recess. Trish and Justin very quickly discovered that taking recess made their release time later.

Children in public school attend school for a certain amount of time each day, so the more recess or play time they can enjoy, the happier they are: it means less actual school work. But children who must accomplish certain tasks before dismissal react differently. They want to do their lessons, and then be free for the rest of the day — this means eliminating recesses or any such "nonsense."

Both Justin and Trish finished a lesson in about two and a half hours of steady work. Every day they were free by 10:30 a.m. After a while I became concerned about these short school hours. When they did return to public school, the longer hours would be quite a change for them. So we struck a bargain: they would stay in school until 11:30, unless they completed two lessons.

We continued school on this principle all four years in the bush. The kids averaged one and a half lessons per day, unless they got snagged on something. The first year, we started the first week of September, and they were finished by the first week in May. Realizing the freedom they gained in the spring, they worked even harder the second year, finishing the end of April. The third year they finished on April 4. And the fourth year even earlier.

The manual consisted of 160 lessons per year, broken into eight units of 20 lessons each. I corrected Trish and Justin's daily work as they went along. At the end of each unit, they took a test. These tests were sent to the office in Nenana to be graded there. The students' final grades were based only on the tests.

I disagreed with this. I thought all work should be considered toward their final grades. The tests, of course, should hold more weight, but the other work should not be disregarded.

Many parents in the bush did not correct their students' daily work, since it did not count toward the final grade. This was unfortunate. Children could learn from their mistakes, and their teachers could identify students' weak and strong areas by grading daily papers.

The greatest experience I encountered in all my teaching was teaching Justin to read. I had never seen that special light in the eye of a student as when he learned to read. Justin was like a horse heading home who couldn't swallow up the road fast enough. The more I gave him, the more he demanded. Indeed, being a first grade teacher in public schools must be extremely rewarding.

I had taught classes with as many as 60 students, and now I taught a class of two. I *always* knew when Trish or Justin did not understand a concept. For instance, Trish was a good student in all subjects except math. I was not aware, during her first three grades in public school, that she was having a terrible time with math. Math was my minor, and I knew it well. We worked more diligently and longer on math than on her other subjects, every day. By the end of the year she was a B- or C+ student. By our fourth year in, she was an A- student in math.

I do wonder if her problem would have been eliminated in a public school. Maybe not. It took a great deal of time and love to help her gain confidence in her math ability.

There are some disadvantages in correspondence education. In science, we were not equipped to do experiments as are most schools. But seeing animals in their natural habitats is more educational than dissecting a frog in a lab. Secondly, children raised in the bush do get plenty of exercise, but they do not get skills in team sports.

Overall, I feel the advantages far outweigh the disadvantages, at least in elementary grades. I am well aware that I am not capable of educating our children in chemistry or physics or shorthand.

Justin began school in the bush in first grade and Trish in fourth. (So in the course of our four years, I have taught grades one through seven.) High school was just around the corner for Trish, when we left the bush. This was one of the biggest factors influencing our decision to return to town.

CHAPTER 4

YEAR ROUND IN THE BUSH —
OUR FIRST WINTER

For the first time we were going to see a colorful fall at the
lake. I watched the leaves slowly change their colors. Some
areas were green and others the bright yellow of birch trees.
From the air it looked as though a painter had spilled his paints
on a huge canvas: blobs of yellow, orange and reddish brown,
interspersed with deep green of spruce trees.

The geese began flying over early one morning. A large
"V" of them came directly over our house, honking and making
such a racket that we quickly jumped out of bed to watch.
About five days later I saw six huge flocks at one time — all
heading south. The lakeshore resounded with echoes of their
calls.

The days began to get colder with a crispness in the air we
enjoyed and treasured. The leaves started falling and carpeted
the forest floor. One day a wind blew gustily, and the trees'
remaining leaves fluttered softly to the ground. Then the birch
trees stood naked to the approaching winter — much like a naked
woman awaiting a new spring dress, a fresh green dress, which
would not arrive for many months.

Jim was putting the walls and floor into our new basement.
Soon it was enclosed, and he insulated the walls. He added
paneling and a woodstove. Then we moved the beds downstairs,
giving us a welcome enlargement in our upstairs living space.
Jim added an enclosed porch to the cabin to create a double

entrance — a necessity in Arctic temperatures. And he added three-inch styrofoam insulation to the roof, preventing heat leakage through the ceiling.

Jim chartered a large plane from Fairbanks to fly in those things we considered necessary for our first winter in the bush. I tried to figure how much food we would consume in nine months. Surprisingly, my estimate came out quite close. On the other hand, I had no idea on the amount of toilet paper a family of four would use in nine months. I was really off with that!

We had three snowmachines flown in. We bought a CB radio and installed a large antenna. We couldn't reach as far as Nenana with it. However, there were two other families wintering on different lakes within a 20-mile radius of us. We could reach them. During severe winter weather of 50° to 60° below zero, we checked on each other, to make sure all was well.

The 16th of September our first snow arrived. It wasn't much, but the snowflakes were pretty. Justin and Trish were glad to see snow covering the ground, even this little, with patches of earth showing through. Of course it all melted the next day; it was just a brief taste of our winter to come.

The smaller and shallower lakes began to freeze before ours. Lake Wien is 250 feet deep in one area. Flying now was impossible. The lake's spray on the floats and belly of the plane during takeoff would freeze immediately, causing dangerous drag and imbalance.

The temperatures were dipping, and it was obvious freeze-up of our lake was imminent. Time to put up the plane for the winter. Jim had sold the Citabria 7GCVC. We now had a Cessna 180 on floats, which we had purchased with a partner. Jim had flown this larger plane, a four-seater, all summer — a special luxury for me. In the Citabria, which is really only a two-seater aircraft, I sat in the back with one child on each knee. Of course it was uncomfortable, but it was a necessity at the time.

The Cessna 180 is an expensive aircraft to fly just for personal use, and we did not have skis for it. Jim decided to put up the 180 for the winter and buy a small Champ (Citabria 7ECA) with another friend of his, Sid. Our main use in winter is flying to town once a week or every two weeks for mail. The Champ would be less expensive to operate for that, and easier to start in the severe cold.

Jim got the nose of the Cessna up as far as possible onto the bank, although the back of the floats still touched the water slightly. He was flown to town. He would return with the Champ on skis after the lake froze. We hoped he would have less than a two-week wait, but we really didn't know, since it was our first freeze-up.

Soon the smaller lakes froze over. A nearby neighbor, Bill Spear, who lives on a shallower lake than ours, landed on ice for the first time that fall. I awoke one morning to see our lake skimmed over. It was a cold day at about 10°; for the first time I had to break a little ice hole to fill the water jug. We carried water to the house in five-gallon jugs. Jim carried two at once, but I carried one. A five-gallon jug of water weighs 40 pounds!

When we lived in Kodiak, we used as much water as the next family. But here we used 15 gallons per day, including laundry, washing dishes and baths. We had a new 30-gallon garbage can in our kitchen (for our water reserve) plus four five-gallon jugs. We also had a five-gallon open bucket on the counter with the dipper in it.

That first freeze did have its humor. The lake froze smoothly, and from the air the ice must not have been visible. A late leaving duck came in for his landing. He landed feet first and skidded along the ice like a figure skater. After regaining his balance, he flew off in a southerly direction!

With the air temperatures below freezing all day, the ice froze in earnest. Almost a half inch was added to its thickness every two days.

Ice froze around and under the back part of the floats on the Cessna 180. No damage was being done, but she looked like a forlorn bird, that definitely belonged in water. Float planes,

The Green Machine on skis.

because of the height of their floats, always look larger and rather awkward out of water. Come spring, she would once again skim across the lake. But for now she must hibernate, as we had no skis for her.

Soon the ice was a good six inches thick — strong enough to support the plane's weight. Jim arrived with the new plane, which we soon named the Green Machine, because of its color.

Then we began work on gathering our wood supply. We really had no idea how much wood we would need.

We decided the best source was the fireburned trees. I taught school all morning, then Jim and I took a snowmachine down the lake. While he cut and dragged the trees to shore, I hooked up three at a time behind the snowmachine and hauled them home. After a good amount was hauled, we returned, for supper must be started. Quite often on weekends, he cut the logs into lengths with the chainsaw, and I split them, or vice versa. The Franklin would only burn split logs.

In November the temperature dipped down to minus 50° for a couple of days. That really scared us. We had experience with northern Minnesota winters at about -30° to -35°, so we thought we could handle the cold. But November was so early for such severe temperatures. During the "cold" months (December and January) we might face real extreme weather. We kept looking at each other and asking ourselves, "What have we gone and done this time?"

At such cold temperatures, birds look as round as snowballs and do very little flying. They stop their singing — much as squirrels stop their chattering.

Quiet is all around. Then there is a tremendous crack! The lake ice cracks from the pressure of freezing. In these super quiet surroundings, it can sound like a cannonball shot.

One must not touch metal with a bare hand or it will be white with instant frostbite. Nor spill blazo (lantern fuel) on your hand as that too will give you instant frostbite. One need only tap a log with an axe at this temperature; it splits as easily as cutting into butter. On the other hand, one must not need to *cut* wood at these temperatures.

During that November cold spell, the man of one neighboring family (20 miles away) tried to cut down a couple of trees. It almost cost him his life. As he started sawing through the tree, it leaned ever so slightly. The tree quickly snapped and fell to the ground — shattering into many pieces. One chunk hit the man and knocked him out. He did not know how long he was out, but it must have been only minutes. He would have frozen to death otherwise. He crawled on his hands and knees to his cabin and was better in a couple of days. This could easily have ended differently, as nature is a very unforgiving mother.

With December, the temperature moderated to a -30°, which is quite tolerable with good down clothing.

We were anxious for our first Christmas. The kids started making tree decorations. The greatest one, an old fashioned green and red paper chain, measured 28 feet by Christmas.

Selecting our Christmas tree turned out to be an all day affair; the right one was hard to find. Trish and Justin decided on one, Jim cut it down, and the kids dragged it the half mile back to the house.

I put the turkey in the oven early on Christmas morning. That was easy; the kids were up at 4 a.m.! We enjoyed home-made cranberry sauce, wild rice sent from Minnesota, pumpkin pie from Halloween pumpkins, and a special bottle of wine that we had saved for months. Out came the hand-cranked ice cream maker, to add the final touch to our first Christmas dinner in the bush. We didn't use the lantern on this special occasion. Candles were set on the table to reflect the happiness we felt.

January arrived. More serious discussion arose as to how we could build a lodge and a few cabins with our remaining money. We could still use our retirement from teaching if we had to. Where to go from here? Which way to turn?

Snow conditions on the lake remained safe for ski planes. The snow wasn't too deep to cause problems. Jim wanted the runway marked with a straight line of boughs along the surface. The first time I tried this I walked out on the lake, dropping boughs about every foot. I stopped after I thought it was of adequate length. I turned around and found the crooked line of a drunkard.

I picked up all the boughs and started again. I concentrated much harder the next time. I stared straight ahead, lining up with a spot on the distant shoreline. I dropped the branches without a downward glance. My straight line runway was much better, but it still left much to be desired.

I just couldn't believe it was that difficult to walk along a straight line on the snow on the ice. Then, just like in a cartoon where a lightbulb appears, the idea hit me: walk backwards.

I collected the boughs again. Once more I began the job, walking backwards, dropping branches. This time it was easy, and it made a very straight line. Now any pilot could easily see where it was safe to land — no overflow or large bumps. Also, the color of the boughs against the white gave the pilot some depth reference.

One evening Justin stepped outside for his bathroom chore before bedtime. He rushed inside saying, "Come and see, quick." Northern lights covered the whole sky. They were dancing all around in continuous motion, with spectacular colors: yellows, greens and blues. The display was breathtaking. We stood out there for about 30 minutes before succumbing to the cold.

In February we were notified that the repossessed lodge and cabins at the other end of the lake were to be sold at auction. All personal property had been repossessed due to non-payment. The land was considered not proved up on and was not included. So here was a lodge and cabins for sale, located 100 miles in the bush from Fairbanks, with no land to go with it. Naturally nobody wanted it . . . except us.

We paid a dime on the dollar and got the bid. It still amounted to a good sum of money, as it included the lodge and furnishings, dozer, ranger, snowmachine, and seven cabins. Now we were really broke. And we had to move all the buildings to be of use to us.

The snow was too deep to do anything. Instead we figured, and worried, about how all this would be done. Our proving up date on our land would come that June!

I stood by the window one day, waiting for the weather to moderate and the actual moving of buildings to begin. I looked out on the winter scene before me. To some, it contains a beauty all its own — and to others, it contains none.

The scene is a black and white picture, giving a strange sensation, a little loneliness in its starkness. The snow on the lake is white. The pine trees look black rather than green. The overcast sky is grayish white.

Late winter — the time of year people in the bush find most difficult. I think, "Should we not be a family, should we not be figuring out how to move buildings, should we not be avid readers, this might be a hard time of year for us too." But we are too busy for such thoughts, and we continue on with the job of living.

*   *   *

In March, Jim flew the Green Machine with our neighbor, Bill Spear, to check a shared trapline about an hour's flight away. As they were taking off to return home, the ski on the right side came off. Dangling by a cable, it came up and hit the windshield, cracking it. The gear leg, which was now only a peg leg, dug drastically into the snow, stopping the plane. Because the plane was going so fast when it was abruptly stopped, the tail lifted until the plane was standing vertically on her nose, breaking the propeller. Then, ever so slowly, she passed the point of precise balance, and over she went — flat on her back!

The temperature was -35° then, and the forecast was for -50° that night. Dangerous conditions for Jim's and Bill's survival, even though neither was hurt in the accident. They heard an airliner overhead. Bill quickly grabbed the radio mike and, tuning to the emergency frequency, radioed an SOS. The airliner, later identified as Japanese, picked up the call immediately and radioed ahead to Search and Rescue.

Bill and Jim were picked up by helicopter within an hour. Home was closer, but regulations required they be flown to the nearest official airport — Tanana.

Then they attempted to reach Bill's wife Becky and me from a CB radio in Tanana. Because of CB radio's limited range, families living in the bush work together to relay messages. We have spoken to many bush families through relays only and never have met them.

The CB operator in Tanana called one bush family, who called another located further in. They then called another, who called us. With this call relay method, we soon received word of the accident.

The weather really turned sour after that — –50° every night. It was another four days before Jim and Bill could be flown home from Tanana. These could have been life-threatening days spent by the downed plane awaiting rescue.

When Bill returned home, he jumped in his plane and flew to town to borrow a prop off another Citabria. He flew that back and picked up Jim on the way. They flew on to repair the downed plane.

Righting the overturned plane was the hardest part. Then they replaced the propeller with the borrowed spare and taped the windshield. The ski had to be rebolted to the gear leg, where the bolt had sheared off, causing the accident. After all repairs were made, Jim flew the plane out.

As spring approached, we knew we faced a huge job — moving all seven cabins plus the lodge. Jim and Bill discussed the move often over the winter, making their plans. First the seven cabins would be moved from their present sites along the far shoreline.

In April, when the snow settled enough on the lake so plowing was not necessary, we hired Bill and the work began. First Jim and Bill built a V-shaped towing bar out of logs. They attached the wide section to the front of a cabin, and the pointed end to the dozer. Each of the cabins in turn was attached and then towed four miles on the ice to our place. This was difficult and time-consuming work.

The two men worked long hours every day, and after a week, there sat seven cabins all in a row along the front of our property. These were quickly towed off the lake onto ground and left as they were, with no regard of leveling. Having accomplished this much, Bill and Jim tackled moving the cumbersome lodge.

There is only a short period of time each spring when the snow is off the ice, yet the ice is still thick enough to hold such weight. The sun beats upon the exposed ice, and in only about two weeks the ice is no longer safe. One week had been used to move the cabins. One week, no more, remained.

It was obvious that the lodge building could not be moved in one piece, with our limited manpower and machinery. Jim and Bill thought half could be towed in the same manner as the

Cabins on the ice in front of our property.

cabins. Granted, even a half of the lodge structure was heavier than a cabin, but they thought the dozer could do the job.

The lodge sat on a small bluff overlooking the lake. The men would move it backwards, down, and around to the shore. A path had to be cut through the woods — the old burned area — from the lodge to the lakeshore. With the last week of safe ice rushing by, the lodge was cut in half. All the picture windows were taken out, and the building stood like a sad skeleton.

The men brought the dozer in and backed it up to the smaller of the two sections. A prayer was said, and the pull began. Nothing happened . . . except that the dozer couldn't budge it. After another couple hours' effort, Jim and Bill realized this procedure just would not work, as it had so nicely for each of the cabins.

The ice was already receding from the shoreline. Constructing a different towing frame, or taking the lodge apart further, would involve days of work. It was clear that the lodge would not be moved on the ice that year. We had run out of time.

That was probably the most discouraging moment of our entire stay. The lodge would sit at the other end of the lake for another year — split in half now and open to the weather. We were very down and would have liked to give up . . . but we did not. We just aren't made that way!

*　　　*　　　*

Two days later Jim was working with the ranger, our small tractor, on the ice. He fell off the machine. He landed very hard on his left elbow, which would be found to be broken. Jim didn't think it was broken at first, so he didn't make a special trip to have it checked. In just a few days he would take the plane to town and wait for break-up to return on floats.

By the next morning he was convinced his elbow was dislocated. That had happened before, when he was in the navy. We called Bill on the CB for help, since Jim couldn't fly our plane. Bill thought he could still make one more takeoff from his lake. Although the ice there was even thinner, because his lake is shallower.

Bill flew over and picked up Jim, then flew him to Tanana where his elbow was X-rayed. The doctor there said the head of the radius had been fractured: the elbow would have to be pinned in a fixed position for life!

Jim wanted to seek another opinion. Billy brought Jim home and then flew on to his own lake for that evening. The next day they would go to Fairbanks.

By morning Bill's lake was unsafe for takeoff. Now it was up to Jim to fly to town by himself in his own plane, with his broken elbow. The stick of the plane is usually controlled with the pilot's right hand. That was no problem, but the throttle is controlled with the left. Jim cheated a little on takeoff. By using his knees to control the stick, he freed his right hand to reach across and push the throttle forward. Landing would be the tricky part, as knee control then is out of the question.

To be noted here is KJNP, a radio station based in North Pole, Alaska, a town just south of Fairbanks. This station has a special service for all people living in the bush. Each evening, and again early in the morning, the station broadcasts messages from friends or relatives in town. These messages are usually quite short — about 40 are read each night — but each message can be very important to the person listening for it. It may relay information about a plane coming out to pick them up — or announce a snowmachiner's safe arrival in town — after five hours on the trail.

For emergency situations KJNP broadcasts messages, on the hour, all day long. The day Jim flew to town with his broken elbow, he called KJNP as soon as he arrived in Nenana. On the next hour I received the message that he had arrived safely. Then I could breathe again.

Jim went to Kodiak to see our family doctor of six years, who had become our personal friend. This doctor's opinion was that immobilization was not called for, but he is not a surgeon. So, together, he and Jim went to see the surgeon there in Kodiak. That surgeon agreed with the first doctor Jim had seen in Tanana — immobilization.

Our doctor then asked, "What would be wrong with trying a cast for three days, removing the cast, then massaging and working the muscles for the next couple of weeks?"

The surgeon considered this option. He said there was a very small chance it would work. Surgery and the pin could always be considered later, if massage did not work. So, of course, Jim chose to try massage first.

He stayed with his finest two friends in Kodiak, two brothers, Sid and Oluf Omlid. Jim had taught with Sid in the high school there, and Oluf taught in the junior high school where I taught. Our three families knew each other very well.

After three days the temporary cast was removed, and massaging of the arm began. Jim spent at least two hours every evening in Sid's sauna, while the Omlid brothers took turns massaging and working Jim's arm. During the day Jim massaged his arm alone, the best he could. The three of them continued this routine faithfully for two weeks.

After those two weeks, Jim's arm was checked. It was diagnosed as definitely healed (although still quite sore). Jim will always be grateful to Sid, Oluf, and our doctor. Their belief, optimism and willingness to work gave Jim a functioning arm instead of a crippled appendage.

While Jim went through his woes in Kodiak, the kids and I had our own excitement that spring. The ice was away from shore and unsafe for anything. Days were warm, school was out, and we were enjoying ourselves immensely.

Outside one day, Trish calmly said to me, "There's another bear, Mom." Sure enough. Right in our yard was another bear.

We all walked inside, and I got the gun. I, just as any mother, wanted to protect my own. No bear would be welcome near my kids.

We knew from experience trying to scare him away was futile. I raised the gun to my shoulder, one shot, and he was dead. I am fairly good with a gun, but I take no pleasure in using one. This time, there was no one to help butcher, so we knew it was up to us. Justin thought we could do it; Trish was skeptical about the results.

My kitchen is notorious for dull knives. I tried many times, but I could not get the hang of sharpening them, and Jim always had something else to do. Thus it was that the sharpest knife we had was Justin's fish fillet knife with a whopping four-inch blade!

Skipping all the gory details, it was a solid six hours later that we proudly hung four quarters of bear meat in our cooler. We peppered the meat, and it would keep almost indefinitely. The kids, both Trish and Justin, were good sports and a great help. We were exhausted, and the only comment I remember was Justin's, "We really did a good job, Mom, but Dad probably would have finished the job in one hour!"

Later I measured the hide: six and a half feet — very large for a black bear. That was the last bear we had to shoot.

The days were so warm by the middle of May, it felt like heaven on earth after our very cold first winter. The leaves began to bud and the trees, almost overnight, grew their green dresses.

A pair of robins appeared — the first we'd seen at our place. Perhaps because we have a larger area cleared? We saw geese every day returning from the south. I was acutely aware that the flocks were much smaller than when they left last fall. On their migration, many were lost, no doubt some to hunters, and some inevitably to natural causes.

When the ice is broken from shore it is very susceptible to the wind. If the wind blows hard enough, the ice will be pushed along one shore with tremendous power: an oozing monster inching along, piling up slowly but steadily with unrelenting force. Spring breakup has a great destructive power, which should not be taken lightly. Where it unleashes its power depends on the direction of the wind. On our lake the wind almost always blows out of the north or south.

While Jim was still in Kodiak working on his arm, I was sleeping in long johns and wool socks and just letting the woodstove go out at night. In the middle of one night I was awakened suddenly by a loud, piercing, continuous noise outside. I leapt from my bed and looked out the window. I saw the wind coming straight across the lake. This was an east wind — very rare on our lake. All the lake's ice was buckling against our shoreline. The eerie sound I could not identify was the ice pressing against, and piling up on, the floats of the Cessna 180!

All I could see was the almost-$10,000 that goes into a set of 180 floats. I shoved my feet into my boots and rushed down to the lake — in only my long johns.

The fronts of the floats were resting on top of a two-foot bank. The backs of the floats were being set upon by the moving ice monster. Oh, to be a "Wonder Woman," so I could just pick up that plane and set it all the way up on the bank!

On one side of the Cessna was our dock with wooden legs. On the other side, about 30 feet out on the ice was a snow-machine. The kids and I had been trying to get it on to land, but we couldn't get it up that two-foot bank. Instead I pulled it further out, on to safer ice, to try again the next day.

I had to save those floats. I grabbed an axe and began swinging. I chopped ice off the backs of the floats. The wind, of course, steadily moved more ice in to shore. A determination of destruction fighting against my own determination to save the floats.

I chopped ice at one float, rushed to the other float to chop, only to see I must rush back to the first float again. It was a noisy atmosphere, because as the ice piled along the shore, it crumbled and crunched. Suddenly, I heard a loud snap! I jumped as if I were shot.

Three legs of the dock had snapped off. I looked to the other side to see what was happening to the snowmachine. It had reached the shore, and the skis were caught in the bank. The ice continued pushing, and the machine was being lifted vertically. Without a pause, I went back to chopping ice. The snowmachine was nothing in value compared to the set of floats.

I had become so exhausted that the axe weighed a ton and my breath came in gasps. The plane actually had inched forward at least a foot. Now the nose was up in the air like the high end of a teeter-totter. The wind continued. The ice marched on. Another of the dock's legs went, "Snap."

By myself — all alone — standing there in my long johns and boots fighting nature, I cried out loud, "Lord, help me please. I cannot endure and you can."

I continued chopping a couple more minutes before I realized . . . the wind had stopped. No wind; no ice moving. Just stopped dead. There are those who will laugh and say it was a coincidence, but I know that He was listening that day, and He did help me when I cried out.

It was the beginning of a spiritual awakening for me — something fairly strong with me up through college. But I slipped badly thereafter.

This was a new beginning. One I could not even express adequately to those I knew. I thought even Jim would not understand; I was afraid he would snicker. I was a coward. As I write this now, I know that he wouldn't have, but that was how I felt then.

After that, about four a.m., I returned to bed, and I did fall asleep again. I awoke about eight. The wind had evidently come up a little, as the plane was now pointing more skyward. I walked down and inspected the floats. They were fine. All that was damaged were the water rudders and one cable. It was nothing.

On impulse I walked along the top of one float to the tip. The addition of my weight was enough to bring the back end up. The front end touched the ground as the bank was acting like a fulcrum. I rigged up a rope around a tree, to tie the plane up, safe from other destruction by the lake ice.

*   *   *

With such a definite and drastic difference in the seasons here in the interior, spring seems warmer and so much more alive with growth than springs I've experienced other places. With the ice away from the shore, but not completely gone from the lake, the kids and I set off for that year's first canoe outing. How wonderful to skim along the lake and see the bottom again. The water was so clear it appeared to invite us for a swim. The kids, in unison, exclaimed swimming a tremendous idea!

I can remember one day, being their age, I asked my mother about swimming. Ice still remained on the lake, but the day seemed especially warm. I was shocked when she said, "Sure, go ahead, but I bet it will be cold, seeing as how the ice is still here." This was a challenge to me, and after all, I was the one who had asked. I did go swimming, and it was an experience that still brings a gasp in the retelling. My breath was gone as soon as I entered the water.

This day though, skimming quietly along the shoreline, I told the kids to drag their hands in the water for a while. After a few minutes, their hands were once again in the canoe, and the question of swimming was not repeated.

In another two days the ice was gone completely from the lake. The kids and I were again out canoeing. This time we paddled toward the south end of the lake. There we saw our first white whistling swans — three of them in the bay. We tried to approach them slowly, but the swans got nervous and soon took off, unfolding and spreading their massive wings. Gracefully they left the water, circled above us for a minute, and then flew a little and landed about a half-mile away. We did not try to creep up on them again.

We spotted a bald eagle on top of a tall spruce tree. Although we often saw as many as 100 a day in Kodiak, this was the first time we had seen this magnificent bird here in the interior. We watched the eagle for a while and then started home. Along the shore Trish pointed out a small bird bobbing along with skinny legs, which, later we identified as yellowlegs, from the sandpiper family.

Even paddling slowly, it seemed we reached home too quickly that day.

CHAPTER 5

"PROVING UP" THE HOMESTEAD

When Jim returned from Kodiak, his arm was still quite weak. He would have to be very careful using it. Again we decided to hire Billy, to help us with the work involved before our proving-up date arrived.

This was a hectic time of year for us. Each day we worked as much as our bodies would allow. The Cessna 180 was turned around and pointed toward the lake. Jim started the engine and gunned it. He actually forced the plane off the dirt bank and

Cessna 180 coming off the bank.

into the water for the first time that year. Next, more brushing was done at the sites for the cabins. We located a cabin at each end of our land and spaced the remaining five in between. The brush was centralized and piled high. On the first rainy day I began a brush burning party.

Jim and Bill continued to work on the cabins; Jim being careful to favor his injured arm. The final location for five of the seven cabins was time-consuming but not impossible. They were pulled with the dozer over logs strung out horizontally in front of them. Then they were jockeyed into their desired positions. The remaining two cabins were going up on the bluff. Those were the tough ones. The bluff was too steep to pull the cabins up with the dozer.

Preparations on the bluff began. First a path was brushed. Logs were prepared to act as "rolling pins" under the cabin. These logs were laid out horizontally ahead of it, and along the cleared path on up the bluff. Jim and Bill jacked up the front of the cabin, attaching two come-alongs. As they cinched these tight, the building began its crawl up the hill. This travel was literally an inch at a time.

One entire day of work was spent only on inching one cabin up the bluff. After preparations were made for the second cabin, another entire day was spent inching it up the bluff. When these final two cabins were in position, they were jacked up. Blocks were put under them until they were solid and level. Porches would be attached in time.

This would prove to BLM that we were utilizing the shoreline of our property: all the cabins were spaced along the shoreline, with a space left for the lodge building.

We also needed to prove that we were using the back section of our property. We decided on a lookout on top of the mountain behind us. We already had a path to the top of that mountain. The view from there included the full stretch of our five-mile lake, Mt. McKinley and the Alaska Range. We would build a lookout where our guests could sit.

Inching a cabin up the bluff.

Jim was gone again on business in town when we hired Billy to help us one more time. I remembered our house on the bluff was difficult — each load of materials seemed heavier on the trip up. But now we were talking . . . on top of the mountain! The distance is probably less than half a mile — but it is all, steep, uphill. And we were in a hurry. Our proving-up date was approaching at a reckless speed. (We once thought five years was plenty of time to accomplish our desires. Now we were finding it quite short.)

The day Billy arrived to start work on the lookout, the temperature was 85 — very hot for hiking up mountains. Bill is a large man of about 6'1", and he is a diligent worker. I figured I could be of some help.

There were twenty 2x6 12-foot boards to haul up the hill, plus six sheets of plywood and various tools. Bill figured he could carry four boards at a time, so off he went. I thought I could carry three. I hiked one-fourth of the way and returned for another three. This is always an easier way for me to haul such a distance. By my third trip I was down to carrying two boards, but I continued hauling until all the lumber and plywood had been moved one-quarter of the distance.

Meanwhile Billy had returned to my pile and started up again. He soon converted to three boards per trip. Then continuing the relay, I hauled my loads farther up. The day was hot and the work exhausting.

About four hours later I calmly announced as we met at the pile, that if I continued one more minute I would surely die of a coronary. Either 1) we could finish hauling it the next day or 2) if he wanted to finish that same day he could haul it himself. It made me smile to hear him say that the next day was soon enough. He was exhausted too.

Jim at the lookout.

The following day he alone finished hauling the small amount that remained, and he began the building. The lookout structure is of a unique design, and guests comment on it often: an octagonal platform with open walls and an octagonal roof.

Four days later, on my birthday — June 19, 1978 — the BLM inspector arrived from Fairbanks to check out our progress. He carefully looked at locations of all the cabins along the shore. He checked out the lodge, even though it was still at the other end of the lake. And lastly he hiked up to our lookout.

He was very pleased and quite proud when he announced, "I have been checking bush places for quite a while, and yours is the finest I have ever seen. You will have no problem obtaining your land!" We were terribly happy. What a birthday gift!

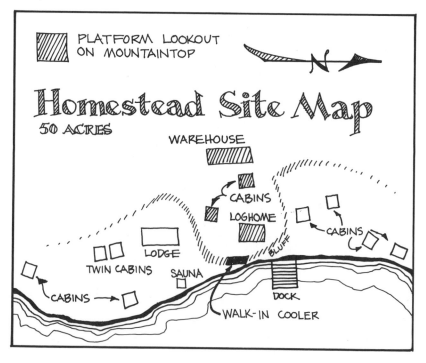

Map of our 50-acre claim.

Later we learned that of the original 12 claims on this lake, seven would not prove up and would lose their land completely. Two claims granted were for five acres. An 80-acre claim was cut down to five and then granted. Still another was a 180-acre claim cut down to 35. Our 50-acre claim came through fine.

During the summer of 1978 we continued using our home as a lodge, and the guests were understanding of the arrangement. One of the cabins had been placed very close to our home. I used this as my "kitchen" and carried meals from there to the "lodge dining room" (our own cabin).

CHAPTER 6

EXPLORING THE NOWITNA

We had been wanting to canoe one of the clear streams in the wilderness of Alaska's interior. The Nowitna River (since designated a Wild and Scenic River) is about a 60-minute flight from our lodge. We expected it to be a good river for our guests' canoe trips. Before we could recommend it, we needed to experience it for ourselves.

After our last guests left in late August, my mom arrived from Minnesota again with Charlotte. Last time they slept in our pole shed, this time we were able to offer them a comfortable cabin.

To prepare for our canoe trip, Jim and Bill each flew one canoe to the river — strapped tightly to one of the plane's floats. Both Jim and Bill have much experience flying exterior loads such as this, but there are many pilots who would never attempt it. It is tricky. If the load has not been tied securely and comes loose during the flight, it can be "the end" for the pilot. The load will begin to wobble and fluctuate in the wind, causing the plane to lose its ability to fly. When flying an external load, no passengers are allowed.

On the day before our trip Jim flew in a load of gear and set up one tent awaiting our arrival. The next morning, Jim first flew in Mom, Justin and Charlotte. Then he returned for Trish and me. Jim knew this area; he had flown over it many times, but it was new territory for me. We all had experience in camping and canoe tripping — even the kids.

Jim flew us above the winding river. It curved back and forth, so we could not judge how many river miles were involved.

I was terribly excited. We had been working so hard all summer, and this would be a vacation for all of us. Soon Jim descended, approaching a small straight stretch in the river. Ever so softly he touched down and then taxied upstream to the spot where he had dropped off Mom, Justin and Charlotte. We unloaded the remaining gear and one excited kid, and Jim taxied downstream to a sheltered bend in the river. He made preparations to leave the plane there while we all left for six days. Billy would meet us at a prearranged place on the river in six days, at 10 a.m. He is as dependable as an old oak tree.

I climbed up the bank and saw Mom working on the tent. I found her sewing shut a huge rip, which ran from the top to the bottom. I asked, "What's up?" She replied, "A bear walked through the tent last night, and I'm sewing the damn thing shut!" Sewing up a tent that a bear had walked into, and then out the door, was nothing to her.

My mother started her American Plan resort, Gunflint Lodge, in northern Minnesota in 1928 and built it up over the next 50 years. *She* has worked 18-hour days, run dog teams, raised a family after divorce, struggled through the Depression, encountered bears and learned what they could do, rebuilt her lodge when it burned to the ground, and put three kids through college. She retired from the lodge after 50 years, handing over the reins to my older brother.

What there was to do, my mom had done. What there was to see, my mom had seen. She has more inner fortitude than any person I have encountered in my life. In Minnesota she has become a legend.

With the tent mended and another tent erected, we made preparations for dinner. We would eat camp food the entire trip, but for this first meal we brought in steaks. This was the true beginning of our week's adventure. There was such a peace —

after flying in gear, setting up camp, and cooking dinner — now sitting on a rock along a fast-moving river with a steak and a cup of camp coffee. The sun set behind the trees, and the air cooled down rapidly. Dishes were quickly washed in the river, and we turned into our tents for the first sleep of the trip.

Jim awakened to a rustle in a nearby bush. He stepped out in his shorts with his pistol and met my mom returning from a call of nature. A good laugh and back to bed!

We began our trip in two canoes: Trish in the center of Mom and Charlotte's canoe; Justin in the center of Jim's and mine. The river ran swiftly at an average of four miles per hour. Thus we were able to figure (after the trip) that we covered approximately 125 miles on the river.

As the river wound back and forth, sandbars formed on each curve. These were quite suitable for camping. Each day we traveled until tired and then just stepped out on shore and set up camp.

Our trip began in heavy woods, but as we progressed along the curves of the river, we entered areas of tundra — a terrain common to much of Alaska.

We got an early start that first morning — off and into the current by eight. By noon we stopped at a sandbar to stretch our legs, let the kids run, and bring out the lunch. We had agreed that we would cook up good, hearty breakfasts and dinners, but have light lunches. So with a cheese and pilot bread sandwich in hand, we strolled along the sandbar to see what we could observe.

We were not the only travelers on this sandbar. We beheld footsteps of bear, moose, wolves and marten. To our delight, we found agates so abundant we literally stumbled over them. Agates are considered semi-precious stones, and we stuffed our pockets like squirrels stuff seeds into their cheek pouches. Then Jim expressed his concern of the added weight when flying back. We promised to fill only our pockets and not our packs.

Within a half hour we all came to the same realization, rather sheepishly. Since we were limited in the weight we could fly back, and since the agates were so available, we'd have to be more selective. Then we started checking our pockets to discard our worst choice before putting in a new one.

These first agates we found were pale yellow, but later ones were darker, more auburn. Sunlight reflected off the surfaces, enhancing the colors. As I write this I check these agates on a nearby shelf — they vary in size from quite small, up to one the size of a softball. Of course, my final collection I considered to be the very best the sandbars had to offer. I'm sure each member of our party felt the same way.

We cleaned up our lunch and proceeded along the river. After we passed a couple of sandbars, we could not stand the suspense. We stopped again. Yes, this sandbar had agates too. Now we were very fussy about the ones we kept. We saw agates for the next 100 miles of river that we traveled.

The second day out we tried our luck fishing. We found the best fishing where a stream fed into the main river. Coming down one stretch, Charlotte had a good strike, saw the fish, but lost it. Mom came up with a large northern pike. After a couple of tries, I hooked into a bright and fighting sheefish. I brought that aboard with Jim's help.

With the current running steadily, it was impossible to stay in one place and fish. If we fished at the Y of an incoming stream, we had only a couple of casts before we were swept further downstream. Turning the canoe around and paddling against the strong current was a real chore, so we continued on our way after catching these first fish. The temptation of having fresh fish for lunch was too great. We stopped to cook it up at the very next sandbar.

Mom and Charlotte were in the lead canoe at this time, canoeing as quietly as possible. We unexpectedly came across a few ducks, so we were even more careful. Because of this, Charlotte only signalled. She thought she heard something special. We cautiously nosed into the bank on our near side of the sandbar, opposite the sound. We landed and stealthily crept up the gravel bar to peer over the other side. There were at least 100 ducks in a little eddy, squawking quite noisily, but contentedly. Inadvertently we made a noise. One duck gave a loud warning call, and a few took off. Like a stampede, with a majority not understanding the cause for alarm, the birds quickly followed the leaders. Soon all were airborne.

Jim quickly cleaned the fish, and we fried them in fry pans over the open fire. We had all eaten northern pike before, but we were anxious to try the sheefish. This was new to all of us. We loved it, but we couldn't say it was better-tasting than the northern.

At almost every gravel bar now we stopped to hunt for treasures. We began with the agates, but soon we were finding artifacts. Jim was first, finding some pieces of old bone. None of us became as perceptive as Jim, a biology major, at finding artifacts. He found many pieces of bones: his greatest find, a camel jawbone complete with teeth. I found an eight-inch piece of fossilized ivory from a mammoth tusk that, 10,000 years before, had been connected to an animal. Trish found a baby tooth — complete and not broken — also of a wooly mammoth. (Finding a whole tooth is quite rare, we learned later.)

Justin, Charlotte and Mom had not done well in their artifact hunting. My mom in particular was quite adamant about all of us "wasting time doing silly things."

Camping again for another evening, the rest went exploring along the shore, as I finished the dishes and went to bed early. They saw large bear tracks, so we knew at least one and probably more bear were around, but we did not see one in the 125 miles we traveled.

Up to this point we had traveled only the main current of the river. This day we explored some of the loops which led off for a distance then rejoined the river further downstream. The current on these loops ran slower, and here we found many active beaver houses. We did not see a beaver but only their handiwork, which is common as they are night workers. In Minnesota beavers build their houses out from shore, and the whole rounded structure is visible. Here the beavers built their houses adjacent to the bank, with about half the house extending into the bank and the other half over the water.

What beavers can do with mud and sticks — their ability of construction — amazes me. Their hard work and determination might be a lesson to those who want others to do the work for them in life.

Once we rounded a corner and came upon many geese. Some were quite young and probably born that spring. One particular goose was unable to fly. Jim and I easily caught up with him, when he tried to swim faster than we could paddle. Jim gently picked him up, then finding no injury, set him back on the water.

We found no rapids to shoot, but there were riffles — shallow areas where we touched bottom slightly. The bowman, especially in the lead canoe, should watch out for water conditions. In one section, Jim and I and Justin stuck to the left side of the river. We didn't have any problem, but Mom, Charlotte and Trish, in the second canoe, decided to run their canoe down the center. In a moment they became high-centered, and the canoe swung around crossways to the current. This can be a serious condition.

Without hesitation Charlotte, who was in the bow, jumped out. While keeping a good hold on the canoe, she turned it in line with the current, pulled it off the rocky bottom and hopped back in. She accomplished this nimble act with an ease that many other grandmothers of 65 would find super human.

Before this, I did not know Charlotte very well. She was a fantastic sport on this trip, and she was always willing to do her share of the work. Charlotte is very kind, always finding the positive in another person. She is a doctor, although not practicing now, and a fine painter.

Charlotte's wish, declared almost daily, was to see an Alaskan moose. She had seen many moose in Minnesota, but they are midgets in comparison. Once we sighted swaying willows, where a moose was retreating into the woods from the river-bank. We had been singing and alerted the moose to our approach. We kidded Charlotte, saying she had seen her moose — she hadn't said she wanted to see a *whole* moose!

That evening, we watched a spectacular sunset. The lower sky, just above the trees across the river, turned a bright pink and deep red for about 15 minutes. When the sun sets at this time of year, (early in September when each day is shorter by six minutes) we can easily feel the approach of fall. We talked a little longer and then eagerly crawled into our sleeping bags of cozy warmth.

About 2 a.m. I awoke to the sound of a beaver's tail slapping the water. Usually this warns of danger, but I have seen beavers slap the water for no apparent reason. Laying awake I listened to an occasional slap as the beavers moved about, foraging and feeding. After this full day, I felt contented with the sounds of nature around me.

On our next two days' travel, the tundra gave way to a taiga area, being more wooded. Birch trees, now starting to change color, were interspersed with evergreens. The colors were still quite mixed: green leaves in abundance but plenty of yellows and oranges with occasional reds. Under the trees were carpets of red cranberries and the taller rosehips so abundant in vitamin C.

During the course of the day we came upon three old trapping shacks. The one closest to shore was just some rotten wood where a cabin had once stood. The second cabin was set high on a bank, back from the river, so only the chimney could be seen.

We beached and eagerly scrambled up the bank to investigate. This was a usable cabin, about 10x12 feet, handmade from

Charlotte (left) and Justine at the trapper's cabin.

logs. There had been a cleared yard, which now stood overgrown. To one side of the house was a low motel arrangement of six individual rooms with doors. One section of the roof was crushed by a large fallen tree, yet this was recognizable as a motel doghouse — much less work than building six separate doghouses. This trapper obviously had a dog team.

The door to the house was not locked. Entering we knew at a glance, that a bear had entered through the window. If windows are not boarded when leaving a cabin in the interior for a time, bears will enter, creating havoc inside.

The cabin had been quite comfortable. There were bunk beds against the far wall and a woodstove in the front corner near the door. A small table sat by the window, now covered with broken glass, with the bench overturned nearby. Food left in the cabin was strewn around. What interested us was a half-finished sled runner being carved from a tree. Obviously the trapper had broken a runner on his dog sled. We guessed the age of this place at not more than five years.

Alaska is full of hearty trappers who build cabins and trap every winter. A flier like Jim would file this location in his brain — a survival shelter for a future emergency.

As we canoed along, we noticed that in many areas the riverbanks were quite high, rising steeply on both sides. We visualized how, when the river flooded, (as it had that previous spring) the sides of the steep banks would break off, uncovering

The motel doghouse.

the artifacts — mastadon tusks, teeth and various bones — which we discovered on this trip.

Now in early fall, the water level was more normal, and so we could see many, many holes going back into the bank. We realized these were homes of bank swallows. This smallest of swallows in North America nests where the ground is soft (must be in a bank). Their feeding areas are close to their nests, which they build at the end of tunnels.

The last part of that day we slipped through an area with high bluffs on either side, rounded a sweeping curve, and beached for the final camp of our canoe trip. The next day Billy would meet us. Here Jim had set up another tent, but there was no sign of it from the river. After searching we found it, flattened, apparently by a raging storm passing through.

Mom and Charlotte went off to fish, and the kids searched for that last special agate or artifact. In this locale the agates were scarce, and the artifacts (although ever present) were harder to find. We ate fresh fish leisurely around the campfire that night. We had seen so much in this heartland of Alaska, and our trip had been such great fun, that all of us were sad at its ending.

In the morning a mist hung in on the river reducing visibility. We were able to see the far shore straight across, but we could not see upriver even a very short distance. The mist was thinning above us, and we began to feel the sun's presence. We knew that as the morning air warmed, the mist would evaporate, and another clear day would follow. We had not encountered any rain on our trip but had watched clouds gather and rain pour over the far hills.

We ate breakfast early, giving us time before our 10 a.m. rendezvous with Billy.

Now Mom just hates to do dishes. She had quite expertly avoided washing them the whole of the trip. That morning we all kept after her until finally she said, "Oh hell, all right, I'll do the damn things." Thus she was kneeling at the water's edge and thought she saw something that resembled an artifact. She reached for something that maybe was a rock, but then maybe it wasn't. She picked it up and called Jim. She had the grand treasure of the trip! A whole adult wooly mammoth tooth 10,000 years old. It was about 12" long, 4" across the top and 8" deep. She was standing there holding this old, old tooth and smiling with such amazement.

Of course all of us wanted to keep hunting, right there, and see if we could match the glory of her find. (Dirty dishes were long forgotten.) But we had to break camp and pack.

Billy arrived right at 10 to pick up Jim and shuttle him back to his plane. Hopefully it was still tied securely where we left it six short days before. The rest of us had about an hour then to make a bigger 'find,' but to no avail. Soon we heard the two planes approaching. Skimming in to two perfect landings, they both taxied to shore. We threw gear in and watched Bill

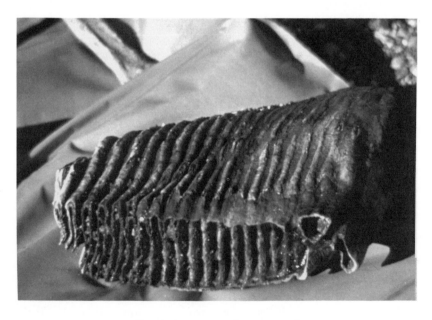

Tooth from a wooly mammoth.

Artifacts and agates.

leave with Mom and Charlotte. Jim then took off with the kids and me. In an hour we were gliding slowly to the water on Wien Lake and home.

Indeed this trip had been most rewarding. The only thing desired and not received was Charlotte's sighting of a *WHOLE* moose.

Mom and Charlotte turned in after dinner to their individual cabin. We planned breakfast at eight, then Jim would fly them back to Fairbanks for their flight to Minnesota. I was up about seven, making breakfast for all, when Charlotte came rushing up so flustered that she could hardly speak. She had just crawled out of bed when she heard footsteps clumping across the wooden bridge on the path to their cabin. Still in her pajamas she went to the door window to look out. There stood a bull moose, complete with large rack, about 10 feet in front of her cabin! He was not aware of the cabin's inhabitants. He looked this way, then that, proudly showing off like a vain male.

Charlotte was beside herself. Should she attempt a picture through the door window and chance a reflection? Or would it be better to open the door? She took a couple of pictures through the window. Then as the moose slowly ambled toward the lakeshore, she opened the door ever so cautiously and took a couple more. The moose turned right and disappeared down the lakeshore.

After breakfast the two women boarded the Cessna 180, and Jim flew them to Fairbanks for their flight to Minneapolis.

From the heart of Alaska to the heart of the Twin Cities — quite a change in one day's time.

CHAPTER 7

OUR SECOND WINTER

That fall Billy, his wife Becky, and their two children returned to town and back to work. They had hoped to make a living by winter trapping, but they found that, although this might sustain a lone trapper each year, it was not enough income to sustain a family of four.

Almost all homesteaders came to the identical conclusion. The cost of living here in the bush interior, where all things must be flown in, is beyond belief. We had seen our share of the hippies come in with the idea of building a log cabin for nothing, in just a couple weeks' time, and then living happily ever after. These failed first and did not prove up on their land.

Then there were the more "stable" individuals who held very good jobs, but like us, decided on this kind of venture for one reason or another. These thought that they, through their savings and a lot of determination and hard work, would make it on trapping. These people took much longer to return to town. Usually they gained some amount of land and a nice bush home. In this region we were the only ones who did not try trapping, opting for the resort instead. We were still hanging on, but only by a thread.

The winter of 1978-79, our second, was looking easier for us. We had one winter under our belts so we knew more of what to expect. And wonder of all wonders, we were to enjoy weekly mail delivery — a luxury.

Once again Jim flew all our winter food in. After using over 20 cords of wood the previous winter, we added a large woodstove in the basement. This stove would not require every piece to be split before digesting as the Franklin did.

School began and was attacked enthusiastically by Trish and Justin as they now realized more fully that the harder they worked, the earlier they would be finished to enjoy the spring. By now Trish was ten and Justin almost seven. They were more responsible, and more definite jobs were assigned to each of the them.

Their day began with school on the dot of eight, running until lunch at 12. After lunch they carried in firewood for the stoves. Justin was responsible for filling the woodbox upstairs and Trish the one in the basement. They took turns filling the Coleman lanterns, an every-other-day chore for them. Then they streaked out the door to ski or toboggan, or to pack down Jim's runway with the snowmachine.

After dinner Justin stacked the dishes, Trish washed and rinsed them, and Justin put them away. In the evening they generally read, carved wood or worked on a craft kit. They were never bored.

Jim and I started teaching them to cross country ski when we were still in Kodiak, and they were four and seven. The time we spent teaching them paid off many times over, as they both became avid skiers.

When Billy and his family moved back to town, we cared for his husky dog until they got settled. He forgot to mention that their dog was very pregnant indeed. So it was, that one night in November, she blessed us with 12 squealing puppies. The kids quickly picked out a rusty brown colored puppy for their own and fell in love with it. They tried to persuade Jim to allow them to keep this puppy; a difficult task, as we already had one dog and one cat. In the end they won with his stipulation that this would be an *outside* dog! They readily agreed. But of course Rusty, by the time he was full-grown, came inside anytime he wanted. He has earned his keep, though. We didn't have a bear in our yard, after Rusty's arrival. And the kids worshipped him.

That month there was a moose season. The regular season is in September of every year, and then, every now and then, there is a November season in certain areas around the state. Jim invited Sid and Oluf Omlid up from Kodiak for a hunt. He wanted to repay them for their time and effort in saving his elbow. Jim met them in Fairbanks and flew them to our home for an overnight. The next morning's temperature was -30°. Even so they flew to the area open for hunting and set up their camp.

Now winter camping isn't my idea of fun. The guys were all wearing long johns, down pants and jackets, insulated bunny boots or Sorel packs. They had good face masks and slept in very good down bags in a tent. They had a small woodstove, and they said they were comfortable.

The law says that one cannot fly and hunt on the same day. So they snuggled in early to begin their hunt the following day. On that first day hunting, they got a moose. Taking care of a large animal at those temperatures becomes quite a chore, with the meat freezing instantly.

The following day another moose was taken. Then Jim flew Oluf and the first moose back to our house. Jim went back for Sid, but they ran out of daylight. So Jim and Sid spent a third night in the tent. Then they returned with the second moose. We kept one moose for our winter meat, and they returned to Kodiak with the other. These fellows often talk about their winter hunting trip, but they have not repeated camping out at those temperatures!

While we were still in Kodiak, I wanted to take a wood-carving class. I asked Jim many times to sign up with me, and he finally agreed. We each carved a few pieces there and learned the fundamentals of woodcarving.

During that second winter in the bush, since we had most of our firewood up for the winter, Jim had time to do something he wanted to do — work more on his woodcarving. By spring he completed a couple of decorative carvings for each of our cabins. Probably from his study of animals and birds through his biology classes, Jim became the real woodcarver of the family. His carvings include ducks, swans, owls, fox, squirrels, and, one of my favorites, a camp robber on the handle of an axe. This was one of his first carvings.

The second winter in the bush we had more snow than our first. That year there were no problems with flying on skis, but this second year, flying became difficult. After snowfalls, a gusty wind built up snow dunes on the lake, much like sand dunes in a desert. The lake was not level, but an open expanse of small knolls. Landing a ski plane and running a snowmachine were both difficult. More snow kept falling, heavy and sticky.

Jim was using a set of wooden skis on his plane. In the fall he had coated the skis' undersides with a black *paint*, similar to that used on downhill skis. That smooth coating slid well on snow and reduced sticking. But as winter progressed, and with frequent landings on the plowed, gravel runway in Nenana scraping off the coating, each takeoff became more difficult.

Jim parked the plane on a small tree laying crossways on the ice. The skis were off the ice and could not freeze to the lake.

Once when Jim was leaving for town, he checked the undersides of the skis to make sure they were clean. After his preflight check, he gunned the engine to get a good running start. The plane came off the log easily, but then slowly lost its momentum — with the engine on full power.

Jim cut the engine and stepped out to start over again. We shoveled long paths in front of each ski. We cleaned around the skis and underneath them as best we could. I stayed just behind a wing strut. Jim climbed in and started the engine again. Holding the strut, I pulled down and back up quickly, rocking the plane so the skis would not stick. As the engine increased its power, the plane moved forward nicely on the 60 feet of shoveled tracks. As soon as the skis hit the unshoveled snow, the skis stuck and the plane stopped.

Our next attempt was the same general process. Two tracks in front of the skis. This time we put plastic garbage sacks over the skis' tips (and as far back as the bags allowed). We had heard that, if desperate, this might work. We were desperate.

Jim started the engine again. I bounced the strut to loosen the skis, and he opened the throttle. As soon as I realized the skis were not sticking, I pushed with all I had from behind one of the wing struts. I was pushing and running faster, as the plane actually picked up speed. At the last moment, the plane lifted off the snow. After pushing so hard while running in knee-high snow, I stood there waving, gulping in huge amounts of air to catch my breath.

That second winter, with those particular skis and the heavy snow, was the most difficult for ski flying. When spring came and Jim took off those skis, he said he'd never use them again. And he never did.

There was an advantage to that heavy and sticky snow of our second winter in the bush. It was just the right consistency for snowforts, snowballs and snowmen. Usually snow in the interior has a granular texture, like sugar or salt and not sticky at all.

One spring morning we awoke to a white wonderland with a fresh, heavy snowfall. Justin and I went outside when school was out for the day. Trish stayed in to read. Justin started by making a small snowball and rolling it all over the yard. It grew too large for either of us to lift, so we rolled it near the house, where we wanted the snowman to stand. Next it was my turn, and I rolled a ball to be slightly smaller. Together we lifted this snowman's chest into place. Justin made the head, and we placed that on top with ease. It now stood about six feet tall.

We carved out arms with mittens in the center section and features on the face. We even added a pair of costume glasses left over from Halloween. I stepped back to look and asked Justin why it had to be a man. Laughing heartily we changed the shape to resemble a woman's body and declared it a masterpiece!

CHAPTER 8

MOVING A LODGE — THE HARD WAY

As spring approached and the time to move the lodge was near, Jim searched in Nenana for someone to help move the building. Jim wanted to be ready for those crucial few weeks, when the lake conditions were right. Jim spoke with a housemover and explained the conditions relating to the building, the distance to move it, and the equipment we had available. The mover said this would be a *cinch*. He estimated five days, including putting the two pieces together again. We hired him.

When the snow conditions on the lake were favorable for the operation, Jim flew him out. After he actually saw the building and the distance, he became quite apprehensive. But he was still willing to try. On the first day of work, snow was plowed around the building and along a path to the lake. The second day, the housemover was running the dozer, and it got stuck in the snow. Then the track came off and a section broke. With the dozer not operating, work stopped. Jim flew the housemover back to town and ordered parts for the dozer.

About 10 days later the parts arrived in Fairbanks. Jim brought them back to the lake and repaired the dozer. Then the housemover decided he didn't want to move that building after all. Now we were really desperate. We had already used up two weeks of good lake conditions.

The next time to town, I was along. Jim and I went to see our good friend Wayne Walters. He was the city police officer, and he knew everybody in town. He suggested two young guys who were hard workers. When we asked where we could find them, Wayne said that they were probably at the bar. We weren't hopeful, but we proceeded to the bar anyway.

This was 11 a.m., so the bar was fairly empty. We sat down with these guys and explained our problem. They had quite a bit of building experience between them, but their expertise was in building, not moving a building.

We talked a long time. They each asked questions which gave us the impression that they knew what was involved. In the end, their recommendation was to take the building completely apart, haul the materials down the lake and build it again! With no breakdowns, they figured the moving would take less than a week, and then rebuilding could begin.

Jim took a big gulp of beer and I took a bigger gulp of soda. We looked at each other, and we thought about that. We had decided that that building was *not* going to be left another year at the other end of the lake. It appeared we had no choice, so we shook hands on it. The following day, the guys were flown into the lake, and they began work that same day.

We agreed on a set price for the job, so any ideas of a time-clock were thrown out the window. For the next five days these guys and Jim averaged 16 hours of work per day each. The two young guys started ripping the building apart, but carefully. They knew these materials were all we had for rebuilding the lodge. Jim built a 4x8' sled to pull behind the ranger. He began hauling materials from the old lodge site to the ice in front of the new lodge site.

After five days the lodge site was empty, except for scraps of tar paper roofing and broken pieces of floor tile. In contrast our end, near where the lodge would be rebuilt, looked like a used lumber lot. The picture windows were neatly and carefully laid out (with a stern warning to Rusty not to walk across them). There were stacks of 2x4s, 2x6s, plywood, ceiling tiles, paneling, T-111 siding, rafters, insulation, kitchen cupboards, a circular fireplace and a large bar cut in half.

Lodge materials out on the lake.

Then all that lumber had to be denailed.

Jim flew the workers back to town. They had a job starting that Monday. But they would come back Friday night to start building. Jim had a few days' business again, so the denailing job fell on my shoulders. The kids had finished school, and that was in my favor.

On Monday morning, I set up two sawhorses on the lake. I threw the first 2x6 across the top, took hold of a good hammer, and began.

Like approaching any job that is huge, I forced myself to concentrate on that one board only and on getting that one "clean" of nails. Without looking around, I then placed that board in my slow-to-grow clean pile, picked up my next board and continued. If I looked up each time and saw just how many remained, I am sure I would have given up.

For three straight days, 10 hours a day, I pulled nails until I felt like a zombie. I was almost finished when Jim returned Wednesday evening. We spent Thursday working together, finishing the denailing drudgery.

On Friday we started dragging the lumber from the lake to our chosen lodge site. Up on the bluff, naturally, but this area is not as steep as it is by our house. I loaded six boards behind a snowmachine and ran up the bluff. Jim unloaded and stacked the boards in a neat pile, while I returned for another trip. We continued this process all day Friday. By the end of the day, a good share of the lumber was up on the bluff.

Our workers were due that evening. George Hobson, the very dependable pilot who managed Nenana Air Service and flew our mail out once a week, would bring them.

Friday got later and later, and no plane arrived. I waited supper. Finally at nine we sat down and ate. Without them, we were really stuck. Jim and I didn't think we had the building knowledge to proceed on our own. We called George on our radio phone. He said the guys did not show up. He would do everything possible to track them down for us.

Saturday, at 11 in the morning, we heard the far-off drone of George's plane. (Yes, we could identify planes by their sounds, after some practice.) George landed and dumped them out. They had a drink Friday night after work in Fairbanks before driving to Nenana. One drink turned into many, and the night wore on. They drove to Nenana Saturday morning and were immediately snagged by George.

I will never know how these guys did it. They looked in bad shape, but with some strong coffee and a good lunch, they started work at one, and didn't quit until 9 p.m. All four of us worked, but Jim and I were definitely the gophers and they the bosses.

We began by 7 a.m. Sunday and worked steadily all day. We had the advantage of pre-cut lumber which Jim had carefully stacked according to size, and by that evening we were able to stand back and see: the foundation of logs completed, the floor down (dimensions 24x32'), the studded walls up, and the rafters in place.

George Hobson's only day off was Sunday, but he agreed to pick the guys up. He arrived late that night to return our workers to town. They would come the following weekend to work and get us to the point where Jim and I could finish on our own.

For the next five days we hauled all the remaining materials up from the lake and piled them around the lodge. The only things remaining on the lake by week's end were the picture windows. Moving those would be safer with four people than two. This time the guys arrived on Friday night, right on schedule.

That weekend the windows went in; the roof and most of the siding were put on. The lodge was looking good. We had located the building exactly where we wanted it, and we had changed the design more to our liking. We could not have accomplished as much without these young guys — two of the finest workers we have ever worked with. They returned to town Sunday evening.

Jim and I finished with the remaining siding, and then we installed the circular fireplace. That last little chore took almost a whole day, as we approached it backwards. By that Wednesday the ice was getting black. It had broken away from the shore in some places, although not yet in front of the lodge. This would be George's last mail day until after break-up.

We used everything salvagable from the original structure, as we were once again broke. All our remaining reserve was used to repair the dozer — well over $1,000. The lodge structure was now basically finished on the exterior, but it needed new roofing material. The idea of leaving the building with a leaky roof was sickening to us, but we just did not have the money.

Amazingly, on that last mail day, Wednesday May 2, 1979, a letter came from my mom. I read it while Jim was showing

George our progress on the lodge. In this letter was a check with a note, "Thought this might come in handy about this time." I hadn't written her except to say we were busting our guts to get things done before break-up.

George, knowing we desperately needed the material, offered to make one more trip the next morning. On his return to town that day, after finishing his mail route, he would obtain our roofing material. There was no extra money in this for George, yet it would take a lot of extra time. But George was a different kind of man. He often did extra things for his clients, and this made him very popular with the people he flew for.

George left to continue his route, and we crossed our fingers.

By now, the ice was receding from the shoreline and becoming crystallized. It was approaching the point of being unsafe for landing. Evenings were still cool enough to firm up the top, but by afternoon it became quite slushy prohibiting the landing of a ski plane. Jim was getting desperate himself to leave the lake with his own plane.

The next morning at 6 a.m., we heard the sound of George's plane again. Not trusting the ice close to shore, he landed out a couple hundred feet. George unloaded the roofing, smiled, and he was off. He had called the lumberyard as soon as he arrived back to town the day before. They trucked the roofing to the airport. George loaded up his plane that same evening. Then he left at 5 a.m. to insure the safe ice conditions.

We could never adequately express our gratitude to him. Many charter outfits are all business and would never consider doing an "extra" for a bush person.

Jim and I pulled the 90-lb. rolls of roofing to shore on the toboggan. By this time there was no snow on the ground; we could not use snowmachines. Jim and I had to carry the roofing up the hill, one roll at a time. I could just barely lift that much, so I waddled much slower than Jim.

Jim watched the ice closely and judged he could stay two more days before leaving with his plane. We worked two long days and finished roofing the building. The lodge was waterproof!

Then Jim left the lake for Georgia to pick up a new Maule aircraft from the factory. We would lease this new plane for the next year. A week after he left on skis, the ice was completely gone from the lake. Planes were landing with floats!

Jim's trip outside to pick up the plane was both exciting and tiring. The plane wasn't ready, as the factory said it would be. He waited two weeks. It still wasn't ready, so he returned home. After another week, the factory guaranteed it to be ready. Jim returned to Georgia and flew the new plane back across the lower states and then up the Alaskan Highway. She was beautiful and, of course, was treated with the respect of a new Mistress by Jim.

Maule M-5 on floats.

CHAPTER 9

FRIENDS, GUESTS AND WORKERS

Jim's instructor's rating had lapsed. Now he was determined to renew it. This entailed becoming proficient in another aircraft and being tested. By proficient, I mean perfect. If the instructor said to a test candidate, "Land there," he meant exactly that. Ten feet off was disallowed. Jim would have no problem taking the test in the Maule, but the FAA ruled the test must be taken in a retractable gear aircraft. It didn't make sense, but it was the way of things. Daily, Jim flew to Fairbanks in the Maule (on floats), took instruction in another aircraft which was on wheels, then flew home in the evening. He was not available for much work on the lodge, so I proceeded at my own pace and ability.

I insulated the building by stapling the batts in place and then stapling clear plastic over that. Next I paneled the kitchen with some of the old paneling. New paneling, ordered for the lounge and dining room, had not arrived. There was a large bar in the lounge of the original lodge. As this was not our desire, I took the bar apart — enough to form my kitchen counters. Next, I put in shelves for all my dishes. Tables and chairs were flown in for the dining room.

In between Jim's daily flying, he moved my stove and double sink down from our home. We opened for business by the middle of June that year. The lodge wasn't finished but it was usable. We expected the paneling to arrive soon. We received word that it was in Fairbanks, awaiting a larger charter plane, which could carry the paneling in whole 4x8' sheets.

Jim was away on business again when two of my friends from Milwaukee came to visit for a couple of weeks. They expected to be on vacation, but I had every intention of having them help me in the hundred thousand things yet to do.

Genie and Ellen are both teachers, so they had the summer free. They are fun-loving college friends of mine, and they arrived just bubbling with enthusiasm. Jim and I were astonished when they presented us each with a T-shirt with "Arctic Tern Lodge" on the front. We immediately put them on.

The morning of their second day here, we decided to clean up the site where the lodge had stood on the north end of the lake. We packed a lunch and headed out with the kids in tow. We took rakes and a shovel and spent the morning making two large piles of roofing debris and broken floor tiling and other scraps. We torched it off and sat down for a tasty lunch. A breeze was coming up, but it was not strong enough to cause concern with our burn piles. We took turns keeping an eye on the fires and exploring around that end of the lake. The breeze started to pick up.

By late afternoon, we felt safe leaving the fires. We heavily soaked the remains and prepared to go home. The five of us had come down the lake that morning by catamaraning two canoes together with our small 2hp motor on my canoe. By now the wind was whipping around and forming frothy white caps on the lake.

With difficulty we got the two canoes off the beach and headed south. Ellen helped push off and then nimbly jumped into one of the canoes and yelled for me to start the motor. It started on the first pull, and we were off . . . we thought.

After about 10 minutes we realized two things: 1) we had gone no more than 25 feet forward, and 2) the canoes were filling with water. We thought it advisable to return to shore before we sank.

There we were on the north end of the lake, and Jim was due to call from town at six that evening. If we didn't answer he would be concerned, so we knew we had to walk home.

We weren't particularly excited about walking the four miles back to our resort after working most of the day. It was rough walking — through swamps, heavy woods, and over a river. We were constantly pestered by mosquitoes swarming around our faces, but we finally arrived home. Jim called at six, and he had no idea what we had gone through to receive his call.

When Jim came home, he brought another friend of mine, Louise Rota, from Seattle. She was a student in the first class I taught. We had kept in touch over the years, as she finished high school, then college, then became a successful teacher. My daughter Trish's middle name is Louise, after her.

Louise was quickly warned by Genie and Ellen how they were being worked after only a couple days' stay. If she wasn't tough enough, she better turn around while she still could. She decided to stay, and then I began working them all in earnest.

Together we dug two new outhouse holes. Just digging holes sounds simple, but in fact it is difficult here because of the permafrost. After many false starts, we learned there is no permafrost where a birch tree stands. Invariably there is near a spruce tree. Makes sense as birch roots go straight down, and those of a spruce tree spread outward for anchoring.

Genie and Louise started work on the "yard" in front of the lodge, which needed lots of work. Ellen and I alone began building an outhouse over one hole, with not much in our favor except determination and strength. We did finish that outhouse, too. Although it is peculiar in one sense: the seat is really too high. To use it, you need to be a very tall person or jump up to the seat!

We would move the old outhouse over the other new hole. We thought if we jacked it up and placed a long pole under each side, four of us could pick it up and carry it. The day of this move, Jim was home. He held one end of a pole; Genie, Ellen and Louise held the others. I was to take pictures, as this struck all of us as being hilarious. On the command, "Lift," they raised the outhouse and discovered almost immediately, it was too tall to balance on such a small base. It was just plain top heavy. Carrying the outhouse wouldn't work.

Our next plan was to lay it down and roll it. Thus it was, the four of them rolled the outhouse and then righted it over the hole, while I frantically took pictures. We all laughed so hard we cried. Unfortunately I had loaded the film improperly. So our pictures of this outrageous scene remain only in our memories.

Our first guests of the summer arrived the first of July. They were very understanding about using an unfinished lodge. In addition to fishing on Wien Lake, Jim flew them to other lakes to fish or flew them sightseeing almost daily. They were good people and took part in our family, rather than remaining outsiders.

When these guests left, we had a week free. (Then it was a steady flow until the end of August.) Genie and Ellen had to leave; their time was up. Louise, who had only three days to go, decided to stay an extra week to help out further. So Louise and I set to work together to get as much done as possible. Jim was still working on his instructor's rating.

Louise and I painted the used tile on the kitchen ceiling. Then the lounge ceiling. We put new ceiling tile in the dining room, although neither of us had done that before. We constructed a double bed for one of the cabins using leftover lumber. We then painted the whole exterior of the lodge building. Lastly we started work on a permanent cement and rock base for the circular fireplace. A frame had been built around the base. We needed to cement rocks in place, and we would make a lip around the cemented area for sitting around the fire.

Jim arrived late and was eating his dinner, when Louise and I mixed up the cement and started working. Jim didn't want to do it as he was very tired. At the same time he wasn't sure Louise and I were capable. Reluctantly, Jim started cementing, and Louise and I handed him rocks. Within a couple of hours we were finished.

On Louise's last day we had guests in again: two ladies who wanted Louise and me to show them a good day. It was a very warm, cloudless day, with only a slight breeze. In all senses, the day was perfect. We all jumped in the boat and started south with the idea of doing the whole lake. (Neither of the women guests had ever caught a fish before.) Louise and I thought we'd start them out fishing, and within an hour, we had caught plenty for dinner. We then put our rods away and proceeded along the east shore.

I was hoping to show them a moose which had been hanging around. Sure enough, about halfway down that side of the lake we saw a huge moose standing along the shore. The ladies were ecstatic, even though they couldn't get their cameras ready before the moose strolled back into the woods. Continuing around the lake, we stopped in another place and picked blueberries for pancakes the following morning.

We returned to the lodge and packed a picnic lunch for a climb to the lookout on the mountain behind the lodge. This was a gasping trip for the ladies, but they were really good sports about it. They were both very pleased with the view of the entire lake. Mt. McKinley and the Alaska Range stood clear and stark, unobstructed by cloud cover. We leisurely ate our lunch and lazed around. We had indeed given the guests a full day of activity.

With great sorrow I watched Louise leave that evening. We had become very close and shared our innermost feelings and thoughts during all the work we had done together. Here, as a female in the bush with mostly men around, it was a rare treat for me to share personal feelings with another. Louise had helped me so much, working side by side, and now the plane lifted off, and she was gone. I was very depressed afterwards, but work helped.

More guests arrived, and now I worked without the help of any other woman. My day began at 6 a.m. and often would run straight through until 10 p.m. as I cooked, waited on tables, baked, did dishes, cleaned cabins, washed clothes and also tried to be a hostess. Jim was flying every day and could not help me. The kids helped as they were able.

The new paneling arrived late one night and was unloaded. Jim had time to put up only five sheets, so I worked on it as I could. The guests went on daily flying excursions, so I would put up a couple of sheets in the afternoon, then go back to the kitchen to prepare for dinner. Our guests enjoyed finding a little more done each day on their return. Finally I completed the paneling, leaving a lot of trimming to do.

We had two "non-guest" free days in August, and we asked George to bring in his family. We wanted to repay him for his extra effort in obtaining and bringing in our lodge roofing. We met his wife Judy for the first time, and she and I found we had much in common. She has her degree in Physical Education, as I have, although she also received her Masters in Elementary Education. She is the only woman I have met, besides my mom, who handles a canoe as it should be. We canoed often those two days they were here, and we became good friends easily.

One day soon after the Hobsons had gone back to town, I was outside the lodge and heard high-pitched yells and the beginning of a scream. The kids had permission to take the boat out by themselves and were fishing in the bay close by. My heart stopped, but my legs reacted automatically and rapidly took me toward them. I thought they had fallen out of the boat.

But I saw two kids in the boat, and Justin was rowing toward me as fast as his little arms could pull on the oars. My heart resumed its normal rhythm, and I sat down to await their arrival.

Justin in the bow and Trish in the stern.

A 15-pound northern, the largest fish either had ever caught, lay on the bottom of the boat. They were both explaining together, so it took some diplomacy to get the full story out, with equal attention to each child.

Seems as though Justin hooked it, and Trish netted it, but she couldn't lift its weight. The fish was flopping madly in her net. Justin dropped his rod and together they lifted the net, with their prize catch, into the boat. They were so excited that they had squealed and slapped each other on the back.

The last week in August, Judy Hobson invited Trish and Justin to town for a week. Justin declined, but Trish accepted. She attended the Fairbanks fair, enjoyed a birthday party and rode the train to Mt. McKinley Park for a picnic. Jim flew Justin to another lake for an overnight of camping and fishing, then to the river where we had canoed the fall before. On this trip Justin found the largest piece of fossilized ivory in our collection. As for me, I slept and relaxed from a hectic and fast summer.

The first part of September Jim suggested that our family do something together. We decided to visit a smaller lake located south of us, which we called Sinclair Lake after Sandy Sinclair, a homesteader there.

Jim had helped Sandy quite a few times, and Sandy had offered in return a stay in his cabin. Sandy was a teacher, already returned to work in Washington. We packed up our sleeping bags and a little food and left.

Sinclair Lake is a pretty lake and quite small — no larger than a half-mile square. We found lots of ducks at one end — the second time that I saw more than 100 ducks together.

Sandy's snug cabin sits low up on a small hill. Unlike some cabins built in the open, his blended into the scenery inconspicuously. Sod was used for the roof, which now had red cranberries growing all over it.

Sandy had, when building his cabin, tired after raising the walls five feet. Then, with insight, he decided to dig down. From the outside the house looked low, but on entering, you stepped down, and the ceiling, then, was of normal height. The floor was dirt but very hard — packed down from use. A woodstove and a small table stood in one corner. Along two other walls were homemade twin beds. Two small windows were the only source of light, but only because Sandy had not flown in larger windows. In the bush, you make do and build with what you have.

We enjoyed staying the night at Sandy's cabin. After waiting for the morning mist to rise, along with hundreds of ducks, we were once again airborne, and this time headed for the Yukon River. Jim had met an old sourdough fisherman on the river during the summer and wanted the kids and me to meet him.

Since it was the first of September, the fall colors were near their peak. From the air, the terrain appeared as a carpet of colors as far as we could see: yellows, oranges, greens. The colors were so vibrant they seemed unreal.

This was my first time approaching the Yukon River — that fast-moving river which I had read so much about in the poems of Robert Service. Now it was a reality for me. The area we approached was a very deep canyon with high rocky cliffs on both sides. We descended with the sun shining brightly on one side and the other side in shadow — a descent in contrast. Jim *greased* the Maule onto the river as lightly as touching a feather. He taxied toward a handmade dock jutting out from the riverbank. A lone figure stood on the dock. It was my first sight of Tom.

He looked about 50, although later I discovered he was in his 70s. He had about a three-day growth of gray whiskers on his weatherbeaten face, and he wore baggy pants with no belt, a once-white T-shirt with a couple of holes and a pair of hard-worn tennis shoes.

Tom was congenial and happy to show us all around. Apologetically he informed us that he had already taken out his fishwheel for the season. He stored it high up on the beach, where it would be safe. During spring breakup, the ice roaring down the Yukon grabbed onto anything it could reach, much like a young child in a candy store for the first time.

He offered to throw in a small gill net and show us how it worked. The kids and I had not seen this done before.

Tom directed us to his boat. This was a well-used flat bottom boat. He had made it from flotsam he rescued from the river. We jumped in, sat on the bottom and tried to stay out of his way. Tom placed a small net carefully on the top front of the boat, and then jumped in as surefooted as a cat. One pull on the outboard, and we began backing away from the rocky shore. We proceeded downstream to an eddy behind a large rock, where he threw one end of the net out and watched carefully as the remainder fed out from his coil with no hint of getting tangled. Tom kept hold of the net's end, ran the boat to the beach, nimbly jumped out and secured that end on a hook he had installed there for that purpose. Then we headed back to the dock.

The dock was anchored to shore but the side in the river was in deep water. On one end stood a well-scrubbed table. At the other end of the dock I saw brushes and pushbrooms used, I learned, to scrub fish slime and remains off the dock surface. Fish remains were always thrown into the river as food for other fish.

Tom offered to give me the grand tour. He had a screened drying house and a large smokehouse (24x30'), both made from flotsam rescued from the river.

There was no way for fishermen along the Yukon to get fresh fish to town to sell. They were forced to dry and/or smoke their catch to preserve it until it could be flown out. The Yukon needed a refrigerated boat traveling up and down the river, to buy fish along the way and deliver it to town.

Tom explained his procedure. He gathered fish via net or fishwheel and returned to the dock to soak them in a desliming solution. Then he cleaned them: heads off, guts out and rib bones removed.

He carried them up the hill in buckets into his screened drying house to soak in another brine solution. The fish were cut into exact, precise strips. Back into the brine for so many more minutes and then hung on racks to dry. When the strips were dried just right (according to his many years' experience) they were taken to his smokehouse. In here the strips were hung again and smoke lazily filtered into the building. He smoked his fish for about two weeks.

Commonly called squaw candy by the natives, this salmon would keep almost indefinitely. How many hours of work went into those smoked strips!

Tom asked us up to his "home" for coffee and a sandwich. We entered his tent, which had at least 15 patches on holes in the roof. He said sparks from his chimney had caused the holes over the years. Inside was a cot with an old sleeping bag thrown on top and a small table close enough so the bed could be used as a chair. The table contained the bare essentials of spices, a well-stained coffee cup and two pieces of silverware. Next to that, but still within reach of his bed, was a small, flat-topped old rusty woodstove which held a dented, black coffeepot.

He filled the battered coffeepot with water and set it on to heat. Then he took a cooked-the-day-before salmon out of his cooler. He and I made salmon salad sandwiches and handed them outside to Jim and the kids. Then we joined them for lunch — a sandwich with a choice of coffee or cocoa.

We all sat on stumps overlooking the Yukon. A cool breeze shuffled the nearby fallen leaves on this crisp fall day that carried a whisper of winter.

After lunch we went back to Tom's set net. We could see parts of the net bobbing, indicating a fish in that section. Tom brought the boat alongside the net and lifted that section until the caught fish came into sight. With gloved hands, he deftly released the fish into the boat bottom and then threw it into a 50-gallon garbage can in the front of the boat. After bringing in many catches, with water and slime accumulating on the boat bottom, it was obvious why he wore tennis shoes.

Soon the net, clean of fish, was hauled in and coiled on the boat's bow. He said we'd have to keep the fish, as he didn't need any more. Jim took the caps off his floats and threw the fish inside — a convenient way to carry fish without getting a fish smell inside the aircraft.

Jim offered an exchange for Tom's hospitality. Arrangements were made for Jim to fly Tom back to town for the winter, a couple of weeks later. Then we returned home, and the next day I canned the salmon into two cases of #2 cans for winter consumption.

Later I was walking downtown in Nenana with Becky Spear. I saw a very well-dressed man across the street, but I didn't return his wave because I didn't know him. He wore dress slacks, a newly pressed shirt and a good looking jacket. He was clean shaven, and his hair was neatly combed.

Becky said, "Hey, there goes Tom," and she waved.

I turned and watched the figure retreat with my mouth still hanging open. What did I expect anyway? Neat clothes on a man working with salmon all summer or fishing clothes on a person in town!

*   *   *

One evening after dinner, Jim and I took a canoe ride on the lake for the last time, before we put the canoes up for the winter. We were out in the middle of the lake but near the swampy south end. We heard a clashing sound, then some snorting. A couple of bull moose were fighting; it was their mating season.

That night was very black, and we couldn't see a thing. The moon was not out, and even after our eyes adjusted to what light there was, we could not see them. We could only hear this once-in-a-lifetime experience. There was another clash of horns, more snorting, some stomping in the water, and lots of splashing.

I was a little frightened, because I could not see the danger, yet I knew the cause of the sounds. We listened for a long time and then paddled home to check on the kids. We listened hard, but we could not hear the moose from the house, so the kids could not share the experience.

The winter before, we installed a woodstove in the basement, trying to burn less wood. That stove was not the answer; it was a nightmare to use. Even with a double damper, it did not burn well. It burned wide open or not at all. We tried dry logs, green logs, split logs, whole logs, and combinations of all of these. Our wood consumption was about 24 cords that year.

We took the Franklin fireplace out and placed it in a cabin, then installed a Fisher woodstove in its place upstairs. In the Fisher, some of the heat escapes naturally (as in the Franklin) but most of the heat is utilized. Also the doors fit snugly for shutting down at night. The Fisher gave us two advantages: we did not have to split wood (which eliminated more hours of work than can accurately be calculated). Secondly, we used about 12 cords of wood for the whole eight to nine months of winter!

CHAPTER 10

ANOTHER SHOCK

In September 1979 we had our feet jerked out from under us, and we at last, almost gave up. A certified letter from the Bureau of Land Management (BLM) arrived. Before I opened it, I had that funny feeling — the same ominous feeling I get when receiving a telegram. Jim signed for the letter and opened it.

The letter stated that we had completed our homesteading requirements; the land would be surveyed within the next year. The survey would cost $7200, and that must be paid in full within 180 days. If not paid in time, all land and anything on it would revert to the government. We went into shock with this letter. We were expecting to pay $1500 for that survey.

In other words, we paid on time or the federal government would inherit a complete American Plan resort by default. We were scared, shaky, nervous . . . and very *MAD*. It just seemed incredibly unfair — after all our efforts, time, and money that went into building our Arctic Tern Lodge.

We went to the BLM office in Fairbanks, where they explained that the increase for this survey was due to rising costs of all things. Yes, they had quoted us $1500, and that was their most educated estimate at that time. Then they dropped another bomb, casually mentioning that after BLM received the money, it would probably take *eight years* for the title to be granted!

As I said before, we aren't quitters — but brother, the thought was lurking there. Where could we get that kind of money? We could not take a loan against our resort, because we didn't have title to the land!

The only thing we owned was half a Cessna 180 on floats. Leasing the Maule over the past year worked well, so we figured we could sell the 180. Now the questions were, "Could our partner buy us out?" or "Could we sell the plane on the market within 180 days?" Our partner could only buy us out with payments on time. Normally we would have no qualms about doing this, but we needed the lump sum. The plane was put on the market, and we crossed our fingers.

Meanwhile I wrote letters: to the state BLM office in Anchorage; to our Senator Ted Stevens, and to our congressman. Senator Stevens worked very hard for us, writing letters to BLM. His office kept in contact with us, sending us copies of all the correspondence.

All this took time, and we were slowly approaching that 180th day in March. By fall we had a buyer for the 180. Payment would be received in November. We were hopeful. Things seemed to be working out for us.

In November the buyer informed us that he couldn't pay for the plane until after fishing started the next summer — too late for us. This really put pressure on us, because we needed $7200 by March. We had nothing else to sell.

Again, we received a letter from my mom with a short-term loan — enough to meet the land survey payment. Our resort was saved!

We paid the BLM in time. In summer, when we received payment on the plane, we immediately reimbursed my mom.

Now that BLM had our money, we demanded the survey be done as soon as possible. As with many federal offices, (their moving speed was similar to a centipede) the land was finally surveyed in September 1980. We were informed the title to our land would be issued by the end of 1981, thanks to Senator Stevens' efforts to expedite the matter.

That fall (1979), we had an interesting experience with our mail. So many bush people had returned to living in town, that our weekly mail delivery was discontinued. That was a luxury enjoyed for only that one winter. As a personal favor to us, George Hobson flew out and air dropped our mail during freeze-up. He flew over very low the first time and dropped a streamer ribbon to judge wind speed and direction. Thereafter, on each pass over us, he dropped some of our mail, which included a sack of letters plus a number of packages. After four such drops, he wagged his wings and headed back to Nenana.

We retrieved all our mail and took it to the house. We excitedly opened everything; it was almost three weeks since we had received word from outside. I was disappointed in not receiving a package from LL Bean. In late August I ordered mitts and heavy wool socks, desperately needed for winter.

I sat right down and wrote them a letter asking about my order. When the ice was solid enough to land on and Jim could fly, my letter went out. Within 10 days I received a letter from LL Bean. They had in fact shipped my order. Since we did not receive it, they duplicated the order. If the first package appeared, please return it. Two days later the duplicate order arrived, and the episode was forgotten.

Eight months later, Justin and Trish were playing by the shoreline where the snow was melting. They found a box from LL Bean. This evidently was the package air dropped the fall before. Although it had been under snow all winter, the merchandise was undamaged.

I wrote another letter to LL Bean and related the whole story. I suggested they just bill me for this and I'd keep it; soon it would be fall again. Instead of the computer response and billing I expected, I received a handwritten note saying they appreciated my honesty. Under the circumstances we could keep the order with their compliments!

Jim tried to pick up the mail once a week himself. He added wheel/skis to the plane, so he could leave our lake on ice and land at the scraped Nenana runway on wheels. Finally when December came, and he still had not obtained his instructor's rating, he flew to California. There it was less expensive, and he acquired the rating in one week.

He returned to Alaska by December 15. In Wasilla he waited for the weather to clear in the notorious Windy Pass by Mt. McKinley. The weather was bad. Jim tried twice, and both times he had to turn back. On his third try, on the 23rd of December, he got no further than Cantwell, at the mouth of the pass. There Jim heard that no small planes had made it through the pass in two months.

Jim called a good friend who lived close to Nenana, Stu Felburg. Stu drove down and picked Jim up. Jim stayed overnight with Stu and his family. The following morning a –50° registered on the thermometer! Stu did have a plane, but no sane pilot would fly at that temperature. On the other hand, this was Christmas Eve.

Stu spent four hours preheating his plane. He stuffed Jim in it, stuffed the Christmas presents around him, and took off for Wien Lake. The flight took 40 minutes.

The kids and I had already decided to postpone Christmas until Jim arrived. We all knew no one flies at a minus 50 degrees. I couldn't believe my ears, when I heard a plane in the distance. Generally, I can hear a plane approaching at least two minutes before the kids can. I watched them closely. Suddenly they stopped, and the funniest expression crossed their faces. Unbelieving, they listened harder. Then they ran outside to hear better. Stu landed and dumped Jim and the gifts out on the ice. He immediately took off before the plane could cool down, and before I could even say, "Thank you." We enjoyed a happy, family Christmas together, which remains special in our memories because of the kindness of this special friend.

A week later the weather moderated to a comfortable 10 below in the afternoon. We, as a family, enjoyed many hours of cross country skiing on the lake. The slender, durable skis slid easily along the packed snowmobile trail. The snow sparkled like a thousand diamonds against the steel blue sky. Rusty bounded ahead, and we stopped to take in our remote winter scene.

In the better weather, Stu returned to pick up Jim and fly him to Cantwell to retrieve his plane. We were once again in the flying business.

We were blessed with the presence of more wildlife this year. We had always seen lots of whiskey jacks (camp robbers) begging for handouts, while chickadees fluttered and pecked at the hard, frozen suet Jim nailed against a nearby birch tree.

One evening, Justin (now seven), walking outside saw a squirrel on the bird tray that looked different to him. We all went outdoors to investigate. Two gleaming green eyes peeped out from the dark branches of the birch tree. The squirrel was momentarily hypnotized by the bright yellow beam of the flashlight. When it came out of its trance, it spread its soft furry arms and glided safely to an adjoining tree. It was a flying squirrel!

Thereafter it was Justin's habit to go outside every evening. He often caught sight of a flying squirrel feeding. One night he saw a marten feeding there and called us out. The marten, silhouetted against the bright moon, stared at us. He slipped noiselessly down the bird tray and melted away into the darkness.

Some time later Trish saw a large animal she couldn't identify. It stood about 30 feet away in the moonlight. In the morning we checked out the tracks and realized they were of a lynx. With sadness we heard later that a nearby trapper had trapped a pair of lynx.

Outside one day with –40°, I frostbit the tip of my nose without realizing it. I returned home from a walk, and Jim exclaimed my nosetip was all white. He warmed it slowly by gently pressing his hands over it. Two days later, slightly swollen, it began peeling. Then I learned that a once-frostbitten part is more susceptible to frostbite in the future.

I tried a face mask, but my glasses fogged over. Staying inside all day for the next three months didn't appeal to me either, so I continued my outside excursions, but I stopped often to warm my nose — such a bother.

By April Jim and our helper began work on a platform base for a water tank. We had a 500-gallon water tank which we hoped to install high enough to gravity feed into the kitchen. When they finished the tower, they stood the tank upright on it, like a proud silver lady.

The test would come after break-up, when our new water pump could be hooked up to fill the tank. Five hundred gallons of water weighs about 4000 pounds! We were not certain the tower could bear that weight.

Near the end of April our helper was across the lake on a snowmachine when, listening, he heard a who-oo-ing high up in one of the tallest trees. Scanning the tree carefully, he located the source of the noise. Looking straight down at him over the edge of a huge nest, was a large owl face. It was a great gray owl. These owls are the largest in North America and are relatively rare. The kids and I often traveled to this nest, but we were never able to see much. The nest was up too high.

CHAPTER 11

OUR LAST YEAR ON LAKE WIEN

When break-up was imminent, Jim left the lake to convert the Maule from wheel/skis to floats. As soon as the ice receded along the lakeshore enough to allow for canoeing, the kids and I were away exploring again.

By following the shoreline very closely, we were just able to make it to the small reedy area at the south end. We generally don't make specific plans for an outing like this: we just let things materialize as they will. Since the reedy area was passable, we proceeded to a narrow stream that led off from there. We had tried to explore this river a year earlier, but the water level was too low. The water was high this time, due to snow runoff, so we paddled forward stealthily and slowly. This river was no more than four feet wide.

Something kept beckoning us, and we three were determined to go as far as possible. Coming around one corner on this narrow river, we met a female mallard with eight very young ducklings. The mother was quite frantic. She flew up and landed behind us. The little ones, hearing danger in the mother's quacks, ducked their heads down and popped under the water like little corks. We skimmed forward and looked back. The family was once again united.

We came to a fallen tree across the river, but the canoe fit under it. Trish, in the bow, lay down as our canoe glided under the tree. Then like bowling pins, Justin and I in turn lay down flat as we each approached the tree. The next section of river was too narrow for the canoe, but we could see a wider section ahead. We got out and pulled the canoe over. Back in, we continued up river.

Ahead the water was shallower. We stopped at a huge beaver dam — about eight feet high — and walked to the top. There was a small pond backed up behind it. On one side there was a large beaver house. We knew it was active, because we saw fresh cuttings along the shore and shiny peeled sticks next to, and on top of, the lodge.

We heaved the canoe straight up one side of the dam and into the pond on the other side. We tried paddling again, but the river was too shallow and narrow. We had to concede that further travel by canoe was impossible.

Then we walked along the bank to see where the river — now really a tiny stream — led us. About a half-mile upstream, we found an abandoned beaver house. Here the water was low enough that the entrance was exposed. It reminded me of an umbrella, with ragged edges and made out of sticks and mud. Since I had studied drawings of beaver houses, I knew what to expect inside. I was eager to explore it.

Obviously beaver are not as large as an adult human being. So too, their house entrances are too small for an adult. But this entrance looked just large enough for an eight- or eleven-year-old kid to fit into. Neither child was eager to enter this dark hole with mud for a base. Whereupon I sat them down, and we discussed just what they might see inside.

The beaver enters underwater into the living room. This front section of the house has a mud bottom and can be damp. Behind the living room is a shelf built up higher. It is packed down hard and usually has dead grass or straw on the floor. In this bedroom the young are born and nursed. The house has thick enough walls that during winter it is actually warm inside from body heat — much as an igloo is.

Justin entering the abandoned beaver house.

Justin said he would try to go in. After his eyes adjusted to the darkness inside, I heard his excited voice, muffled by the thick walls. He found a higher shelf at the back, and yes, dead grass was still on it. Then Trish wanted a turn. Justin crawled out, on muddy knees, and she crawled in to explore.

This discovery was one of the kids' special experiences in the bush. Though they returned to this beaver house to show others, this first time remained the most memorable for them.

We backtracked to the canoe and on down the river. Soon we were in the main lake again and headed for home. The wind had shifted, pushing the ice against our side of the lake. Just halfway home, our way was blocked by ice, and we had to beach the canoe. We dragged it onto shore, away from the pushing ice, and walked the remaining mile home undaunted. The experience was well worth it.

A week later, the kids were fishing, and I was at the lodge by myself. All was quiet, but suddenly I heard walking splashes along the shore. A cow moose was eating along the shore, taking a step or two after each bite. Amazingly, there were ducks along the shore there, and these animals paid no attention to the others. The ducks actually swam around the legs of the moose. I had never seen such nonchalance of one animal to another. Perhaps the moose stirred up material from the bottom of the lake, and this interested the ducks.

I watched this for a while — close to 30 minutes, and I named the cow moose, Matilda. She was seen often the rest of that summer in various areas along the lake. She was always barren and seemed recognizable by her looks — although moose do look a lot alike. She appeared to be the same one that Tracy Shawn and I had seen two summers before.

By early June, with the ice gone until sometime in October, Jim arrived home with the plane on floats again. This time he flew in Judy and her two girls. George had to work in town for the week, and she came to enjoy my way of life and work with me. She was glad to help prepare for the new season and glad to be away from town for a while.

The stove and sink were moved again from our house to the lodge, and we *moved* to the lodge now for meals. Judy and I washed all the dishes that had stood all winter. A tedious job that Judy helped make fun. As Jim and our helper drained and seeded the "lawn," Judy and I spent hours relocating dirt to plant flowers. We bordered our new flower gardens with rocks

Matilda, our familiar cow moose.

and then transplanted some flowers and planted seeds of others. This was our experimental year to discover which flowers survived and where they grew best.

Jim and our helper hooked up the pump and filled the Serene Silver Lady, standing erect on her tall wooden log frame, with two tons of water. The frame held. A hose was hooked up to the tank running to the sink in the lodge. Wonder of wonders, I experienced my first running water on Wien Lake!

Examining the tower two days later, Jim found cracks developing, saying the weight was too great. The tank was quickly drained and pushed off the tower. A stronger platform was built, and the Silver Lady was reinstalled, refilled and hooked up again. I enjoyed water from the tank all summer long.

Not wanting to waste anything by discarding the first tower, Jim decided to build a small Alaskan cache. This would weigh only a few hundred pounds; the tower could hold it easily. And the cache would add atmosphere to the place.

So while Judy and I continued working on the yard, the cache was built. Small trees were cut and peeled, and within three days the roof was being put on. Sod was added along with moss to the roof. When Jim attached a rack of moose horns to the front, it looked quite picturesque.

The Alaskan cache in winter.

We added trim to the interior of the lodge, and more decorations went in; wood carvings on the walls, mounts of deer, goat, and sheep, and a large Kodiak bear rug. We hung crossed snowshoes and antique cross country skis that were handmade in 1928. My authentic Chippewa tickanoggin, made for me by an Indian friend when I was pregnant with Trish, hung in one corner. Jim's handmade cribbage board inlaid with Trish's baby mammoth tooth and Justin's fossilized ivory was added. We built a front porch on the lodge and once again awaited our first guests of the summer.

Mom arrived in July with two paying guests. Charlotte was back with her husband this time — a renowned brain surgeon in the Twin Cities, who had just retired. This time as guests, they flew somewhere with Jim every flyable day, returning each night to the comfort of our lodge and their individual cabin.

Another couple of our guests were enjoying flying as often as possible. They made one 6 a.m. sightseeing trip of Mt. McKinley National Park on an especially cloud-free day. Jim indicated all the peaks and major glaciers, and they also saw moose, caribou, bear, sheep and wolves. Jim planned to take Mom and her friends on the same trip another morning, but the weather did not cooperate.

Eight-year-old Justin, my mom's namesake, experienced one special day fishing with them. He took Mom out in one canoe, and our helper took Charlotte and her husband out in another. Bets were made on the first fish, the most fish and the largest fish of the day.

Suddenly Justin hooked a good one. He played the fish with some expertise, and my mom netted it when it showed signs of being tired. This was a beautiful northern pike weighing 18 pounds — a record weight for Wien Lake all summer! He was delighted to catch the first *and* the largest.

Later that summer we had an interesting time with a family from Switzerland who were our guests. The parents both knew English very well, although their two daughters (just the ages of Trish and Justin) spoke only German. The kids were all eager to be friendly, and it was touching to watch their communication through actions and sign language. Almost immediately they started a game of Hide and Seek which continued at intervals over the next week. One player counted in German; the next in English. By the end of the week our kids were easily counting in German and the Swiss kids in English!

Trish and Justin took them to our beaver house, and those two girls were game enough to go inside. They ate peanut butter and jelly sandwiches for the first time and requested them for every lunch thereafter. Peanut butter is not available in Switzerland. Everyone went fishing, and they were excited with the results.

Shortly after dinner one day of their stay, the father and one daughter left with Jim to see how many bears they could see. They flew around a radius of 20 miles and were elated to count 13 bears. (And yet we had none around our place, since Rusty had joined our household.)

As they flew over a nearby lake, they noticed the sun reflecting off a stovepipe that Jim had never seen before. They decided to land and investigate. They walked into the woods in the direction of their sighting. On the far edge of a clearing they spied what appeared to be a mound of dirt with a stovepipe sticking out of the top and a door facing them. It was some form of handmade abode.

The Swiss father was concerned that an old trapper's remains might be inside. He stayed back with his daughter while Jim investigated. There was no one inside. Breathing came easier, and all three began exploring.

The "house" was made with a small 6x8' frame of unpeeled poles set about eight inches apart. The frame was covered with sod blocks about four inches thick and covered with moss. Behind the house they found where the sod blocks had been cut. Four-inch thickness of the sod gave good insulation for cold

The camouflaged sod "house."

winter weather. Enough time had passed that saplings were growing from the walls and roof, camouflaging the home — it looked like a small hill.

Inside the dwelling was a bunk, one very small table, a relatively new woodstove, one cup and a coffeepot. Jim located two frying pans and three pots hanging in a nearby tree along with an old rusty saw and axe. The occupant, when he left, expected to be gone awhile. He hung these items outside so the leftover cooking smells would not be inside, enticing a bear to enter.

Nearby was a cache, which had collapsed over the years, and some old canvas, possibly the remains of a tent the trapper had used while making his home. There was an old, rusty wood-stove made from a barrel cut in half. A hole was burned in the barrel, from so much use.

This dwelling may have been a *line shack*. Old time trappers placed five or six shacks around the bush about one day's walking distance apart. The trappers walked their lines, staying over nights in the shacks, and checking their trapline every week. Modern trappers frequently use snowmobiles, and their lines are shorter.

After those guests left that summer, Jim flew me over to see that dwelling — one of the highlights of my experiences in the bush. It did my heart good to see the hard work that went into that simple, but functional dwelling! That trapper had done what we all must do here in the bush: make do with what we have. No one would call it a beautiful home, but it was very snug and adequate for what he wanted.

By that summer the kids felt they were ready to really work, and they were a tremendous help. I delegated the daily cleaning of cabins to them. They worked as a team. Trish was responsible for making the beds and sweeping the floors. Justin shook the rugs, changed the towels, cleaned the table and ash-tray and dusted. I still did the many other jobs, but I was not nearly as tired as the summer before.

We were continually aware that the social aspects of life are necessary for all people. We tried to fill that gap for our kids, while we lived in the bush. That summer Trish had a friend stay for one week, and Judy Hobson with her two girls were here for a week in June. The Swiss guests were here a week, with two children the same ages as Trish and Justin. That was followed by another friend in for a week.

Finally Trish, now 11, was invited to Wasilla. She took the train alone from Nenana to Wasilla, a trip of nine hours, where she was met by a friend of mine. Trish learned how to crochet hats (she gave a new one to each of the men in our lives that Christmas) and also attended the State Fair in Palmer. When she took the train back to Nenana, Justin and Jim met her. She returned home and gave me a new black kitten, which joined our family.

With the fall canning, I added four cases of salmon, three cases of blueberry jam, one case of sauerkraut, and half a case of carrots to our larder for the winter. The kids again picked cranberries to total half a gunny sack, to be hung and later frozen.

Moose season arrived in September. Early one morning Jim stepped out of the house and heard splashing along the lakeshore. Right in front of him stood a two- or three-year-old bull moose with odd-looking, deformed horns. Jim got his gun, and one shot later, we had our supply of meat for the entire winter.

It was almost too easy that year, but then the work began. The moose was dragged to the dock and up on dry ground. I had been present many times for butchering bear, but never for a moose. I was astonished at its size, now that I was so close. Besides having deformed horns, the moose was blind in one eye. After butchering, Jim showed me where four ribs had been broken and healed over. This young moose had been in a horrible fight at some time.

By evening the four quarters were hanging to age, along with the ribs, heart, liver and backstraps. After it hung for a week, we spent two days cutting and wrapping the meat. Three days later, Jim flew the meat to town to a freezer. Our days were not cold enough yet to keep meat frozen.

The timing of the annual moose hunting season is a problem for people living in the bush. Often in September (during moose season), nights are freezing, but daytime temperatures warm up considerably. If a moose is taken at this time, the meat will spoil and be wasted.

On the other hand, if one shoots a moose in October (out of season), the meat will keep and be used. The weather is cold enough to keep it frozen. But shooting a moose out of season is a serious offense in Alaska, often carrying greater punishment than shooting a person.

Some laws are so difficult to understand, and this particular one seems unfair to people living in the bush.

*　　*　　*

At the north end of our lake is a handmade airstrip. It is so small and crude that it is only used on very rare occasions. It sorely needs to be lengthened and leveled. Five planes have landed there: one crashed and is still there; another crashed and was repaired over a period of two weeks and flown out; a third landed and broke its landing gear (being repaired in one day). Only two have landed and taken off safely. One of these last was Jim flying in a Super Cub late in October when freeze-up was very late. He had flown the Maule out three weeks before to be fitted with wheel/skis.

He buzzed over our house, and I paddled the four miles to meet him with the canoe. I remember so well coming to the shore, and seeing him stand there with a happy smile — so very glad to be home. Nearby were packages from the mail and on top, two large, bright orange pumpkins for the kids for Halloween.

The kids had an exciting Halloween — carving scary faces into their pumpkins and inserting candles to light up their jack-o-lanterns in the dark. We carefully separated the seeds from the stringy material, and baked them, salted, to make a snack food similar to salted sunflower seeds.

After the jack-o-lanterns sagged, I scraped the pumpkin meat out. Measuring into one-pie amounts, I set one aside for a pie that evening, and froze the rest in individual containers.

Jim planned to take Justin, almost nine, to Kodiak for a deer hunt. It was late fall and the time to leave was fast approaching. They would have to takeoff from the primitive airstrip, as the lake would skim over on any night.

The weather was not flyable, but I suggested we canoe down the lake with the gas they needed to refuel the plane. Then if the lake did skim over before the weather cleared, he and Justin would have to walk down, but at least they would not have to carry the gas. Jim vetoed the idea and said he would wait another day.

During that night the lake did skim over. The next morning the weather was cold and almost "zero, zero," meaning no visibility and not flyable. Jim was determined to get the gas down there by some means other than carrying it.

He loaded the canoe and we "shoved" off. The canoe rode up onto the one-inch-thick ice, broke through due to its weight, and moved about two feet forward. It was soon evident to both of us that traveling four miles in two-foot gulps would take too long. We backtracked to shore.

Then Jim took out the motor. We had already drained it and put it up for the winter. He filled it with gas and pulled the cord. It remained in that position, too cold to recoil. Then he took that motor and another (for a spare) into the house.

After the motors warmed up and with both full of gas, Jim attached one on the sidebracket of the canoe and lay the other one on the bottom. The motor started with the first pull, and we headed down the lake. One tank of gas was usually enough for a round trip, but we weren't taking any chances that day.

The canoe rose above the ice and broke through just as when we were paddling. It was still slow going but faster than paddling. If the motor did not die on us, we should reach the north end successfully. We figured the trip back would be easier, retracing our path through the ice.

The motor ran out of gas just as we reached the north end. It had used twice as much gas as normal, due to our slow progress. Quickly we hauled the plane gas up to the airstrip and refueled the plane. Then it was ready for takeoff when the weather allowed. By the time we got back to the lakeshore, our path was already skimmed over. But we were not worried.

Jim changed motors on the canoe, and we pushed off for what we thought would be a quick return home. One pull on the cord and . . . it did not start. The motor would not recoil, and it looked like a naughty child with his tongue stuck out. The extra motor was too cold.

We had two options open to us: walk home or try paddling through the skimmed-over path. I voted for paddling, thinking it was the lesser of two evils. Jim agreed.

We started off and made fair progress. The ice wasn't too thick. But the more time it took, the thicker the ice became. By halfway point, I (in the bow) had to slam the paddle very hard into the ice for a toe-hold, and then pull with everything I had. Jim did the same in the stern, only pushing.

I was becoming absolutely exhausted. My arms each weighed a ton. My knees were numb from receiving the brunt of force, as I slammed the paddle into the ice. It was cold, and I was sweating, and panting, and wondering why I hadn't voted to walk. The further we progressed, the thicker the ice, the harder to slam and pull, and the more exhausted we both became.

We were really in a predicament. The ice was almost impenetrable, yet not thick enough to hold our weight. If only we could get out and walk home. How easy that sounded. If we did not proceed, we'd just freeze in. We neared a point of land and considered heading to shore. However, the ice was two inches thick there, where we had no path. We figured it was "easier" to continue onward.

Jim suggested we change places — he would pull and I would push. That was a little relief for each of us. Eventually we reached home. Our paddles, not usable after that, were chewed to a pulp. I just crawled up the hill, and Trish, bless her heart, made a marvelous dinner that night for all of us.

That was Thursday. Friday was not flyable either, but Saturday dawned bright and sunny. The ice was four inches thick along the shore and, by keeping very close to shore, I was able to snowmobile Justin and Jim down the lake and drop them at the plane. I returned home, again creeping along close to the shoreline.

They took off with ease and headed toward Nenana and on to their second annual father/son deer hunt. The year before when Justin was eight, he got his first deer — a buck with a five-point rack. He used a gun with a shortened barrel, which he could handle better.

When Jim and Justin returned from their hunt, they landed on the ice without incident. That was the latest, yet fastest freeze-up we experienced on Lake Wien.

Rusty was a full-grown dog then, and he often took off alone chasing rabbits for an hour or so in the afternoon. One morning we noticed the left side of Rusty's face was swollen like a balloon. Trish said he looked like Frankenstein on a bad day. We both checked him over very carefully and couldn't find a cut, wound, or any sign of blood. After much thought, I decided maybe Matilda had kicked him in the face. (Although we had never known him to chase moose, and he had plenty of opportunities to do so.)

When Jim and Justin returned, Justin was concerned about Rusty. Jim checked him over carefully, and he could find nothing. Four days later Rusty's wound opened and began to drain. Each morning I washed Rusty's face and used disinfectant. The hair on that side of his face started to fall out. Then one day a porcupine quill flowed out with the drainage; the answer was given to us.

If a dog tangles with a porcupine, he will usually get his whole face full of quills. They must be removed, one by one, with pliers. It is painful for the dog; the quills are barbed. If the quills are not removed, they work themselves inward until they reach a vital organ, and the animal dies. Rusty must have received only one or two quills, as there were none showing. This one penetrated inward to his skull and could go no further.

Rusty was terribly sick for two weeks. We considered putting him out of his obvious misery, but Justin was too attached to him. Jim and I decided if Rusty was going to die, it would not be from us. Slowly, ever so slowly, he mended, and the hair grew back on his face. He received a scar from the encounter, but he wore it like a badge, signifying his recovery.

*　　*　　*

A trapper came by one day to show Trish and Justin a great gray owl. He found it caught in a trap, by just a toe. The owl was in shock, but otherwise in good shape. I shivered in the biting wind and stared at the drunken-looking owl standing on the trapper's arm. The owl stared back at me with unblinking, fierce yellow eyes.

Justin stepped up and held out his thin, shaking arm. The trapper set the owl on Justin's arm and told him to flap it up and down a little. Justin did as he was told, and the owl unfolded its great wings to balance itself. But it was still too unsteady to take flight.

We kept the owl in a cabin for a day while it recovered its senses. Then Jim took it to the top of the ridge behind us. The mighty owl spread its giant wings and gracefully soared away.

That December, our last winter in the bush for sometime, was the most severe: two weeks of -40° and then two weeks of -60°. Previously, when we experienced cold weather — all the way to 68° below — it was for a couple of days only. Then it warmed up to a tolerable -30°. With four weeks of extreme weather, the walls began to close in on us.

The kids could not get out and run around in the afternoon, nor ski, nor toboggan; they could only stay inside. I could not take my daily walk on the lake. Jim could not work outside. Rusty could not run and chase around. Even the birds, at those extremes, fly very little. They did not arrive at the bird tray as usual.

Then on December 23, we received word that Jim's mother had died in Missouri. Jim could not make plane connections in time for her funeral, due to the Christmas rush. She was a grand person, a fine mother-in-law, and the sadness of losing her capped our cabin fever. That was the worst month our family ever experienced.

Mother Nature is never to be outguessed nor, do I believe, completely understood. The first week in January she did a complete turnaround and, within two days, sent the temperatures from minus 60° to 20° ABOVE zero. That balmy weather continued for six weeks! Unheard-of for January.

The kids were soon out on the ice making snow survival houses described in a survival book, and we were all happy again.

CHAPTER 12

FAREWELL TO THE BUSH

When we decided to stay in the bush during winter and teach our own children, we said that we would leave and place them in public school when Trish reached junior high. This year I am teaching Trish seventh grade. So we extended one year beyond our original plans. Next fall we will enroll them in a public school.

Both Trish and Justin are well aware of the special experiences they have enjoyed these past four years. Although we will return each summer to run our resort, it will not be quite the same. So many of our special experiences were in the early spring or late fall.

The children are not afraid to return to school. Perhaps, like me, they have very mixed feelings about it. Mixed or not, it is something we feel we must do. We owe it to both Trish and Justin.

Keeping children in the bush all the time would be an injustice to them and their future (whatever that may hold) — unless one could afford to take them out on vacations once a year to see educational things. If, in their future, they decide to make bush life their way of life, either running the resort or something else, they will decide that as a choice, and not because no other avenues are open to them.

Financially, moving back to town will be a shock for us. In 1977, when we still lived in Kodiak, we spent $1000 per month and lived very modestly. Recently a friend of mine gave me a complete rundown of expenses for her family of four living in town. In 1981 (a short four years later), expenses will run about $1600 per month.

For these past four years, we have had no house payment, a minimal electric bill (blazo for our lanterns), and almost no heat bill (one new Fisher stove). We expect our move back to town will be no less difficult than our move into the bush.

A question often asked of me is what I missed that was available in town. Most people are sure they could not live without television, but we had already eliminated that from our diet in Kodiak. We were all too addicted to staring at that noisy box, and we sold our set. After our withdrawal period we found ourselves reading many exciting books, playing games as a family, and enjoying good conversations together more than ever.

Most people cannot stand the isolation of bush living. It only brought our family closer together. I sometimes missed visiting with female friends though. The only things I really missed were daily showers, and selfishly perhaps, the times Jim would take me out to fancy steak dinners on our anniversary, Mother's Day and my birthday.

Last night after the dishes were done, I took the waste water out to dump. I heard the distant hooting of an owl — a sound that reflects my mood. I will miss this life more than words can express. Perhaps Jim and I will return, after the kids finish school, and live here once again during the winter months.

— *Spring 1981*

EPILOGUE

And so we left our place on Wien Lake after our decision to put the children back in public school.

After much letter-writing and interviewing, we ended up taking a teaching job on the Aleutian Chain at Unalaska. Jim signed up for teaching all the science classes, grades 7-12, and I for all the math classes, grades 7-12. The school had just under 200 students, Kindergarten through 12th grade. About one-third of the students were native, and the rest were mostly whites, with a very small percentage of other ancestries.

The Aleutian Chain is a series of islands stringing out to the west from the mainland of Alaska. The weather is probably the worst in the world. One hundred-knot winds are not uncommon, and rain is constant. During World War II there was a large base on this island, as there were all through the islands. There were more military personnel lost in this area due to weather, than fighting.

Unknown to many Americans is the fact that the Japanese actually had a foothold for a short time on these islands. All the lands were retained and the Japanese were off these islands midway through the war.

During our years at Unalaska, we have seen the community grow quite a bit. Like Kodiak, Unalaska is a fishing village with canneries. Bottom fisheries are now used commercially with recent addition of Seremi plants.

When we arrived here, Justin was in fifth grade and Trish in eighth. We did not know we would be here so long.

Trish graduated as Valedictorian in 1986 and went on to attend college at the University in Fairbanks. She transferred to the Anchorage campus her last year to be closer to her fiance.

Justin graduated in 1989 as Salutatorian and enrolled at Arizona State University at Flagstaff that fall. He hopes to someday fly for a living. To that end he has almost finished his private pilot license requirements. After getting to solo on floats, he was hooked completely.

As to our resort . . . we put a great deal of thought into it. We tried to teach in the winter and run the resort in summer after moving to Unalaska. It didn't work out very well. After a lot of soul searching, we put the resort up for sale.

We sold the resort on an escrow arrangement in 1986. By 1988 we had to repossess for nonpayment. We filed for repossession, and then the buyers filed for bankruptcy. It was a year in the courts before we got our resort back.

It had taken so long through the courts, that we weren't sure we would get into the resort that summer. So, we planned only one month there and planned to spend July and August visiting my mother and family.

In spring of 1989, with mixed emotions, we flew in once again and landed on Wien Lake. We did not know what we would find. We were scared to look, yet happy to be back.

When we first landed, Justin was standing by me. We were just looking from the dock and could see only *some* of the situation. I must have shown a lot on my face, for he turned to me and said, "Don't worry Mom, it can and will be cleaned up again." Great wisdom from the mouth of my 18-year-old son.

The buyers had left the fall before with all the dining room tables and the kitchen full of dirty dishes, which attracted the bears. The bears broke through a picture window and damaged everything in the lodge. There was garbage all over the yards, equipment scattered all over, boats left in the water to freeze over winter, and dirty beds and linens in all the cabins. Many items were missing: such as all the cabins were missing their stoves. It was a traumatic time for all of us.

It was hard work, but we just all got in and dug. Soon we could see the kitchen floor, and the stove was hooked up and working. That was a start, and the second night we were enjoying fresh fish from the lake again, and seeing the great majestic mountain in all its beauty. The mountain has always had a soothing effect on our problems and emotions.

With six of us working 12 hours a day, seven days a week, we were able to clean up the place pretty well in our allotted month that summer.

Our future is unsettled now. Both Jim and I are retiring from teaching after 25 years in that profession. We have tossed around several ideas now that the resort is back in our hands, but nothing definite has yet materialized.

P.K.S.
May 1990

APPENDIX:

COOKING IN THE BUSH

Many outstanding books have been published about various aspects of cooking. Like many homemakers, I use recipes from more than one cookbook and "make do" with the things I have. Some things I learned during my years in the bush may be helpful to others.

Many people who live in the bush cook all their meals over a woodstove, which is very economical. It just takes time and experience to learn to regulate the temperature. I have cooked over a woodstove myself and found it very rewarding. Naturally it requires more effort than cooking with gas or electricity. I used a propane stove with Jim flying in the necessary propane bottles.

The most important thing to learn about cooking in the bush is to use what is available, experiment, and try again. I tried to think ahead and make things during the summer that I could use during the winter months. One needs to be like a chipmunk: when the harvest is plenty, prepare for the times of scarcity.

BERRIES

In late July the blueberries come ripe. We generally ate quite a few fresh. Then I canned up the amount of jam that I thought we could use during the winter. Some years there is also an abundance of raspberries. We found our preference ran to raspberry jam, so I made up twice as much raspberry jam as blueberry. The first winter I put up 12 quarts of raspberry jam and six quarts of blueberry. We used all the raspberry jam, but only one jar of blueberry. In following years the raspberry crop was poor, so we only canned enough for Christmas. We still put up blueberry jam — about a case.

Jam is one of the easiest things to put up for winter use. I use Sure-gel and follow the recommendations for times and proportions. The berries are cleaned, placed in a pot with so much water and sugar, and boiled. Sure-gel is added, and then the jam is poured into waiting sterilized jars. Melted wax is placed over the top to seal them.

Rosehips are ripe in late August. I tried to make rosehip jelly once, but I did not have the proper equipment to separate out the seeds. It was a mess. I found it very time-consuming, and one gets little for a large amount of picking. On the other hand, rosehips *are* one of the most abundant sources of Vitamin C found in the bush.

Cranberries blanket the forest and come ripe the latter part of August also. They can be found almost anywhere. If hung in a ventilated sack after picking, (like a gunny sack) they will keep well all winter, frozen outside. I hung ours in one of the cabins, and we ate off those all winter. My family particularly likes them in sourdough pancakes for breakfast, in the same way many people enjoy blueberries. In spring when the cranberries thawed, and if I still had some left, I canned them up just like blueberries. I used them until they ran out. If the kids had picked enough, they lasted until the cranberries became ripe again, the following August.

MUSHROOMS

Mushrooms are quite abundant during summer also. They can be added to any favorite recipe. Harvesting mushrooms did require buying a good mushroom book and learning to identify the poisonous ones. Soon, without any effort, we could tell which ones should not be picked. (In our area at the lake it was only one kind.) We enjoyed all the rest. I have tried blanching and freezing them for later use, but I have not found that worth the effort. We just used them fresh — they taste so much better then also.

FISH

Northern pike is the most common fish in our lake, so I have cooked it in many different ways. Our favorite is still fried — using a light batter. I use two cups flour, one cup cornmeal, two eggs, a dash of salt, and enough milk to make a medium thick batter. I dip the fish in the batter and then fry it in hot grease. (Bacon grease is the best, but it is not always available.) Cornmeal gives the fish a golden appearance quickly, appealing to the eye.

To bake this fish, lay the fillets in a well-buttered baking dish and spread a generous amount of mayonnaise across the top of the fish. Bake at 350° for 30 minutes. This dish is similar in taste to halibut. It is quite bland-looking, however, so I present it with something which has color. If I have parsley available, so much the better, but I have used fresh leaves from a birch tree, and the effect is the same.

Still another favorite recipe for northern pike is also baking fillets in a buttered baking dish but covered with Velveeta cheese. Cover this and also bake for 30 minutes. Another tasty dinner without too much effort and with good coloration and eye appeal.

Each year Jim brought me salmon from the Yukon River, which was an added treat for us. I have canned up lots of this fish. I invested in a good canner and bought my own cans. Canning meat must be done with great care, but it is not too difficult. All the cans and also the lids must, of course, be sterilized. One teaspoon of salt and a tablespoon of oil are put in the empty can. The fish, after being cleaned, is cut into lengths that fit in the can with ¼" space left at the top. Pack them fairly tightly, and wipe the rim of the can very carefully. Seal with the lid and using the canner. Check that the seal is done properly, and that there is no wrinkle in the seal. The cans are then placed in a pressure canner (buy a good one if you are going to do this) and then pressured for so many minutes at certain pressure, depending on the size of can used.

When I did my #2 cans, I pressured at 10 pounds for 90 minutes. When the cans are removed, the ends have a "bulged" look. Then they are placed in cold water, where they should "suck in" on the ends and look like a normal can from the grocery store.

Salmon canned at home is like any other canned product from a store — it has a very long shelf life. I can up whatever Jim brings me. I always have enough left over to never skimp. And I just keep the cans to use the following year. They also make very good Christmas presents.

Of course salmon is excellent when cooked fresh. Salmon steaks are probably our favorite way of eating this meat fresh. After the fish is gutted, I just cut crossways straight through the fish every inch or so. I lay these steaks on the broiler. I melt butter, adding a little lemon and some Worcestershire sauce. I paint the steaks with this mixture and push them under the broiler for about five minutes on one side. Then I turn them over, repaint them, and broil for another three minutes.

I also serve Peroke (Russian for *salmon pie*). First I cook ½ cup rice, fry up half a pound of bacon, and cut up one small onion and one carrot (if available). I put all this in a bowl with a can of salmon and mix thoroughly with two eggs. I make a regular pie crust in a pie pan and add the filling. Then, as with any pie, I cover with a second crust and bake for about 45 minutes until golden brown. I cut and serve in wedges, just like pie. This is very tasty and a different way of serving a fish dinner.

For lunches, I make salmon salad or salmon patties (similar to hamburgers). For the patties, I flake already-cooked salmon into a bowl, add two eggs, a little salt and about ½ cup cracker crumbs. Then I fry the patties like hamburgers.

For salmon salad (similar to tuna salad), I flake the salmon meat into a bowl, this time adding mayonnaise, onions, pickles, salt and pepper, with a dash of Worcestershire sauce for good measure.

I did can up some sheefish one year. I found that to be so much like canned tuna, that our guests couldn't tell the difference.

All kinds of fish can be baked whole and served whole, for guests to cut anyway they wish. Using a favorite stuffing mix, this is quite simple, and similar to stuffing a turkey. Baked whole fish is especially appealing for a festive occasion (or smorgasbord, in my situation).

MEAT

As with almost all people living in the bush, our main source of meat during winter was shooting a moose in the fall. Moose can be cooked just like regular beef, except that the fat of moose is not eaten. (Nor does one cook meat with fat on it. All fat must be trimmed off during butchering.)

We ground our own hamburger. At first I used a small handgrinder, and the job took two days. It was hard work, but then I had enough hamburger to last the winter. Using or buying an electric grinder would be worth it. We couldn't afford to buy one at the time.

Because I did not have suet to add during grinding, the meat was quite lean, but had a good flavor. I added a little grease when frying the moose hamburger. Another time I had the opportunity to add suet. Then I found it didn't enhance the taste any. Thereafter I did not concern myself with it.

Baking a moose roast like a regular beef roast can make it tough. With some experimenting, I found a way to make it tender. I placed the roast in a kettle of hot water, with some salt, pepper and a few onions thrown in for flavoring. Often I also added three or four cubes of beef bouillon. I left this on our woodstove most of the afternoon, and we would have a tender, tasty "roast" for dinner. This was similar to cooking the meat in a crock pot.

The first time I did this, I cooked it too long, and the meat just fell apart — it was so tender. Thereafter I cooked it for about three hours. The meat held together like a good roast, but it was still easily cut with a fork.

Our moose steaks I cooked by pounding them slightly first. I used lemon pepper for seasoning, dipped them in flour, and fried them in oil (or bacon grease, when available).

Due to our strenuous activity, our bodies demanded a certain amount of fat in our diet. Since we could not eat the fat on the moose, and fish has none, we craved bacon and/or bacon grease in our diet.

Bear meat is a very good meat also. It can be cooked like moose or like regular beef. The only difference is that one must not eat this meat rare or even medium pink. It must be cooked well done, to eliminate any parasites that may be present.

SPROUTS

During our first summers at the lake, the only food we missed (and craved when returning to teaching in the fall) was fresh items — mainly lettuce.

Soon I found I could grow alfalfa sprouts with ease. Two gallons growing all the time kept us in "lettuce" — as much as we could eat.

I used a large glass jar, a gallon jar, and placed ¼ cup alfalfa seeds in the bottom. I covered that with water and let it sit overnight. The following morning, I drained the water out, added fresh water to rinse, and drained it again. Then I was well on my way. I covered the top of the jar with a clean cloth punched with knife slashes and attached with a rubber band. Every day I rinsed the seeds and inverted the jar. In seven to 10 days, I had a whole gallon of sprouts to enjoy.

We didn't have tomatoes and cucumber to add to our tossed salad. We just added something that we did have. My tossed salad in the bush consisted of my sprouts, peanuts, raisins, and sunflower meats and/or cubes of cheese. We never tired of this salad.

BREAD AND PIE CRUST

My bread and pie crust recipes are very simple and not very time-consuming. Bread: 4 Tbs. sugar, 4 Tbs. Crisco, 4 tsp. salt, 4 cups boiling water (dissolves the whole mess). I added another 4 cups of cold water, then 4 Tbs. yeast. Next comes enough flour to make the right dough consistency. The nice thing about this recipe is that I can so easily make larger or smaller quantities, because of the simple proportions.

Pie Crust: 2 cups Crisco, 4 cups flour, 2 Tbs. salt, and just enough water to be able to roll the dough out (about ¾ cup or a little more). I have found that sprinkling a thin layer of sugar on the crust, just before baking, gives it a nice flaky texture.

SOURDOUGH

Sourdough recipes abound in many cookbooks. I have tried many of them, but I still prefer sourdough pancakes to anything else. Sourdough starter is essential to the bush person. The best bet is to get a small amount from a friend who already has sourdough. Although there are samples on the market which can be bought.

Jim particularly likes sourdough pancakes with cranberries. He says it *sticks to the ribs*, whereas a breakfast of eggs doesn't seem to last as long in his stomach while working. Some people use sugar in their sourdough pancakes. I find that sugar makes them too sweet — sourdough is meant to have a sour-like taste.

In my sourdough recipe I do use eggs — although the old-time trappers and miners surely didn't have eggs to use on the trail. As a family, we use a good amount of eggs, and I found that they keep for a long time in a cool place. I bought a whole case in the fall, and the eggs kept for the three to four months it took us to use them up. Then I bought another case which lasted until summer.

Sourdough Pancakes: The night before, add 2 cups flour and 2 cups water to the starter. Mix this to a smooth consistency and leave to stand until morning. In the morning set aside ½ cup of this mixture for the next time — this is the new *starter*.

To the rest, add 2 eggs, 2 tsp. baking powder, 1 tsp. baking soda and a dash of oil (to keep them from sticking). I add cranberries, blueberries, or even bananas for variety.

*   *   *

We have a crank ice cream maker given to us for Christmas one year. We found that to be a special treat during the winters. We got ice from the lake, the kids cranked, and ice cream was enjoyed by all!

GLOSSARY

agate — A semi-precious stone, often quite colorful. All kinds of jewelry pieces are made from cut agates.

airplanes — See Citabria 7ECA, Cessna 180, Maule M-5.

Alaskan cache — A traditional Alaskan storage shed placed on stilts to prevent trespassing by bears and other predators.

American Plan Resort — A resort which includes both room and board in their prices. In an American Plan Resort the meals are served either family style or individually. We served ours individually and tried to be more individualized in the presentation.

Arctic tern — This rather small gull-like bird ranges from 14-17" in size. It is whitish in coloration with a very black cap and forked tail. In appearance it is quite similar to the common tern. The female lays two spotted eggs in a shallow depression sometimes lined with grass (which is the way the nests we saw were built) on a reedy platform. Arctic terns winter in the Antarctic Ocean and summer as far north as the Arctic Ocean — making a round trip migration totaling as much as 22,000 miles and they see more daylight than any other living creature. There were many Arctic terns nesting on Wien Lake. We found a hurt one and tried to help it regain health, but we lost it in the end. This episode prompted us to name

Arctic tern (cont'd)
our resort after the Arctic tern — always flying and always courageous.

bald eagle — Our national bird. These birds are between 30 and 43" in size with a wing span of 78-96". The young or immature bird of less than five years has a brownish color to its head and body while the mature bird, over five years of age, has the well-known white head and black body. Eagles formerly bred throughout North America, but now only breed in Alaska, parts of Canada, northern United States and some in Florida. Although this bird is endangered in many areas, in Alaska it is quite prevalent. It is primarily a fish eater.

bank swallow — A common bird in Alaska, similar to the barn swallow of the central United States, but smaller. Bank swallows are the smallest swallows in North America — just 4½ to 5½". They are brown above and white below with a distinct band of brown across their upper breast. They nest in river banks, building their nests at the end of tunnels going back into the bank.

blazo — fuel used in our lanterns and stoves.

BLM — Bureau of Land Management, an agency of the federal government managing land claims.

bush — an area of Alaska that is usually not accessible by road, but almost always accessible by plane.

central interior — The area of Alaska located in the center of the state, north of the Alaska Range and south of the Brooks Range of mountains. If one imagined a dart

central interior (cont'd)
board on the shape of the state of Alaska, the central interior would be the bulls-eye.

Cessna 180 —A single engine four-seater aircraft commonly used on floats and skis in Alaska. This aircraft is very popular because of its rugged construction and load-carrying capability.

Cheechakos — Newcomers to the state of Alaska. The term has much the same connotation as "greenhorn" does elsewhere.

chickadee — A small bird, standing about four inches tall. It is white with a dark head and chirps as if to say its name. Chickadees are plentiful and cheerful, especially during the winter months.

Citabria 7ECA — An excellent ski plane used to haul supplies during the winter months. This is a tandem two-seater aircraft. We referred to ours as the "Green Machine."

draw knife — Used to peel bark from downed timber, a draw knife is a steel blade about 12 inches long, with a sharp edge like a knife and a handle on each end. One grasps the handles and pulls (or draws) toward oneself along the log.

Fisher stove — A name brand of woodstove, one of the best on the market today. This stove can be stoked up well at night and then turned down and controlled so it will give off heat for at least 12 hours. It is an ideal choice for heating in the bush, where other sources of heat are not available.

fishwheel — A waterwheel designed to scoop out fresh water fish from a river. In Alaska they are used primarily by Alaskan native peoples.

Franklin stove — A name brand of woodstove, which has the appearance of a small fireplace. It has an open front with a fire screen, similar to a fireplace. It is an excellent stove for its picturesque appearance but is not ideally suited as the sole source of heat for a cabin.

great gray owl — This owl is gray in coloration, has a very rounded head which lacks ear tufts, and huge gleaming yellow eyes. It usually nests in an abandoned hawk nest and lays from two to five white eggs. It is the largest member of the owl family, being from 24 to 33 inches in size, with a wing span of five feet. One of the most elusive of American birds, it was discovered in America by Europeans — before they realized that the species also occurred in Europe.

Green Machine — Nickname for our plane, the Citabria 7ECA.

Gunflint Lodge — The resort purchased as a fishing camp in the 1920s by my grandmother, which my mother operated and built up until her retirement. It is located along the Canadian border of Minnesota, 150 miles north of Duluth. Gunflint Lodge is very well-known and respected all over the midwest.

Homestead Act — An Act of Congress which opened up lands in the west for homesteading in the mid-1800s. This Act was in effect in some areas all the way up to 1964. When Alaska became a state in 1959, it was possible to gain land through the homestead process.

KJNP — A radio station located in North Pole, Alaska with a stronger transmitter than other radio stations. This station can reach further into the interior, and it is a special gift to those who have no other means of communication. This station will also send special messages to people in the bush and does tremendous service to all kinds of people. The letters stand for "King Jesus North Pole."

loon — An aquatic bird with a distinct call heard often in the wilds. Some consider its call lonely. Others, like myself, feel it is the call of the wild, and hearing it out in the bush makes them excited and contented.

lynx — A wild cat, similar to the bobcat, found throughout Alaska and Canada.

marten — A beautiful mink-like animal with an amber red-colored fur. It is the creature most trappers seek (in this area) being trapped extensively for its fur.

Maule M-5 — Another popular four-seater aircraft valued for bush operation because of its high performance in short field capacity.

northern pike — A fish abundant in many Alaskan fresh waters and those of other states as well. Very good-tasting, but often not appreciated due to the extra row of 'Y' bones found in each fillet. After I learned how to clean this fish removing those bones, our guests loved the taste.

pilot bread — A commercial product for sandwiches that is round, about four inches in diameter. This product lasts a very long time without molding as fresh or store-bought bread does. It is especially good for camping, fishing and "out-back" type living.

proving-up date — An end date set when one first applies for land under the Homestead Act. Certain qualifications for obtaining that land must have been met and adhered to by this deadline, or the claim becomes null and void. In our case we had five years from the date of our application to "prove" that we had an American Plan resort doing business and it was utilizing the land we had put a claim on.

ranger — A track vehicle often used on a farm, but it can be used on ice or tundra as we used it. With a sled hitched to the back, it can haul tremendous loads.

Sea-Land Service, Inc. — A shipping company which transports goods between Alaska and Seattle and then transfers the goods to a land vehicle. This company does a great service to the Alaskan people.

sheefish — A large whitefish found in the rivers and streams of northwest Alaska.

snowmachine — A track vehicle used over snow in winter. Used extensively in Alaska on traplines, for travel, and for carrying cargo.

sourdough — 1) a long-time resident of Alaska, usually an Alaskan who has been in the state most of his life. The opposite of Cheechako. 2) Type of bread or pancakes made from sour dough starter, which can be used for years and years. Each time the starter is used, a portion of the "new" dough is set aside for the next time. A strong and durable food / or a strong and durable person.

squaw candy — Another name for smoked salmon strips.

taiga — The dominant vegetation of central Alaska; a Russian word meaning "small trees."

tickanoggin — A packboard used by the Indians to carry their young children. A Chippewa Indian friend of mine made one for me as a gift. We used it when Trish and Justin were quite young.

trapline — A path (called a line) through the woods or along lakes or both, where a trapper set his series of traps in winter to catch wild animals, usually for their value as furs.

tundra — A common terrain in Alaska. Usually treeless areas which have just grass growing (and often many kinds of flowers and berries) but with a spongy bog underneath. Tundra is difficult to walk on, especially if it is real moist (which it often is).

Whiskey Jacks — Another common name for the Canadian Jay, which is gray in color and about eight inches tall, when sitting on a branch. Also known as "camp robbers," as they can become quite bold, easily taking food out of one's hand or robbing the camp of anything — edible or not.

Wien Airlines — One of the first of Alaska's famous bush airlines, started in the 1920s. It was said that one of the Wien brothers liked so much to fly in and fish on a certain lake in central Alaska, that the lake, Wien Lake, was named after him.

yellowlegs — A small bird in the sandpiper family, 9½ to 11" in size. They nest in bogs or marshes and usually lay four eggs.

ABOUT THE AUTHOR

Pat Kerfoot was born in Minnesota in 1942 and grew up in the northwoods of Minnesota along the Canadian Border. She graduated from high school in 1960 and went on to Wisconsin State University in LaCrosse, WI to obtain her B.S. degree in Physical Education and Mathematics in 1964. She then began teaching in Tenino, Washington, where she met 'her' Jim, who was also a teacher.

In June of 1965 she married Jim Shoffner. After two more years teaching school and another year when they both attended college working on their Masters' degrees at Ellensburg, WA, they packed up their worldly belongings and headed for Alaska.

Pat and Jim taught another eight years in Kodiak. Then Pat taught another four years — this time her own children, elementary grades while living in the bush — while both she and her husband Jim built up and started Arctic Tern Lodge.

Then Pat and Jim returned to teaching for another nine years, this time on the Island of Unalaska located on the Aleutian Chain. There Pat taught math grades seven through 12, while their two children finished high school and went on to college.

In 1990, both Jim and Pat retired from teaching after each putting 25 years into that profession. They look forward to spending some more time at their resort in the summers and some vacation time during the winter months.

WANT TO ORDER THIS BOOK?

Use this form to order copies of *At Home in the Heart of Alaska,* or other titles by Women's Times Publishing:

___ *AT HOME IN THE HEART OF ALASKA*
    by Pat Kerfoot Shoffner   Foreword by Justine Kerfoot
    Modern Day Pioneers   ISBN 0-910259-07-0 146p, paper . .$9.95

___ *WOMAN OF THE BOUNDARY WATERS*
    by Justine Kerfoot   Foreword by Les Blacklock
    Canoeing, Guiding, Mushing and Surviving
                            ISBN 0-910259-03-8 200p, cloth. .$14.95

___ *INGEBORG'S ISLE ROYALE*
    by Ingeborg Holte
    Family life in a commercial fisherman's family in the early 1900s
                            ISBN 0-910259-01-1 97p, paper . . .$7.95

___ *KIDS' NORTHWOODS ACTIVITY BOOK*
    by Jane Lind   Illustrations by Liz Sivertson
    Innovative nature activities for ages 5-12. Glossary, 3-color pencil set.
                            ISBN 0-910259-06-2 26p, spiral . . .$4.95

___ *I WALK ON THE RIVER AT DAWN*
    by Joanne Hart   Drawings by Betsy Bowen
    Poems of Winter   ISBN 0-910259-05-4 38p, paper . . .$5.95

___ *IN THESE HILLS*
    by Joanne Hart   Drawings by Jayne Gagnon
    Poems and Drawings of Grand Portage, Minnesota
                            ISBN 0-910259-04-6 22p, paper . . .$3.75

- -

Please add $1.50 for first book, 50¢ for each add'l book to cover mailing costs. Minnesotans please add 6% sales tax.

To: Women's Times Publishing, Box 215, Grand Marais, MN 55604

Name _____

Address _____

City_____State_____ Zip_____

Prices subject to change without notice.
Bulk purchase inquiries invited.

Dysle**x**ia

The SEN series

Dyslexia

Second Edition

Gavin Reid

continuum

Continuum International Publishing Group
The Tower Building
11 York Road
London
SE1 7NX

80 Maiden Lane
Suite 704
New York
NY 10038

British Library Cataloguing-in-Publication Data
A catalogue record for this book is available from the British Library.

ISBN: 0 8264 9236 3

Typeset by Fakenham Photosetting Ltd
Printed and bound in Great Britain by Ashford Colour Press Ltd, Gosport, Hampshire

Contents

Introduction

I wrote my first book on dyslexia in 1993. At that time the priorities were to lobby government for recognition of dyslexia, to develop an awareness of dyslexia among teachers and to promote extended specialist training in the field of dyslexia. Although the priorities are still very similar to what they were all those years ago, the progress that has been made to meet these targets has been considerable.

There has been significant progress in the scientific field regarding the nature and the origins of dyslexia – particularly in genetics, where a number of possible genetic permutations associated with dyslexia have been identified. In other areas too, our understanding of the reading process and the skills associated with language and learning has been revisited many times, and interventions strategies have been revised and contextualized for learners with dyslexia. Indeed, it has been recognized that many of the strategies and programmes long advocated for children with dyslexia can be useful for all. This has been acknowledged in government reports on reading in the UK, the USA and New Zealand.

It is encouraging that in most countries there has been recognition of the need to develop policies for dyslexia at both national and local levels. There are some excellent examples of policies for dyslexia in the Republic of Ireland and in Northern Ireland in particular, as well as in other countries. I mention Ireland as an example as it has been obvious that governments there have shown a dedication to dealing with dyslexia at all levels, and the rhetoric of policy has been supported by the essential follow-through in staff development programmes and in classroom practices.

Dyslexia

Having presented courses on dyslexia in over 30 countries, I have noted the progress and the desire among practitioners and policy-makers to establish and develop knowledge and expertise in dealing with dyslexia in the classroom. It is impressive to witness the endeavours in some areas with few resources (such as in Africa), which are attempting to ensure there is adequate training and knowledge in schools in relation to dyslexia. At the same time it is equally impressive to note how in other countries, such as Scotland, dyslexia and other specific learning difficulties have been seen as a priority area and supported with funding to enable innovative intervention, research and training programmes to be developed. This pattern has also been seen in many areas of the USA, too numerous to mention in this introduction. In Tennessee, for example, the Tennessee Center for the Study and Treatment of Dyslexia at Middle Tennessee State University has been developing training programmes for teachers since 1993, as well as offering diagnostic and consulting services. There are many examples of this type of excellence in practice.

Additionally, there are also instances of independent 'centres of excellence' developing, which are complementing the work done in the school system. For example, the Red Rose School, in Lancashire, UK; Learning Works in Wiltshire, also in the UK; the REACH Learning Center in Vancouver, Canada; and Fun Track Learning in Perth, Australia (see Appendix 1) are just a few of the organizations that have done a great deal to develop excellence in meeting the educational and social needs of children with dyslexia. Interestingly, the *International Book of Dyslexia* (Smythe, Everatt and Salter 2004) features 53 countries, all showing a commitment to tackling dyslexia.

This book is therefore timely. The effect of the impetus shown in recognition and training in dyslexia has been to increase the needs of classroom teachers and parents to be fully acquainted with the area. This book is therefore geared towards that end, that is, to provide classroom

2

teachers with a range of strategies for recognizing and teaching students with dyslexia.

Chapter 1 recognizes that there is confusion around the use of the term 'dyslexia', and attempts to clarify this. It highlights the need to identify the barriers that confront students with dyslexia, and suggests that dyslexia should be seen as a difference rather than a deficit.

Chapter 2 focuses on assessment of dyslexia and indicates quite strongly that assessment is a process, and one that involves more than the use of a test. There is an emphasis on empowering teachers to develop diagnostic phonological assessment for identifying difficulties in reading and spelling, and to take learning differences into account by looking at learning styles and learning preferences. There is also a strong emphasis on the need to link assessment to intervention.

Intervention is the theme of Chapters 3, 4, 5 and 6, which look at individual specialized approaches as well as curriculum adaptations and differentiation. There is also an emphasis on learning and study skills. Intervention is more than dealing with reading; it needs to focus on the whole child, and particularly the learner's social and emotional needs.

One of the areas of current confusion relates to the perceived overlap between dyslexia and other specific learning difficulties. This is dealt with in Chapter 7, where it is recognized that many of the interventions for different specific difficulties are very similar, sharing the same priorities and principles. The most crucial element in this, irrespective of the label, is 'constructive communication' between home and school. This is crucial if any form of intervention is to be successful.

The role of parents is the theme of Chapter 8. Parents have a significant role to play, and it is essential that this role is fully appreciated. This is particularly important in order to enhance the work of the school, and to minimize any anxieties that may arise from the challenges the young person with dyslexia faces within and outside school.

Chapter 9 provides suggestions for staff development, as well as some follow-up suggestions that might be helpful for parents. Those within the school who have knowledge of dyslexia can provide information and support to others. Staff development is therefore a crucial area if the target of a full understanding of dyslexia in every school in every country is to become reality. The book also contains appendices with contact details for over 30 countries, as well as some useful websites.

The aim of the book therefore is primarily to empower teachers to recognize that they have the skills to deal with dyslexia. What they need is the knowledge to develop an understanding of children with dyslexia: an understanding of their needs and their skills, as well as of the challenges they face in education and in the world at large. An understanding of children with dyslexia is at the heart of this book. It is hoped this will transmit into constructive and effective practice in school, and allow all people with dyslexia to develop to their full potential, academically and socially, so that they can have a 'sense of belonging' in today's inclusive communities.

1

Understanding Dyslexia

Dyslexia is a term that can be surrounded by confusion and ambiguity, which can give rise to anxiety for teachers and parents. It is the aim of this book to clarify the confusion surrounding dyslexia and provide strategies for identification and teaching. There will be an emphasis on making the curriculum accessible for children with dyslexia within an inclusive educational setting, through the use of learning styles and differentiation.

Defining Dyslexia

There is a range of definitions that are currently used to describe dyslexia. Most of the definitions include the following aspects:

◆ the neurological and genetic causes of dyslexia

◆ the characteristic difficulties associated with dyslexia, such as phonological, visual and auditory processing difficulties

◆ the associated characteristics of dyslexia – difficulties relating to memory, time management, processing speed, organization, and sequencing and planning

◆ the need for over-learning and specific teaching approaches

◆ the overlap with other conditions such as dyspraxia, dyscalculia and ADHD.

5

Characteristics of Dyslexia

There are a number of core characteristics of dyslexia that are important for identification and assessment, including reading, writing and spelling difficulties. These can be noted particularly when the learner is progressing well in other areas and seems to have a good oral understanding. Often, poor reading (decoding) contrasted with good comprehension can be an indicator of dyslexia.

> Children with dyslexia can often have good listening comprehension skills.

Barriers to Learning

Accessing the curriculum can be dependent on accessing print, but it is important that children with dyslexia are able to access materials using other means. The presentation, content and layout of worksheets is an important factor, and the use of visuals, space on page and font style and size are all important, as well as ensuring the content can be understood and that the tasks are achievable.

> The layout and presentation of worksheets are as important as the content and the tasks.

These barriers can be overcome through differentiation as well as through the use of specialized resources. There are some specific programmes for dyslexia (discussed later in this book), but often the answer lies not in a specific resource but in the teaching and learning process. Differentiation is part of this process, as are interactive question-and-answer sessions, and the building of confidence and self-esteem.

Dyslexia Research

The research field of dyslexia has many different dimensions. There are research activities in different aspects of neurology/brain structure; neurological processing; the cerebellum; the visual cortex; and speech and language processing and the processes involved in learning. Cognitive psychologists are involved in studies involving memory and dyslexia, as well as the role of processing speed and the cognitive routes to literacy acquisition. This can present a confusing picture for teachers who are seeking straightforward explanations of dyslexia and guidance for practice. It might therefore be useful to view dyslexia as a difference rather than as a deficit: that is, a difference in how the child processes information.

Children with dyslexia can have a different and individual way of processing information. Difference does not mean deficit!

Dyslexia as a difference

Dyslexia can be described as a **difference** in the following ways:

♦ how information is processed

♦ the strategies that are needed to learn effectively

♦ the speed of processing

♦ the style of processing.

Children with dyslexia usually have a visual, right-brained global processing style, so it is important to acknowledge the characteristics and the strengths of this style.

Three factors: neurological, cognitive and educational

There are three factors that can help provide an understanding of dyslexia:

♦ neurological/brain

♦ cognitive/learning

♦ educational/environment/learning experiences.

Neurological/brain

There is now considerable evidence that there is a neurological basis to dyslexia. This means that the brain structure and the neural connections needed for processing information may develop differently in dyslexic children, so that dyslexic children and adults will learn differently and find some types of processing tasks, such as those involving print and language, more challenging than other learners.

There are two hemispheres in the brain – the left and the right, and generally speaking each hemisphere is more adept at processing certain types of information. Usually the left hemisphere processes language and the small details of information, such as print. This means the left hemisphere is important for decoding tasks that are necessary for accurate reading.

The right hemisphere tends to process information that incorporates a more holistic stimulus. This would involve processing pictures and other types of visual information. The right hemisphere also usually deals with comprehension, and some aesthetic aspects such as the appreciation of art and music. Some neuro-psychologists, such as Dirk Bakker in Holland, have related this to reading and have suggested that right hemisphere readers can become 'sloppy' readers, but may have good comprehension (Robertson and Bakker 2002).

It is often the case that while children with dyslexia can show skills in right hemisphere processing, they may have difficulty in processing information using the left hemisphere. The skills necessary for accurate reading tend to be left hemisphere skills, such as, for example, being able to discriminate different sounds in words. These skills are called phonological skills and they are essential for identifying the clusters of letters that make certain sounds, such as 'ough' as in 'tough' and 'ight' as in 'right.' It is now widely accepted that children with dyslexia have a weakness in phonological skills, and this will certainly affect their ability to read fluently, especially when they are young (Snowling 2005). There is, however, evidence that if intervention to teach phonological skills takes place at an early age, the acquisition of literacy can become easier.

Identification and Intervention

When identifying dyslexia, it is preferable to have both a rationale and a strategy for the assessment. Often a suspicion of the presence of dyslexic difficulties can be identified through observation, or through the results of routine assessments. This information, however, needs to be contextualized, so that an overall picture of the child's profile can be seen and any evidence of dyslexia can be noted. It is important that the identification is linked to intervention. Some general aspects relating to the purpose of an assessment include the following.

Identification of the learner's general strengths and weaknesses

It is important to identify the strengths as well as the areas of weakness. This can be helpful in developing a programme and suggesting appropriate strategies. For example:

Dyslexia

Strengths:

◆ Good visual skills

◆ Excellent expressive vocabulary

◆ Good in team games

◆ Good understanding of language.

Weaknesses:

◆ Difficulty remembering spelling rules

◆ Difficulty reading aloud

◆ Slow reading speed

◆ Difficulty organizing work.

A programme for this child could therefore ensure that he or she gets the opportunities to use visual skills and participate in team games. The strengths can be used to develop interest in a topic, as well as to develop skills in the weaker areas.

Indication of the learner's current level of performance in attainments

This can easily be obtained from standardized assessment. It is important to have this information as it can help to monitor progress, and be used to note the discrepancy between the child's reading/spelling age and his or her chronological age. It is important not to rely too much on standardized data of this type, but they can provide a guide.

An explanation for the learner's lack of progress

This involves identifying aspects of the learner's performance in reading, writing and spelling that may typify a 'pattern of errors':

- identification of specific areas of competence
- understanding of the student's learning style
- indication of aspects of the curriculum that may interest and motivate the learner
- specific aspects of the curriculum that are challenging for the child.

Specific difficulty: Reading

Difficulty in recognizing and remembering sounds in words
Example
Letter combinations that make sounds, such as 'ph' and 'th' found in a word like 'elephant', can be difficult. Other confusions can be noted in words like 'necessity'. I have an example of an 18-year-old with an IQ of 120 who still experiences these difficulties. His pattern of errors can be noted in the words below:

Physicion
Predujuce
Nessecity
Comision

Substitution of words with similar meanings when reading aloud
This is called semantic confusion. Words that have similar meanings, such as 'bus' and 'car', can be confused when reading aloud. This, however, means that the reader does understand the text and is reading for meaning and context rather than focusing on reading accuracy. Sometimes it can be difficult for the child with dyslexia to read for accuracy and meaning at the same time, and for some it may be more effective to focus on reading for meaning. This would mean that language

11

experience and pre-reading discussion are important to ensure that the reader has a good idea of what the text is about.

Difficulty with rhyming, for example remembering nursery rhymes and the sequence of the rhyme
This can be used in an early identification programme. Some children can become quite adept at joining in at nursery rhymes, but are not able to recite these on their own. This type of activity should be included in any early identification procedures that are used in the classroom.

Children with dyslexia may not only forget the actual words in the rhyme, but also get some of the lines confused and out of sequence.

Reverses, omits or adds letters or words
This is quite characteristic of dyslexia, as it indicates that the child is reading or writing using context. Children who have difficulty in decoding often compensate by over-relying on context.

Loses the place when reading
This is also very common and can indicate the presence of a visual difficulty. Sometimes complete lines can be omitted. A ruler that masks the line below can be used, but this can also restrict the opportunities and the flow necessary for reading in context. A good resource is the transparent ruler with a colour transparency.

Difficulty with the sequence of the alphabet
This can make using a dictionary very time-consuming and frustrating. There are some alphabet games that can be used to help with this. This colour-coding of groups of letters can also be helpful: the alphabet can be divided into seven sections, with a different colour for each section.

Difficulty pronouncing multi-syllabic words, even common ones
Words like 'preliminary', 'governmental' and 'necessity' can be easily mispronounced and misspelt. The use of colour-coding can also help with this.

Poor word attack skills – particularly with unknown words
This can be a problem when tackling new, unknown words. If the child has poor word attack skills then he or she is likely to read the word visually, and not break the word down into its constituent parts. This can be a difficulty when learning new vocabulary.

Reading speed slow and hesitant and often with little expression
This happens because children with dyslexia spend a great deal of effort on reading accuracy, which can result in a loss of emphasis on meaning and expression. It can also make reading speed quite slow, and a loss of reading fluency can therefore be evident. This is a major concern, as reading fluency can be linked to reading comprehension. It is important that comprehension is given a prominent position in a reading programme for children with dyslexia.

Reluctance to read for pleasure
With most skills, practice can develop competence. This is the case also with reading. It is important that reading takes place every day, even if it is only magazines. Reading for pleasure can result if reading is daily, and particularly if the reader chooses his or her own reading material.

Reading comprehension better than single word reading
This can often be the case for children with dyslexia. This is because they read for meaning and context. With single word reading there are no contextual clues available. To ascertain the actual level of decoding, therefore, a single

word test would be better than reading a passage. The use of non-words is also a good method of testing actual decoding skills.

Confuses words which have the same or similar sounds (such as 'their' and 'there', and 'access' and 'assess')
This is very common in children with dyslexia, which is why when they are doing written work, time should be allocated for proofreading so that they can check these potential errors. The best way to remember these words is to use them: through usage, automaticity can occur. The more they are used, the more likely it is that the differences between these commonly confused words can be learnt and consolidated.

Specific difficulty: Spelling

Difficulty in spelling
Examples include remembering spelling rules, making phonological errors in spelling (for example 'f' for 'ph'), letters being out of sequence, inconsistent use of some letters with similar sounds such as 's' and 'z', difficulty with word endings (for example using 'ie' for 'y'), confusion or omission of vowels, and difficulty with words with double consonants such as 'commission'.

These types of errors can be quite characteristic of dyslexia. One of the difficulties with spelling is that once a word has been habitually misspelt, it is difficult for the child to unlearn the error. This means that many of these errors can persist throughout all stages of school and beyond.

Specific difficulty: Writing

Inconsistent writing style
This can often be noted in the inconsistent use of capital letters and small letters. Often these are used wrongly and there is little or no pattern to how they are used.

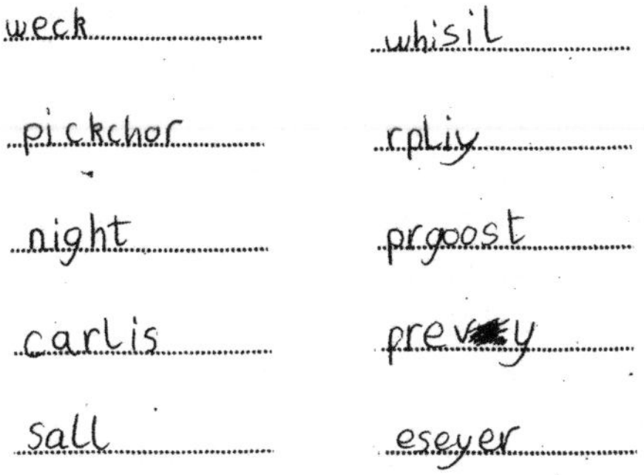

weck ....   whisil ....

pickchor ....   rpliy ....

night ....   prgoost ....

carlis ....   prevey ....

sall ....   eseyer ....

Figure 1 Spelling pattern of a dyslexic boy aged 10
with an IQ of 110

*Slow writing speed and perhaps reluctance to write a
lengthy piece*
This may be the result of not being able to generate
sentence and grammatical structure very fluently, as well
as of a difficulty in finding the most appropriate words
to explain things. Because this can take some time, the
written piece can take longer than might be expected.

It is helpful to provide a framework for the written piece
as well as the key words that are to be used. This can
speed up the writing process.

Unusual writing grip or sitting position
This can often indicate a visual/perceptual difficulty,
or dyspraxic-type difficulties that can affect hand–eye
co-ordination. Special adapted pencils with rubber or
spongy grips can help. It is also important to recognize
the importance of good posture when writing and using
a keyboard.

Specific difficulty: Memory

Poor short-term and working memory intervention
This means that there can be difficulties in remembering
lists of information, even short lists, or short instructions. It

is important therefore to provide one piece of information at a time, otherwise the child will become confused.

Poor long-term memory/organizational difficulties
These two factors can be linked. Long-term memory is to a certain extent dependent on good cognitive organization. That means being able to organize information at the point of learning. The use of strategies to categorize information will make recall easier and strengthen long-term memory. The use of personal memory strategies is therefore important for children with dyslexia. They may show poor organization of their timetable, materials, equipment and items needed for learning, such as having difficulty remembering and organizing their homework notebooks.

Specific difficulty: Movement

Difficulty with coordination and tasks such as tying shoelaces; bumps into furniture, trips and falls frequently
There can be an overlap between dyslexia and dyspraxia (which is a difficulty with motor and movement control). Some of the factors associated with coordination difficulties can provide clues in early identification of dyslexia. These factors can often be noted at the pre-school stage.

Specific difficulty: Speech development

Confusing similar sounds; poor articulation; difficulty blending sounds into words; poor awareness of rhyme; poor syntactic structure; naming difficulties
Speech difficulties in the early years can also be an indicator of dyslexia. Not all children with dyslexia will have speech difficulties but those who have will usually have the phonological difficulties associated with dyslexia.

It is important to recognize that many of these specific difficulties can be seen in a continuum from mild to severe, and the extent and severity of these difficulties will have an impact on the assessment results and the subsequent recommendations for support.

Information Processing

Dyslexia is a difference in how some children process information. Information processing describes the interaction between the learner and the task. The information processing cycle has three components. These are:

◆ **input** – auditory, visual, tactile, kinesthetic

◆ **cognition** – memory, understanding, organizing and making sense of information

◆ **output** – reading aloud, talking, discussing, drawing, seeing, experiencing.

Children with dyslexia can have difficulty at all three stages of this cycle. It is important therefore to draw on information that relate to these three stages. For example, one can ask whether the same difficulties are experienced if the material is presented visually as opposed to auditorily; or perhaps the individual can learn more effectively if he or she is able to experience the learning through the kinesthetic modality. Although related to teaching approaches, it is crucial that this is acknowledged in the identification and assessment process, as it is important that reasons for the difficulty are sought, and further, that a clear link can be forged between assessment and teaching approaches.

Dyslexia: Some Key Points

Dyslexia is individual

This means that children with dyslexia may have slightly different characteristics from each other. These characteristics can have a varying impact on the child. In some children this may not be too noticeable, but in others it can be very obvious. Dyslexia therefore can be evident along a continuum, from mild to severe.

This of course means that what works for one dyslexic child may not work successfully for another.

Dyslexia relates to how information is processed

This means that dyslexia involves more than reading: it affects learning and how all information – and that includes oral instructions – is processed.

It is important to recognize that the cycle of learning called the 'information processing cycle' is important. It can help us to understand the difficulties experienced by children with dyslexia. This cycle applies to how we take information in, how we memorize it and how we display to others that we know the information.

Children with dyslexia can have difficulty displaying knowledge and understanding in written work

In schoolwork, children usually display what they know through the written mode. Yet this may be the dyslexic child's weakest way of presenting information. Writing can be laborious and tedious for the dyslexic child. However, it can be made easier and more enjoyable if he or she is provided with a structure for writing and perhaps even the key words. One of the important points to consider here is that we need to identify and acknowledge the specific strengths of each child with dyslexia.

Children with dyslexia can have difficulty learning through the auditory modality (i.e. through listening)

There are many ways of learning, particularly today with computer games and other electronic learning and leisure tools. Yet in many cases we still rely on what is called the auditory modality: that is, the person's ability to listen and understand through sound, rather than through pictures (visual) or through experience (kinesthetic). Most of the research indicates that children with dyslexia have a phono-logical difficulty – that is, they have difficulty with sounds, and remembering the sound combinations and sequence of sounds that make up a word. Listening may therefore not be the easiest means of acquiring information. Usually it is better if children with dyslexia can see the information to be learnt.

Children with dyslexia have difficulty remembering information

This can apply to short-term and working memory and means it can affect the remembering of oral instructions, especially if a list of items is presented. The short-term (or working) memory can only hold a limited amount of information at any one time, but children with dyslexia can have difficulty in remembering even a limited amount accurately, so it is best to provide only one instruction at any one time.

Children with dyslexia can have difficulty organizing information

Whether we are aware of it or not, we always make some attempt to organize new information. We might group new items to be remembered into one category, and when we are recalling information we generally do so in a fairly organized way, so that a listener can understand. This can be especially important if we are recalling a sequence of events. Children with dyslexia can have some difficulty in organ-izing information, and this can affect both how efficiently information is remembered, and how they can present the information to others. This can affect their performance in examinations unless additional support is made available.

19

Dyslexia

Children with dyslexia need more time to process information

This is very characteristic of dyslexia: usually children with dyslexia will take longer to process information because they may take an indirect route to arrive at an answer. This emphasizes the individuality of dyslexia and the right hemisphere way of processing information that children with dyslexia often use.

Children with dyslexia usually have difficulty reading and spelling accurately and fluently

You will note that the word 'usually' is mentioned here. This is because not every child with dyslexia will have difficulty in reading and spelling. Some children can compensate for a reading difficulty by becoming very adept at using context, and tend to read for meaning. These children may still however show some of the other characteristics of dyslexia, particularly those aspects that relate to information processing, such as memory and organization.

Similarly, they may have difficulty in reading but not in spelling or vice versa. This again emphasizes the individual nature of dyslexia, which means that different children can show dyslexic characteristics to a different degree.

Although the degree of dyslexia can differ, the indicators are usually fairly constant; but these can also depend on the age of the child. It is possible to note some of the indicators of dyslexia before the child attends school, that is, before he or she starts to learn to read.

It is important to recognize that dyslexia occurs within a continuum and that there can be shared and overlapping characteristics between dyslexia and other specific learning difficulties.

Summary

This chapter has

♦ recognized that there is confusion around the use of the term 'dyslexia'

♦ suggested that differentiation and acknowledgement of learning styles can help access the curricular needs of students with dyslexia

♦ identified the barriers and suggested that dyslexia should be seen as a difference rather than a deficit.

2

Identification and Assessment

Process and Strategies

Dyslexia should not **only** be identified through the use of a test: assessment for dyslexia is a process that involves much more than this. The assessment needs to consider classroom and curriculum factors and the learning preferences of the child, as well as his or her specific difficulties and strengths.

Specifically, assessment should consider three aspects: difficulties, discrepancies and differences, and these should relate to the classroom environment and the curriculum.

Assessment for dyslexia is a process that involves more than a test.

Difficulties

The main problem for children with dyslexia usually relates to the decoding or the encoding of print. This may be due to difficulties in

♦ acquiring phonological awareness

♦ memory

♦ organization and sequencing

♦ movement and coordination

♦ language problems

♦ visual/auditory perception.

Discrepancies

The discrepancies may be apparent

♦ in comparing decoding skills with reading/listening comprehension

♦ between oral and written skills

♦ in performance within the different subject areas of the curriculum.

Differences

It is also important to acknowledge the differences between individual children with dyslexia. The identification process should therefore also consider

♦ learning styles

♦ environmental preferences for learning

♦ learning strategies.

> Assessment should inform teaching.

Diagnostic Assessment

Miscue analysis during oral reading

The strategy known as miscue analysis is an example of a diagnostic assessment. It is based on the 'top-down' approach to reading, which suggests that, when reading, the reader has to make predictions as to the most likely meaning of the text. Such predictions are based on how the reader perceives the graphic, syntactic and semantic information contained in the text.

Miscue analysis is the process that occurs when a teacher listens to a child read, and notes the mistakes or 'miscues'. Miscues can arise from symbolic, syntactic or semantic errors.

♦ *Symbolic* errors mean that the child has misread the actual letter(s), and this can be a result of a visual difficulty.

♦ *Syntactic* errors occur if, for example, the child reads a word as 'of' instead of 'for'. This indicates that the child does not have the grammatical structures of sentences but can make a fairly good stab at the symbolic features of the word – even though it is still wrong.

♦ *Semantic* errors are quite common with children with dyslexia, as they indicate that the reader is relying heavily on context. An example of a semantic error would be reading the word 'bus' instead of 'car'.

The important point is that this can provide impetus to a more diagnostic approach to the assessment of reading. This approach was further emphasized by Marie Clay in the Reading Recovery programme (Clay 1985), which also uses miscue analysis as one of the fundamental approaches to diagnosing a child's reading level.

One of the important aspects about miscue analysis is that it can help the teacher make deductions about the reader's understanding of the text. For example, if the child read 'the poor horse bolted his food' instead of the 'the scared horse bolted fast', this would indicate that he or she has little real understanding of the text apart from the fact that it concerns a horse. This would most likely indicate a difficulty with the semantics of the text, since the guess does not properly fit the context. The syntactic flow of the sentence appears to be OK, and there is some attempt to represent the symbols. Other types of errors often noted in miscue analysis and the significance of these are discussed below.

Omissions
These may occur if the child is reading for meaning rather than the actual print. He or she may omit small words that do not add anything significant to the meaning of the passage.

Additions
These may reflect superficial reading, with perhaps an over-dependence on context clues.

Substitutions
These can be visual or semantic substitutions, and they may reflect an over-dependence on context clues.

Repetitions
These may indicate poor directional attack, especially if the child reads the same line again. They may also indicate some hesitancy on the part of the child, perhaps because he or she is unable to read the next word in the line.

Reversals
These may reflect the lack of left-to-right orientation. They may also indicate some visual difficulty, and perhaps a lack of reading for meaning.

Hesitations
These can occur when the reader is unsure of the text and perhaps lacking in confidence in reading. For the same reason that repetitions may occur, the reader may also be anticipating a difficult word later in the sentence.

Self-corrections
These occur when the reader becomes more aware of meaning and less dependent on simple word recognition. It is important to recognize the extent of self-corrections,

as this can indicate that the child does have an under-standing of the passage.

Children with dyslexia can show most of the miscues noted above, especially as often they read for meaning and therefore additions and substitutions can be quite common.

Assessment should be diagnostic so that the information can support the selection of teaching approaches.

Phonological Assessment

To a great extent, this can be carried out by the teacher using adapted materials, or indeed by observation of the child's reading pattern. Phonological assessment covers the following areas:

♦ non-word reading

♦ sound recognition

♦ syllable segmentation

♦ recognition of prefixes, suffixes and syllables

♦ rhyme recognition and production

♦ phoneme segmentation (such as blending, recognition of initial and final phonemes).

There are standardized phonological assessments available and recommended for use in an assessment for dyslexia. One such assessment available in the UK is the **Phonological Assessment Battery (PHAB)**. This consists of five measures:

♦ alliteration test

♦ rhyme test

- naming speed test
- fluency test
- spoonerism test.

This technique is very suitable for assessing dyslexic difficulties. There is good evidence that dyslexic children have difficulty with rhyme and alliteration, and some researchers have indicated that naming speed is in itself a significant feature of dyslexic difficulties (Wolf and O'Brien 2001; Fawcett and Nicolson 2001).

The Phonological Assessment Battery (Frederickson, Frith and Reason 1997) can be accessed by all teachers and is available from www.nfer-nelson.co.uk.

Screening/Baseline Assessment

There are some issues that can be raised in relation to screening and baseline assessment:

- What is the most desirable age (or ages) for children to be screened?

- What skills, abilities and attainments in performances should children be screened for?

- How should the results of any screening procedures be used?

It is important that the results of screening and baseline assessments are used diagnostically, and not to label children prematurely. There are some screening tests that have been developed specifically to identify the possibility of dyslexia. These can yield very useful information but should be used in conjunction with other data, obtained from observations made by the teacher of the child's work, and of progress in class and in different areas of the curriculum. Some examples of these are shown in Appendix 2.

Checklists

There are many variations in checklists for identifying dyslexia (which in itself highlights the need to treat them with considerable caution). Checklists are not, in any form, definitive tools for diagnosis of dyslexia, but can be used as a preliminary screening to justify a more detailed assessment. Some checklists (such as those shown below) can provide a range of information that may produce a picture of the child's strengths and weaknesses. Even these, however, are still very limited, and no substitution for a comprehensive and contextual assessment.

Checklist: Reading

	Comments
Sight vocabulary	
Sound blending	
Use of contextual clues	
Attempting unknown vocabulary	
Eye tracking	
Difficulty keeping place	
Speech development	
Motivation in relation to reading material	
Word naming difficulty	
Omitting words	
Omitting phrases	
Omitting whole lines	

Checklist: Writing

	Comments
Directional difficulty	
Difficulty associating visual symbol with verbal sound	
Liability to sub-vocalize sounds before writing	
Unusual spelling pattern	
Handwriting difficulty	
Difficulty with cursive writing	
Using capitals and lower case interchangeably and inconsistently	
Poor organization of work on page	

This form of assessment can provide some general data on the broad areas of difficulty experienced by the child – for example, the teacher may decide the child has a pronounced difficulty in the use of contextual cues; but this does not provide information as to why this difficulty persists and the kind of difficulties the pupil experiences with contextual cues. Does the child use contextual cues on some occasions, and under certain conditions? The teacher must carry out further investigations to obtain some further explanations of the difficulty.

Checklists/screening can be good starting points but they have limitations.

Discrepancies

An approach to assessment that can be readily carried out by the teacher involves noting discrepancies between different components of reading. This kind of assessment can include using:

29

- decoding tests (non-words reading test)
- word reading tests
- phonological awareness tests
- listening comprehension tests
- reading comprehension tests.

The information gleaned from this type of assessment strategy can be used to note any obvious discrepancies between achievement in the different tests. For example, a child with dyslexia may have a low score on a decoding test, and particularly one that involves non-words, while scoring considerably higher in the listening comprehension test.

Differences

It is important to obtain information on the differences as well as the difficulties and the discrepancies. The interactive observational style index shown below can provide some pointers on the kind of information that can be useful.

Interactive observational style index *
Emotional

- Motivation
  - What topics, tasks and activities interest the child?
  - What topics does the child speak about confidently?
  - What kinds of prompting and cueing are necessary to increase motivation?
  - What type of incentives motivate the child: leadership

---

* Adapted from Given and Reid (1999), Reid (2005).

opportunities, working with others, gold star, free time, physical activity, etc.?

◆ Does the child seem to work because of interest in learning or to please others – parents, teachers, friends?

◆ Persistence

   ◆ Does the child stick with a task until completion without breaks?

   ◆ Are frequent breaks necessary when working on difficult tasks?

   ◆ What is the quality of the child's work with and without breaks?

◆ Responsibility

   ◆ To what extent does the child take responsibility for his or her own learning?

   ◆ Does the child attribute his or her successes and failures to self or others?

   ◆ Does the child grasp the relationship between effort expended and results achieved?

   ◆ Does the child conform to classroom routines or consistently respond with non-conformity?

◆ Structure

   ◆ Are the child's personal effects (desk, clothing, materials) well organized or cluttered?

   ◆ How does the child respond to someone imposing organizational structure on him or her?

   ◆ When provided with specific, detailed guidelines for task completion, does the child faithfully follow them, or work around them?

Dyslexia

Social

♦ Interaction

  ♦ Is there a noticeable difference between the child's positivity and interactions when working alone, one-to-one, in a small group, or with the whole class?

  ♦ When is the child's best work accomplished – when working alone, with one other child or in a small group?

  ♦ Does the child ask for approval or to have work checked frequently?

♦ Communication

  ♦ Is the child's language spontaneous, or does he or she need prompting?

  ♦ Does the child like to tell stories with considerable detail?

  ♦ Does the child give the main events and gloss over details?

  ♦ Does the child listen to others when they talk, or is he or she constantly interrupting?

Cognitive

♦ Modality preference

  ♦ What type of instructions does the child most easily understand (written, oral, visual)?

  ♦ Does the child respond more quickly and easily to questions about stories heard, or read?

  ♦ Does the child's oral communication include appropriate variations in pitch, intonation and volume?

  ♦ In his or her spare time, does the child draw, build things, write, play sports, or listen to music?

♦ When working on the computer for pleasure, does the child play games, search for information, or practise academic skill development?

♦ Does the child take notes, write a word to recall how it is spelt, or draw maps when giving directions?

♦ Given an array of options and asked to demonstrate his or her knowledge of a topic by drawing, writing, giving an oral report, or demonstrating/acting, what would the child choose?

♦ Under what specific areas of learning (reading, maths, sports, etc.) is tension evident, such as nail-biting, misbehaviour, distressed facial expressions, limited eye contact, etc.?

♦ Sequential or simultaneous learning

♦ Does the child begin with step 1 and proceed in an orderly fashion, or have difficulty following sequential information?

♦ Does the child jump from one task to another and back again, or stay focused on one topic?

♦ Is there a logical sequence to the child's explanations, or do his or her thoughts 'bounce around' from one idea to another?

♦ When telling a story, does the child begin at the beginning and give a blow-by-blow sequence of events, or does he or she skip around, share the highlights, or speak mostly in terms of how the movie *felt*?

♦ When asked to write a report, does the child seek detailed directions or want only the topic?

♦ What types of tasks are likely to be tackled with confidence?

♦ Impulsive or reflective

  ♦ Are the child's responses rapid and spontaneous, or delayed and reflective?

  ♦ Does the child return to a topic or behaviour long after others have ceased talking about it?

  ♦ Does the child seem to consider past events before taking action?

Physical

♦ Mobility

  ♦ Does the child move around the class frequently or fidget when seated?

  ♦ While learning, does the child like to stand or walk?

  ♦ While working, does the child slump, or sit up?

  ♦ Does the child jiggle his or her foot a lot?

  ♦ Does the child become entangled in his or her chair when working quietly?

♦ Food intake

  ♦ When working, does the child snack, chew on a pencil or bite on a finger?

  ♦ Does the child seek water frequently?

  ♦ Does the child chew on his or her hair, collar, etc. while working?

♦ Time of day

  ♦ At what time of day is the child most alert?

  ♦ Is there a noticeable difference between morning work as compared to afternoon work?

Environment

◆ Sound

  ◆ Under what conditions is the child relaxed but alert when learning – noisy or quiet?

  ◆ Does the child seek out places to work that are particularly quiet?

◆ Light

  ◆ Does the child squint in 'normal' lighting?

  ◆ Is there a tendency for the child to put his or her head down in brightly lit classrooms?

  ◆ Does the child like to work in dimly lit areas, or say that the light is too bright?

◆ Temperature

  ◆ Does the child leave his or her coat on when others seem warm?

  ◆ Does the child appear comfortable in rooms below 68° Fahrenheit?

◆ Furniture design

  ◆ When given a choice, does the child sit on the floor, lie down, or sit in a straight chair to read?

  ◆ When given free time, does the child choose an activity requiring formal posture or informal posture?

Metacognition

◆ Is the child aware of his or her learning style strengths?

◆ Does the child analyse the environment in regard to his or her learning with questions such as:

  ◆ Is the light level right for me?

- ◆ Am I able to focus with this level of sound?
- ◆ Is the furniture comfortable for me?
- ◆ Am I comfortable with the temperature?

◆ Does the child demonstrate internal assessment of self by asking questions such as:

- ◆ Have I done this before?
- ◆ How did I tackle it?
- ◆ What did I find easy?
- ◆ What was difficult?
- ◆ Why did I find it easy or difficult?
- ◆ What did I learn?
- ◆ What do I have to do to accomplish this task?
- ◆ How should I tackle it?
- ◆ Should I tackle it the same way as before?

Prediction

◆ Does the child make plans and work towards goals, or let things happen as they will?

◆ Is the child willing to take academic risks, or does he or she play it safe by responding only when called upon?

◆ Does the child demonstrate enthusiasm about gaining new knowledge and skills, or does he or she hesitate?

◆ Is there a relationship between the child's 'misbehaviour' and difficult tasks?

Feedback

◆ How does the child respond to different types of feedback: non-verbal (smile), check mark, oral praise, a

36

detailed explanation, pat on the shoulder, comparison of scores with previous scores earned, comparison of scores with classmates' performance, and so forth?

♦ How much external prompting is needed before the child can access previous knowledge?

This type of information can help to inform teaching and can be used before embarking on the developing of differentiated materials. It should be recognized that not all learners with dyslexia will have the same learning behaviours. It therefore follows that the type of intervention and the presentation of materials will differ. For that reason it is important to obtain as much information as possible on the learner's preferences.

The Principles of Assessment

Some general principles can be noted in carrying out an assessment:

♦ The lack of availability of a test must not prevent a child's dyslexic difficulties from being recognized – many of the characteristics can be quite obvious in the classroom situation.

♦ Teachers must have an understanding of dyslexia so that these characteristics can be recognized.

♦ Appropriate materials and teaching programmes need to be developed that are based on the results of the assessment.

Summary

♦ Assessment of dyslexia is a process that involves more than using a test.

♦ The assessment process needs to consider the difficulties, the discrepancies and the differences.

Dyslexia

♦ Teachers can develop a diagnostic phonological assessment that is contextualized for the classroom.

♦ Assessment of reading, spelling and expressive writing should be diagnostic.

♦ The differences and the child's preferences in learning styles need to be taken into account.

♦ Assessment must have a clear link to intervention.

3

Teaching Approaches

This chapter will describe some appropriate teaching approaches for use with children with dyslexia. There are many excellent commercial and established teaching programmes available. Many of these utilize similar principles and strategies. These will be discussed in this chapter and some examples of programmes will also be shown to highlight these principles and strategies. The chapter divides teaching approaches into three broad areas: individualized approaches; curriculum approaches; and whole-school approaches.

In determining the most appropriate approaches for children with dyslexia, a number of factors must be considered. These include:

♦ The context – this includes the provision, the type of school, class size and the training of the staff as well as the age and stage of the learner.

♦ The assessment – this provides an indication of the strengths and the difficulties experienced by the learner. This type of profile is important initial information needed to develop an appropriate programme.

♦ The curriculum – what are the expectations being placed on the learner? To what extent is the curriculum accessible and differentiated?

♦ The learner – what motivates the learner? What do we know about his or her learning style? How can we use this information to develop a programme?

> Programmes and strategies need to be individualized for the child with dyslexia to take into account the learning context and the learner's strengths and weaknesses.

Programmes and Strategies

The various types of programmes and strategies that can be used are outlined below.

Individualized programmes

These programmes are usually:

♦ highly structured

♦ essentially free-standing

♦ one to one

♦ a main element of the overall strategy for teaching children with dyslexia.

Curriculum strategies

These usually:

♦ utilize the same principles as some of the individual programmes

♦ can be used more selectively by the teacher

♦ can be integrated within the normal activities of the curriculum.

Whole-school approaches

These approaches:

♦ recognize that dyslexia is a whole-school concern and not only the responsibility of individual teachers

◆ focus on consultancy, whole-school screening, and monitoring of children's progress.

Early identification is a key aspect of a whole-school approach.

Individualized Programmes

Most individualized programmes incorporate some, or all, of the following principles.

Multisensory

'Multisensory' means that they utilize visual, auditory, tactile and kinesthetic modalities. Multisensory methods utilize all available senses simultaneously. This can be summed up in the phrase 'hear it, say it, see it and write it'. These methods have been used for many years and are a key component in the Orton–Gillingham (OG) programme and in most other phonic programmes.

Over-learning

They ensure that **over-learning** is present, as this is necessary to achieve automaticity. Over-learning is deemed necessary for children with dyslexic difficulties. The short- and long-term memory difficulties experienced by dyslexic children mean that considerable reinforcement and repetition is necessary.

Structured

They are highly **structured** and usually phonically based, and are **sequential and cumulative** (see below) – which means that progression can be easily noted.

The structured approaches evident in programmes of work for dyslexic children usually provide a linear progression, thus enabling the learner to complete and master a particular skill in the reading or learning process before advancing to a subsequent skill. This implies that learning occurs in a linear developmental manner.

Sequential

There is usually a progression in the approach. It is necessary for children with dyslexia to master sub-skills before moving to more advanced materials. Hence, a sequential and cumulative approach may not only provide a structure to their learning, but help to make learning more meaningful and effective.

Key components of a teaching programme

The following are some of the key components of a reading programme for children with dyslexia:

♦ bottom-up emphasis on phonics

♦ emphasis on listening skills

♦ opportunities for oral work

♦ recognizes the importance of discussion

♦ phonic skills a key focus

♦ whole-word recognition skills

♦ develops sentence awareness

♦ includes comprehension-building activities

♦ looks at reading and spelling connections

♦ develops skills in creative writing

♦ provides opportunities to develop imagination and creativity

- ◆ ensures practice in the use of syntactic and semantic cues

- ◆ places an emphasis on learning the 44 phonemes of the English language, and a knowledge of the 17 vowel sounds and the 27 consonant sounds

- ◆ includes development of pre-reading skills such as visual and auditory perception

- ◆ provides opportunities to practise visual and auditory discrimination

- ◆ facilitates practice in fine motor skills

- ◆ ensures knowledge of spatial relationships

- ◆ ensures a knowledge of colour, number and directions

- ◆ includes game activities

- ◆ develops syllable segmentation

- ◆ develops rhyme judgement and rhyme production

- ◆ alliteration, onset and rime, and phoneme segmentation.

IDA matrix of programs

The International Dyslexia Association have produced a short matrix of multisensory structured language programs indicating the type of programme, delivery, the level of phonic instruction, how each program deals with fluency, comprehension, written expression and text construction, and the level of training needed for the program. The programs included in the matrix are OG (www. OrtonAcademy.org), Alphabetic Phonics (www.ALTAread. org), Association Method (www.usm.edu/dubard), Language! (www.SoprisWest.com), Lexia-Herman Method (www.Hermanmethod.com), Lindamood–Bell (www. Lindamoodbell.com), Project Read (www.Projectread.com),

Slingerland (www.Slingerland.org), Sonday System (www. SondaySystem.com), Sounds in Syllables, Spalding Method, (www.spalding.org), Starting Over, Wilson Fundations and Wilson Reading (www.wilsonlanguage.com).

(Source: IDA, www.inter-dyslexia.org)

Materials

Some supplementary materials that can be used in association with teaching reading include:

♦ wall friezes

♦ code cards and flashcards

♦ word books, copymasters and workbooks

♦ cassettes and songbooks

♦ games and software

♦ videos and interactive CDs/DVDs

♦ interactive whiteboards.

Examples of programmes

Orton–Gillingham

Programmes based on this approach have become a central focus for multisensory teaching for children with dyslexia. The programmes offer a structured, sequential, phonic-based approach that incorporates the total language experience and focuses on letter sounds, the blending of these sounds into syllables and words, reading, spelling rules and syllabication. The approach rests heavily on the interaction of visual, auditory and kinaesthetic aspects of language. Orton–Gillingham lessons are success oriented with the goal of the student becoming a self-correcting, independent learner (Green 2006).

Orton–Gillingham lessons, according to Henry (1996, 2003; see also Green 2006), can incorporate spelling and reading and usually include activities such as:

◆ card drills – these involve the use of commercial or teacher-made cards containing the common letter patterns to strengthen the visual modality: phonemes (sounds) for auditory and kinesthetic reinforcement, and syllables and whole words to help develop blending skills

◆ word lists and phrases

◆ spelling of phonograms in isolation, as well as of phonetic and non-phonetic words

◆ handwriting – with attention to pencil grip, writing posture and letter formation. This also includes tracing, copying and practice, and making phonetically correct cursive connections such as 'br', 'bl'.

◆ composition – encouragement to develop writing sentences, paragraphs and short stories.

Henry (2003) also maintains that lessons take place as a 'dynamic discussion session with the teacher acting as facilitator as well as instructor'.

The process

1. To begin with, ten letters are taught – two vowels (a, i) and eight consonants (f, l, b, j, h, m, p, t).

2. Each of the letters is introduced with a key word.

3. Once the child has mastered the letter name and sound, the programme then advances to introduce blending of the letters and sounds.

Green (2006) suggests that blending can begin as soon as the child knows two letters that can be blended together.

For example, after learning the short vowel 'a' as in apple, and 'm' as in mitten, the child can blend to read 'am'. The task is to teach children to smoothly blend sounds together and to hear the word. Therefore, it is not acceptable to hear 'a-m'. The child must hold the vowel to the consonant and hear 'am'.

There are two important factors in teaching blending. First, it is important to begin blending with phonograms that can hold their sound continually, such as 'mmmmmmmmmmmmmmmm', as opposed to a stop consonant such as 't'. The following sounds are continuous: m, s, n, f, h, l, v, z; their sound can be held. Blending will start with vowel (v)–consonant (c) and cv, and grows to cvc, ccvc, ccvcc, finally getting to polysyllabic words. Second, blending sounds together should only be done with phonetically correct phonograms.

To help a child achieve proficiency with blending it is helpful to have him or her practise with drills before reading actual words. Torpedo drills are easy to prepare and use all the modalities. An example of a torpedo drill is shown below. Note there are only continuous consonants in the first column, and all sounds should be known to the child. Using a crayon to torpedo phonograms together, the child should be saying the sounds aloud while blending them and then producing the word they have made. The words a child makes from this blending exercise can be nonsense or martian words.

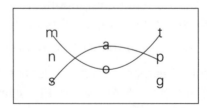

4. The visual-kinesthetic and auditory-kinesthetic associations are formed by the child tracing, saying, copying and writing each phonogram. Children are taught phonograms,

spelling concepts and rules so they can read and spell unknown words that follow the same spelling pattern

5. Reading of text begins after the child has mastered the consonant–vowel–consonant words to a higher automatic level, i.e. when he or she can recognize and use these words.

The programme is more suited to one-to-one teaching, but the key principles of over-learning, automaticity and multi-sensory approaches are very apparent in Orton–Gillingham, and these principles can be utilized within the classroom curriculum.

There is also considerable scope in this programme for building metacognitive skills and developing comprehension-building exercises (Green 2006). The dynamic aspect is important, and Zylstra (2005) has shown how creativity in developing games can complement, expand and clarify many of the language skills in OG lessons (some of these games are shown in Figures 2 and 3). Zylstra has developed a considerable range of games to be used in conjunction with the OG approach. These include alphabet ideas (falling into order, fish for formations), general lesson aids (pumpkin SOS spelling game, Valentine SOS order games), morphology ideas, phonogram ideas (super vowel hopscotch, Why Mr Y game), spelling rule ideas (policeman e rule, ruler of the kingdom) and syllabication ideas (Lion division, Pony Division, vowel team football). (Source: www. stepintophonics.com; www.reachlearningcenter.com)

> Learning to read needs to be fun – games can make it fun.

Hickey Multisensory Language Course
The Hickey Multisensory Language Course (Augur and Briggs 1992) recognizes the importance of the need to

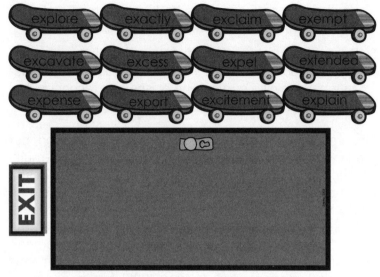

Cut out the door and the strips of skateboard ex- words. Tape the three ex- word strips together, end-to-end. Use an exacto knife to cut a small slit about 1 inch long along the right side of the door, beside the door knob. Allow your student to read the ex- words as you pull them "out of, or from" the exit door.

Figure 2 Morphology game for 'ex' prefix
Reproduced with permission from Zylstra (2005)

learn the letters of the alphabet sequentially. The dyslexic child will usually have some difficulty in learning and remembering the names and sequence of the alphabetic letters, as well as understanding that the letters represent speech sounds which make up words.

The process

The programme is based on multisensory principles and the alphabet is introduced using wooden or plastic letters; the child can look at the letter, pick it up, feel it with eyes open or closed and say its sound. Therefore the visual, auditory and tactile-kinesthetic channels of learning are all being utilized with a common goal.

The programme also suggests some activities to help the child become familiar with the alphabet. These include:

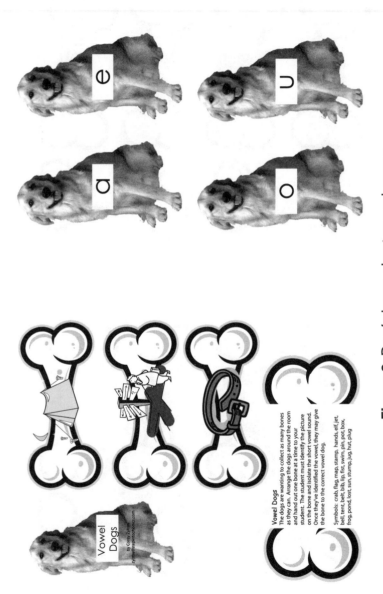

Figure 3 Dog's bone short vowel game
Reproduced with permission from Zylstra (2005)

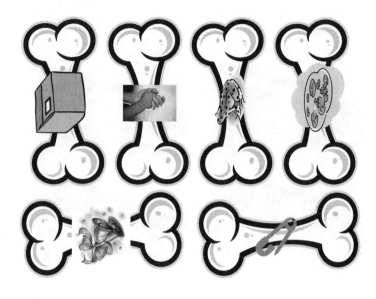

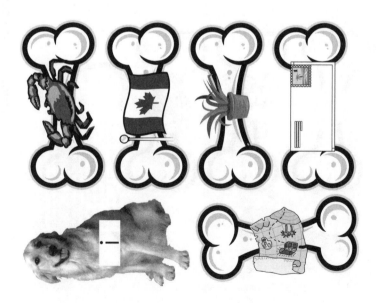

Figure 3 Continued

50

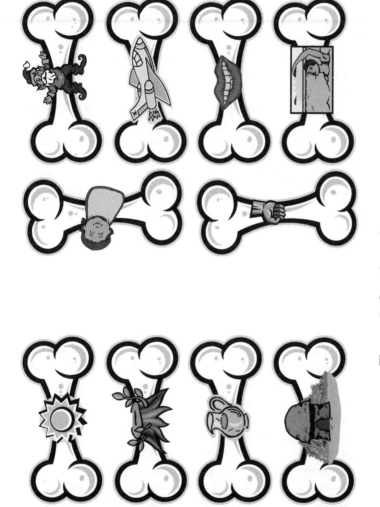

Figure 3 Continued

51

Dyslexia

- learning the letters sequentially
- learning the positioning of each letter of the alphabet
- naming and recognizing the shape of the letters.

These programmes involve games and the use of dictionaries to help the child become familiar with the order of the letters and the direction to go: for example, he or she needs to know that 'i' comes before 'k', and the letters in the first half of the alphabet and those letters in the second half. The alphabet can be further divided into sections, which makes it easier for the child to remember the section of the alphabet in which a letter appears, for example:

A B C D
E F G H I J K L M
N O P Q R
S T U V W X Y Z

The Hickey Language Course includes activities related to sorting and matching the capital, lower-case, printed and written forms of the letters; practising sequencing skills with cut-out letters and shapes; and practising positioning of each letter in the alphabet in relation to the other letters (this involves finding missing letters and going backwards and forwards in the alphabet).

The course also indicates the importance of recognizing where the accent falls in a word, since this clearly affects the spelling and rhythm. The rhyming games can be developed to encourage the use of accent by placing the accent on different letters of the alphabet. This helps to train children's hearing to recognize when a letter has an accent or is stressed in a word.

The course includes reading and spelling packs that focus on securing a relationship between sounds and symbols. This process begins with single letters, and progresses to consonant blends, vowel continuations and then to complex letter groupings.

The reading packs consist of a set of cards; on one side the lower-case letter is displayed in bold, with the upper-case (capital) letter shown on the bottom right-hand corner, in order to establish the link between the two letters. The reverse side of the card indicates a key word which contains the sound of the letter, with the actual sound combination in brackets. Rather than providing a visual image of the key word, a space is left for the child to draw the image. This helps to make the image more meaningful to the child and also utilizes and reinforces visual and kinesthetic skills.

The spelling pack is similar in structure to the reading pack. On the front of the card the sound made by the letter is displayed in brackets, while the back contains both the sound and the actual letter(s). Sounds for which there is a choice of spellings will in time show all the possible ways in which the sound can be made. Cue words are also given on the back as a prompt, in case the child forgets one of the choices.

Spelling is seen as being of prime importance by the authors of the programme, since they view it as an 'all-round perceptual experience'. The multisensory method used involves the following process: the child

♦ repeats the sound heard

♦ feels the shape the sound makes in the mouth

♦ makes the sound and listens

♦ writes the letter(s).

This process involves over-learning and multisensory strategies.

Dyslexia

Alphabetic Phonics

The key principles found in the majority of individualized programmes for dyslexic children – multisensory techniques, automaticity and over-learning – are all found in the Alphabetic Phonics programme. Additionally, the programme also recognizes the importance of discovery learning, with opportunities for this throughout this highly structured programme.

The programme, which stems from the Orton–Gillingham multisensory approach, was developed in Dallas, Texas, by Aylett Cox. She has described Alphabetic Phonics as a structured system of teaching students the coding patterns of the English language (Cox 1985).

Cox asserts that such a phonic-based programme is necessary because around 85 per cent of the 30,000 most commonly used English words can be considered phonetically regular and therefore predictable. Thus learning phonetic rules can allow the child access to the majority of the commonly used words.

The process

Alphabetic Phonics provides training in the development of automaticity through the use of flashcards, and over-learning through repetitive practice in reading and spelling until 95 per cent mastery is achieved.

1. An alphabetic activity, which emphasizes sequence and directionality.

2. Introduction of a new element or concept, which begins with discovery and is reinforced with multisensory techniques.

3. Training in automatic recognition of letter names, through flashcard presentation (Reading Decks).

4. Training in recognition of letter sounds, by having students pronounce the sounds for a letter or letters presented on flashcards (Spelling Decks) and then naming and writing the letter or letters.

5. Practice in reading and spelling (10 minutes allotted for each). Each task is continued until student reaches 95 per cent mastery, as measured by the Bench Mark measures.
6. Handwriting practice.
7. Practice in verbal expression, first oral and later written, focusing on various skills (e.g. sequencing ideas, creative expression, vocabulary, syntax).
8. Listening to good literature and building comprehension skills, while reading instruction focuses on decoding skills.

The programme also incorporates opportunities to develop creativity in expression and in the sequencing of ideas.

The programme is highly structured, with daily lessons of around one hour. Lessons incorporate a variety of tasks, which helps to keep the child's attention directed to the activities and prevents boredom.

In this programme, reading comprehension instruction does not begin until the student has reached a minimal level of accuracy in relation to decoding skills. Cox, however, does recognize that children will learn and retain new vocabulary more effectively and efficiently through experiential learning, and that this is particularly applicable to dyslexic children.

The principles and practices of this programme, such as structure, multisensory technique, emphasis on automaticity, emphasis on building comprehension skills, experiential learning and listening skills, and in particular recognition of letter sounds, can have desirable outcomes. These can readily be adapted and implemented into teaching programmes devised for different needs and contexts.

Dyslexia

Synthetic Phonics

A number of studies (Johnston *et al.* 1995) have indicated the merits of synthetic phonics. The Rose Review into the teaching of reading in the UK (DfES 2005) also indicated the merits of this approach. The report discusses the differences between synthetic phonics and analytic phonics.

The process

Synthetic phonics refers to an approach to the teaching of reading in which the phonemes (sounds) associated with particular graphemes (letters) are pronounced in isolation and blended together (synthesized). For example, children are taught to take a single-syllable word such as 'cat' apart into its three letters, pronounce a phoneme for each letter in turn – /k, æ, t/ – and blend the phonemes together to form a word. Synthetic phonics for writing reverses the sequence: children are taught to say the word they wish to write, segment it into its phonemes and say them in turn, for example /d, ɔ, g/, and write a grapheme for each phoneme in turn to produce the written word 'dog'.

Analytic phonics on the other hand refers to an approach to the teaching of reading in which the phonemes associated with particular graphemes are not pronounced in isolation. Children identify (analyse) the common phoneme in a set of words in which each word contains the phoneme under study. For example, teacher and pupils discuss how the following words are alike: 'pat', 'park', 'push' and 'pen'.

Studies suggest that the synthetic phonics programme is an effective method of teaching reading. Many of the approaches suggested for teaching reading to children with dyslexia utilize a synthetic phonics approach. One such programme is discussed below.

THRASS

THRASS is an acronym for Teaching Handwriting Reading And Spelling Skills. It is a whole-school phonics programme for teaching learners, of any age, about the building blocks of reading and spelling: that is, the 44 phonemes (speech sounds) of spoken English and the graphemes (spelling choices) of written English.

The process

The programme teaches learners that, basically, when spelling we change phonemes to graphemes, and when reading we change graphemes to phonemes.

The programme is very comprehensive and has an excellent user-friendly website (www.thrass.com) with free downloads. The components include speaking and listening skills, phonemes and key graphemes and letter names, and it is suitable for all ages.

The THRASS pack consists of four resources for teaching essential speaking, listening, reading and spelling skills. The THRASS Picture Book, THRASS Picture Cards, THRASS Workbook and THRASS Spelling Tiles can be used in classes by teachers and assistants. The resources can also be used by parents, at home, to support the introduction, revision and assessment of the THRASS keywords and basewords.

If when using the Workbook and Spelling Tiles additional help is required in identifying the phonemes (speech sounds) of English, then the first section of the THRASS Phoneme Machine, the 'Phoneme Grid', can be used. It is downloadable, without charge, from the THRASS website. This is an excellent resource that enables the user to produce the sounds of each phoneme simply by clicking on the lips of the symbol.

The Slingerland Programme

The Slingerland Programme is an adaptation of the Orton–Gillingham Programme. Essentially, the programme was developed as a screening approach to help minimize the difficulties experienced by children in language and literacy. The Slingerland Screening Tests accompany the programme and are usually administered in the early stages of education.

The programme shares similar features with other programmes. Multi-sensory teaching permeates the programme, which begins by introducing letters of the alphabet.

The process
Writing
This is the first step and usually uses the following order:

♦ tracing

♦ copying

♦ writing in the air

♦ simultaneously writing from memory and saying the letter.

Letter sounds
This involves naming the letter, then the key word associated with the letter, and then the letter sound.

Blending
This is introduced with oral activities and may involve repetitive use, and blends with kinesthetic support to reinforce the material being learnt.

Decoding
In decoding, students begin with three letters c–v–c, for example words such as 'bay' and 'way'. They are required to:

♦ pronounce the initial consonant

♦ then the vowel

- then blend the two
- pronounce the final consonant
- say the whole word.

Vowel digraphs and vc digraphs are taught as units, although Slingerland maintains that consonant blends are usually learnt more easily.

Sound Linkage

Sound Linkage (Hatcher, 1994, 2004) is an integrated phonological programme for overcoming reading difficulties. In addition to a section on assessment it contains ten sections on teaching, each dealing with a specific aspect of phonological processing. For example, Section 3 deals with phoneme blending, Section 5 deals with identification and discrimination of phonemes, and some other sections deal with phoneme segmentation, deletion, substitution and phoneme transposition.

The process

Although Sound Linkage can be used as an individual structured programme, each section contains a series of activities that can be used to support mainstream curriculum work with dyslexic children. The activities are clearly presented and no complex instructions are necessary. Many of the activities are, however, not new, and many teachers will be aware of the importance of them. To have all these activities in a methodical package, linked to assessment, with a clear overall rationale is an appealing feature, and provides a good example of a programme that can be used within the curriculum.

Step Into Phonics

This is a structured guide for sequential phonics based on the Orton–Gillingham approach for multisensory teaching. Developed by Lois Lindsay and Corey Zylstra, Orton–Gillingham Tutor Trainers, Step Into Phonics is an easy-to-use manual that aids in lesson preparation while offering a wealth of information about phonograms, spelling rules, syllables and non-phonentic words (www.stepintophonics.com).

Reading Recovery
Reading Recovery is an early reading and writing intervention programme, developed by Marie Clay, which focuses on children who after one year at school have lagged significantly behind their peers in reading and writing (Clay 1985). Clay originally introduced the programme in New Zealand, but it has now been shown that the programme can be successfully transferred to other countries and contexts.

The programme aims to boost the reading attainments of the selected children over a relatively short period (around 12 to 20 weeks), with specially trained teachers carrying out the programme, seeing children on an individual basis for 30 minutes every day.

The process
The programme centres around the individual child's strengths and weaknesses as assessed by the actual reading programme. It is not, therefore, structured around a set of principles and practices to which the child has to be accommodated, but rather the programme adapts itself to the child's specific requirements and needs. It utilizes both bottom-up and top-down reading approaches and therefore encourages the use of decoding strategies through the use of phonics, and awareness of meaning through an awareness of the context and language of the text.

The programme aims to produce 'independent readers whose reading improves whenever they read' (Clay 1985). There is an emphasis, therefore, on strategies that the reader can apply to other texts and situations, and there is evidence that gains made in the Reading Recovery programme are maintained over time.

For some children the Reading Recovery programme may need to be supplemented by additional sessions, which could include:

♦ re-reading familiar books

♦ taking a running record (see 'Identification' opposite)

♦ reinforcing letter identification

♦ writing a story, thus learning sounds in words

♦ comprehension of story

♦ introducing a new book.

It is also important that the child is helped to develop a self-improving system. This encourages the child to:

♦ be aware of his or her own learning

♦ take control and responsibility for this learning.

The goal of teaching reading is to assist the child to produce effective strategies for working on text, and according to Clay this can be done through focusing on the practices of self-correcting and self-monitoring.

The process
The main components of the programme include:

♦ learning about direction

♦ locating and focusing on aspects of print

♦ spatial layout of books

♦ writing stories

- learning sounds in words
- comprehension and cut-up stories
- reading books
- using print as a cue
- sound and letter sequence
- word analysis
- fluency.

A typical Reading Recovery lesson would include an analysis of the child's decoding strategies, the encouragement of fluent reading through the provision of opportunities to link sounds and letters, the reading of familiar texts, and the introduction of new books.

Identification

Since the programme provides an intensive input to those children lagging in reading, it is vitally important that the identification procedures are sound in order to ensure that the children who receive the benefits of this programme are those who would not otherwise make satisfactory progress.

The lowest-achieving children in a class group, after a year at school at around six years of age, are admitted into the programme. Clay believes that by the end of the first year at primary school it is possible to identify children who are failing. She suggests that this can be achieved through systematic observation of children's learning behaviour, together with a diagnostic survey.

The systematic observation takes the form of noting precisely what children are saying and doing in relation to reading, so the focus is on reading tasks rather than specific sub-skills such as visual perception or auditory dissemination. In order to identify the child's reading behaviour Clay has developed a diagnostic survey which involves taking a 'running record' of precisely how the child is performing in relation to reading. This type of analysis of children's errors in reading can provide clues in relation to their strengths and weaknesses in this area.

The diagnostic survey includes directional movement (which looks at general directional concepts, including motor coordination, impulsivity and hesitancy), error behaviour (focusing on oral language skills, speed of responding and the use of semantic and syntactic context), the use of visual and memory cues, the rate of self-correction, and the child's preferred mode of identifying letters (alphabetic, sound or cueing from words). The survey also includes details of the child's writing skills. This is particularly important since it may provide some indication of any reading problems as well as language level and message quality.

> It may be necessary to use a combination of approaches: no single approach will be successful for all children with dyslexia. It is important to obtain a comprehensive assessment in order to help in the selection of approaches.

Curriculum Approaches

In addition to the impressive number of individualized programmes available for children with dyslexia, there is also an abundance of support materials that can be utilized by teachers to complement teaching programmes within the curriculum. Conceptually, most of the individualized programmes have much in common, emphasizing areas such as structure, multisensory aspects, over-learning and automaticity. Curriculum approaches do not necessarily provide an individual one-to-one programme, but can be used by the teacher to help the child develop competencies to facilitate access to the full range of curriculum activities.

Some of these curriculum approaches are discussed below.

Phonological Approaches

There is strong evidence to suggest that phonological factors are of considerable importance in reading (Stanovich 1991; Snowling 2000, 2005). Children with decoding difficulties are considerably restricted in reading because they are unable to generalize from one word to another. This means that every word they read is unique, indicating that there is a difficulty in learning and applying phonological rules in reading. This emphasizes the importance of teaching sounds (phonemes) and ensuring that the child has an awareness of the sound/letter correspondence. Learning words by sight can enable some children to reach a certain standard in reading, but prevents them from adequately tackling new words and extending their vocabulary.

> Children with dyslexia need a phonic programme to give them the basic foundations of literacy.

If children have a phonological awareness difficulty they are more likely to guess the word from the first letter cue and not the first **sound**; that is, the word 'kite' will be tackled from the starting point of the letter 'k' and not the sound 'ki', so the dyslexic reader may well read something like 'kept'. It is important, therefore, that beginning readers receive some structured training in the grapheme/phoneme correspondence; this is particularly necessary for dyslexic children who would not automatically, or readily, appreciate the importance of phonic rules in reading.

Creativity and the 'gifted' dyslexic student.

One of the pitfalls about teaching a structured reading programme to dyslexic children is that the programme can often be so structured that it stifles creativity and indeed comprehension. It is important that teachers are aware of this and establish teaching procedures that can accommodate the 'gifted' dyslexic to ensure that a preoccupation with decoding does not result in a lack of development of thinking and comprehension skills. Silverman (personal correspondence 2005) suggested, following a presentation on developing learning skills with dyslexia children given by the author (Reid 2005), that these approaches are very similar to those she recommends for gifted children. Silverman has produced a number of books on visual/spatial processing and creativity for learners who have a different way of learning. It is important that these types of approaches and the different way of learning that underlies them are accepted by all. Further, Silverman's approach also accommodates the needs of the whole child, looking at the importance of positive relationships with peers, coping with their differences and making appropriate career choices. Silverman's websites are www.gifted development.com and www.visualspatial.org.

The area of giftedness focusing on the learning needs of children with dyslexia is very much the focus of the work of Yoshimoto (2005), who has developed programmes and strategies for the gifted dyslexic following the Orton–Gillingham programme. This ensures that crucial thinking and learning skills are developed alongside the basic decoding skills needed by all dyslexic children, and essential for reading fluency. Yoshimoto suggests that gifted dyslexic learners can have:

♦ superior listening skills

♦ expansive vocabulary

Dyslexia

- excellent general knowledge
- good abstract reasoning skills
- unusual capacity for processing information
- good problem-solving skills
- the skills to be creative, original thinkers
- artistic or musical talents.

At the same time, Yoshimoto claims that they also have a:

- low self-concept
- propensity to use humour to divert attention away from perceived failure
- low frustration tolerance
- tendency to react poorly to criticism
- increased likelihood of refusing to perform tasks in order to avoid failure.

An example of a model for gifted dyslexic students is shown overleaf.

> It is important to extend the thinking skills of learners with dyslexia. This should not be restricted on account of their reading difficulties.

Spelling

Liberman and Shankweiler (1985) have shown that a clear difference exists in the performance of phonological tasks between good and poor spellers. This implies that successful spelling is related to children's awareness of the underlying phonological structure of words. This is supported by Rohl and Tunmer (1988), who found that good spellers were better at phonemic

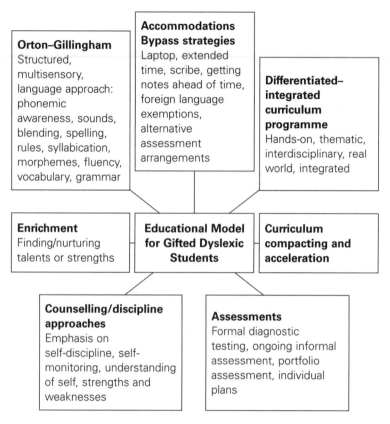

Orton–Gillingham
Structured, multisensory, language approach: phonemic awareness, sounds, blending, spelling, rules, syllabication, morphemes, fluency, vocabulary, grammar

Accommodations Bypass strategies
Laptop, extended time, scribe, getting notes ahead of time, foreign language exemptions, alternative assessment arrangements

Differentiated–integrated curriculum programme
Hands-on, thematic, interdisciplinary, real world, integrated

Enrichment
Finding/nurturing talents or strengths

Educational Model for Gifted Dyslexic Students

Curriculum compacting and acceleration

Counselling/discipline approaches
Emphasis on self-discipline, self-monitoring, understanding of self, strengths and weaknesses

Assessments
Formal diagnostic testing, ongoing informal assessment, portfolio assessment, individual plans

Figure 4 A model for gifted dyslexic children
From Yoshimoto (2005)

segmentation tasks than older children matched for spelling age.

Further, Bradley and Bryant (1991) showed that measures of rhyme judgement and letter knowledge in pre-school children were good predictors of subsequent performance in spelling. Thus children who can recognize words that sound and look alike tend to have a good memory for spelling patterns. Indeed, Bradley and Huxford (1994) show that sound categorization in particular plays an important role in developing memory patterns for spelling. Bradley

Dyslexia

(1989, 1990) has shown that rhyming is a particularly useful form of categorization for developing spelling skills, and that practice in sound categorization through nursery rhymes and rhyming word games in early language play helps spelling. This can be noted in the simultaneous oral spelling technique developed by Bradley (see below).

Many children have problems remembering 'chunks', such as 'igh' in 'sight' and 'fight'. If children cannot do this, then every word will be unique. Phonological aspects are important in the development of reading and spelling skills. This seems to have considerable importance, particularly for dyslexic children, who do not automatically relate the sounds to the visual images of print. Exercises in phonological awareness are therefore of great importance, not just to assist with reading but also to help with spelling, by allowing children to learn and understand sound patterns and to recognize how these are transposed into print.

Simultaneous oral spelling

1. Have the word written correctly, or made with the letters.

2. Say the word.

3. Write the word, spelling out each letter as it is written, using cursive script.

4. The child needs to:

   ♦ see each letter

   ♦ hear its name

   ♦ receive kinesthetic feedback through the movement of the arm and throat muscles.

5. Check to see if the word is correct.

6. Cover up the word and repeat the process.

Continue to practise the word in this way, three times a day, for one week. By this time the word should be committed to memory. However, only one word will have been learnt.

7. This step involves the categorization of the word with other words which sound and look alike. So if the word that has been learned is 'round', the child is then shown that he or she can also spell 'ground', 'pound', 'found', 'mound', 'sound', 'around', 'bound', grounded', 'pounding', etc. Therefore, he or she has learned six, eight or more words for the effort of one.

A strategy that can be helpful for spelling suggested by Lee Pascal is shown below:

♦ Spell the word aloud as you write it down.

♦ Look at the word.

♦ Cover the word with a piece of paper.

♦ Try to see the word on the paper.

♦ Copy the word as you see it.

♦ Check to see if you have spelt the word correctly.

♦ Have a ten-minute break, then repeat the exercise above.

♦ A few hours later again repeat this.

♦ Then repeat this at various times over the next few days.

♦ Add a new word to the list each week and repeat the sequence.

Although spelling can be problematic for children with dyslexia, it is important that this should not restrict their expressive writing in any way. Do not use a red pen or crosses to correct spelling; doing so will discourage and dishearten the learner.

Counselling Approaches

Hales (2001) suggests that considerable scope exists for personal counselling of the dyslexic individual. This would allow people with dyslexia the opportunity to talk through their fears, and some attempts could be made to help to match 'self-image' with reality, since often dyslexic children have a self-image that presents a distorted and unrealistic picture of themselves. Hales points out that while there is no specific personality disorder that affects dyslexic children independently of other factors, there is still a strong case for considering closely the individual and personal aspects of children and adults with dyslexia. Indeed, he argues that it may be important to consider counselling and social support of the 'dyslexic person' before dealing with the 'dyslexic difficulty'.

Effective provision for dyslexic employees in the work situation can also reduce potential stress in the workplace, and help facilitate the performance of a large number of competent and experienced individuals to work up to their full potential.

Some strategies to help facilitate the emotional development of the young person with dyslexia include:

♦ ensuring that the child's difficulties are accurately described in order to remove doubts, anxieties or prejudices

♦ ensuring agreement between the significant adults in the child's life, such as parents and teachers

♦ ensuring the child has a voice, is understood and has a trusting relationship with those adults.

The case for an approach to the teaching of reading that incorporates counselling is very strong. Counselling can perform a dual role: it can be utilized to help with interaction with children with dyslexia, in order to foster skills in learning, and can also be seen as integral to the implementation of a teaching programme and conducted simultaneously with teaching.

There are some excellent self-esteem programmes available that can be successfully utilized for dyslexic children. These include the Mosley (1996) 'circle time' activities.

> Self-esteem can be the most crucial predictor of success in reading.

The use of visualization

Bell (1991b, 2005) suggests that one has to be wary of the 'cognitive cost' of some analytic phonic programmes – a cost which is reflected in a weakening of the gestalt (right) hemispheric skills. The gestalt hemisphere is usually associated with visual imagery, creativity and comprehension.

The stress and effort that is necessary for children with dyslexia to fully engage their cognitive resources and to develop phonological skills is so great, according to Bell, that a weakening of the gestalt hemisphere results as resources are diverted from the right hemispheric functions to concentrate on the left hemispheric skills of decoding and phonological processing. This results not only in a restriction in the use of visual imagery, but also in a stifling of the development of skills in comprehension, and perhaps in creativity.

Bell's well-known programme 'Visualizing and Verbalizing for Language Comprehension and Thinking' deals with this aspect. This programme provides a comprehensive procedure for the use of visualizing to promote and enhance reading and comprehension. The stages outlined by Bell include picture imagery, word imagery, single sentence, multiple sentence, whole paragraph and whole page. Additionally, the programme provides an understanding of the functions of the gestalt hemisphere and useful strategies for classroom teaching.

Paired Reading

Paired Reading is a well-established and successful method that can be utilized by learners with dyslexia and their parents or carers. There are a number of reasons why paired reading is successful, including the following:

- Failure is not a factor, because if the child 'sticks' at a word, the adult says the word almost immediately.

- The experience of gaining enjoyment from the language of the text helps reading become pleasurable and increases the desire to read.

- Children are provided with an example of how to pronounce difficult words and can simultaneously relate the auditory sound of the word to the visual appearance of that word.

- Children can derive understanding from the text because words are given expression and meaning by the adult, and discussion about the text follows at periodic intervals.

Paired Reading can be useful as:

- a strategy to develop motivation and confidence in reading

- an aid to the development of fluency and expression in reading

- a technique which can also enhance comprehension on the part of the reader.

The process

Paired Reading involves the adult (tutor) and the child (tutee) reading aloud at the same time. It is however a specific structured technique. Both adult and child read all the words out together, with the tutor modulating his or her speed to match that of the child, while giving a good model of competent reading. The child must read every word, and when the child says a word wrongly, the tutor just tells the child the correct way to say the word. The child then repeats the word correctly, and the pair carry on. Saying 'no' and giving phonic and other prompts is forbidden. However, tutors do not jump in and correct the child straight away. The rule is that the tutors pause and give the children four or five seconds to see if they will put it right by themselves (see Figure 4).

It is intended only for use with individually chosen, highly motivating non-fiction or fiction books which are **above** the independent readability level of the tutee. Topping

Figure 5 Paired Reading

suggests however that the name has been a problem: the phrase 'Paired Reading' has such a warm, comfortable feel to it that some people have loosely applied it to almost anything that two people do together with a book. One of the important aspects of Paired Reading, and indeed any reading activities, is praise: the adult should look pleased when the child succeeds using this technique.

Whole School Practice and Policy

What is meant by whole school policies? Clearly they embrace an acceptance to meet the needs of all children in the school. Further, the term indicates an acceptance that the responsibility for certain pupils does not reside exclusively with trained specialists, but rather with all staff under the direction of a school management team.

The implications of this are two-fold:

♦ First, identification and assessment procedures need to be established and monitored to ensure that children who may present with specific learning difficulties, even in a mild form, are identified at an early stage.

♦ Second, the school needs to be resourced in terms of teaching materials and training of staff to ensure that the educational needs of children with all specific learning difficulties are effectively met.

As these children progress through the school it is important that each new teacher they meet has at least some training and understanding of specific learning difficulties/dyslexia. Additionally, the school will need to possess a teacher with a high degree of specialist training to complement the class teacher input and to provide consultancy and training to staff and management.

Thinking skills programmes are an example of a type of programme that can be undertaken from a whole school perspective, irrespective of a child's particular skills or abilities. Many of these programmes involve children in decision-making and problem-solving activities without having to read long instructions. This ensures that the dyslexic child can participate virtually on the same terms as other children in the class.

Summary

♦ There is a vast range of different types of teaching approaches that can be used with dyslexic children.

♦ It is fair to say that no one single approach holds the key to completely dealing with dyslexic difficulties.

♦ Many of the programmes and strategies described in this chapter can be used together and can be complementary to other teaching and curriculum approaches.

♦ Irrespective of the type of provision used for dyslexic children, it is important that at all times every opportunity is taken to help them access the full curriculum. This can present real difficulties for some dyslexic children, but the challenge can be met through careful planning, utilizing the skills of teachers and being aware of the abundance of approaches and strategies available.

♦ It is important to recognize the abilities and the creativity of children with dyslexia. It can be too easy to restrict their creative process and progress through a preoccupation with improving attainments in literacy.

4

Planning for Learning

Many of the challenges experienced by children with dyslexia arise from difficulties with information-processing. This includes reading, spelling, writing, language-processing, organization and speed of processing. There is no shortage of programmes to deal with these difficulties (see the previous chapter and Reid 2003): but one of the drawbacks is that, by necessity, they often single out, or even isolate, children from others in the class. This may have a negative effect on the child's self-esteem, and further, it may mean the child missing out on some aspects of the mainstream curriculum. It is appreciated however that some children with significant difficulties in literacy will benefit from some type of specialized input. There are many tutorial and extended teaching and learning centres in most countries that provide this (for details, see the Appendices), but good examples of how it can work in practice can be seen in the work of the Red Rose School in England (www.redroseschool.co.uk), the REACH Learning Center in Vancouver, Canada (www. reachlearningcenter.com), and Fun Track Learning in Perth, Australia (www.funtrack.com.au).

Specialized provision can complement, and help the child access, the mainstream curriculum. There needs to be a balance between curriculum needs and specialized individual input.

For the main part however the onus is on the teacher to prepare and present the curriculum in a dyslexia-friendly manner. This will require effective differentiation in the preparation of materials. These need to consider the classroom and environmental factors, such as learning styles and the classroom layout, as well as the content of the materials.

> It is important that interventions take a curricular and classroom perspective and focus not only on the child, but on the learning and teaching context.

Interventions and Dyslexia

The debate

There is an ongoing debate regarding the 'special' type of teaching that is required for children with dyslexia. This is encapsulated in the views presented by Norwich and Lewis (2001). In their paper they question the claims that differential teaching is required for children with special educational needs, including dyslexia. They claim that the 'unique differences position' (p. 313), which suggests that differentiated teaching is needed for this group, has little supportive empirical evidence, and suggest that the approaches for children with dyslexia are in fact adaptations of common teaching approaches. Conner (1994) argues that specialist teaching approaches for dyslexia are little different from teaching literacy to any pupil, although arguably there seems to be more of a preference for bottom-up approaches relating to phonological awareness, as well as for structure and over-learning. Reason *et al.* (1988) also question the differences in specialist approaches, indicating that individual differences within the dyslexic students are the most crucial factor in relation to utilizing specific teaching approaches. Given this controversy and debate, it may be more productive to identify specific approaches by examining the barriers to learning experienced by the child. This would imply that each child is individual and the specific barriers may be different for different children. One way of dealing with this is through the use of individual education plans, as these can identify the barriers, identify strategies and approaches to overcome these barriers, and contextualize these within the learning and the classroom situation.

Individual Education Plans – implications for children with dyslexia

Individual Education Plans (IEPs) can provide a means of ensuring the needs of children are met within the educational setting. The principles used in an IEP can be applicable to all education systems in all countries.

In order for an IEP to be used appropriately it should, as a minimum, contain details of:

♦ the nature of the child's learning difficulties

♦ the special educational provision to be made

♦ strategies to be used

♦ specific programmes, activities, materials

♦ any specialized equipment

♦ targets to be achieved

♦ the timeframe for any specified targets

♦ monitoring and assessment arrangements

♦ review arrangements (with dates).

Planning for learning

In some schools the class teacher may be supported by specialist teachers such as resource teachers, learning

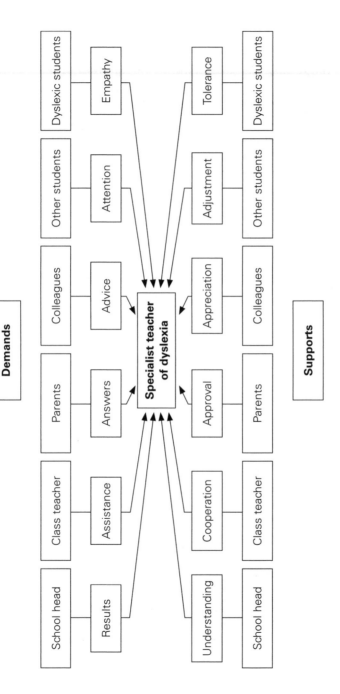

Figure 6 Demands on and support for specialist teachers

support staff and special needs coordinators (the titles vary from country to country but often the demands on this group are the same (see Figure 6). Nevertheless, the responsibility for planning and preparing class work usually rests with the class teacher. It is important therefore that class teachers have some awareness of dyslexia, but equally it is important that consideration is given to the role of planning and preparation in meeting the needs of dyslexic children, within the class and curriculum context.

> Dealing with dyslexia is a whole school concern and not the responsibility of any one person.

Planning for learning should include

♦ consultation

♦ deciding how the information is presented

♦ deciding how materials and tasks are developed.

There are many fundamental factors that can be incorporated into the planning and presentation of curricular materials and tasks. Some of these are discussed below.

Planning

Knowledge of the child's strengths and difficulties
This is essential, especially since not all children with dyslexia will display the same profile. It is therefore the best starting point, as often strengths can be used to help deal with weaknesses.

For example, dyslexic children often have a preference for visual and kinesthetic learning, and a difficulty with auditory learning. Therefore, phonics, which relies heavily on sounds, and therefore the auditory modality, needs to be introduced together with visual and experiential forms of learning. The tactile modality involving touch and feeling the shape of letters that make specific sounds should also be utilized, as well as the visual symbols of these letters and letter/sound combinations.

Consultation
The responsibility for dealing with children with dyslexia within the classroom should not solely rest with the class teacher. Ideally it should be seen as a whole school responsibility. This means that consultation with school management and other colleagues is important, and it is equally important that time is allocated for this. Information from previous teachers, support staff, school management and parents is necessary, and such joint liaison can help to ensure the necessary collaboration to provide support for the class teacher. Importantly, this should be built into the school procedures and not be a reaction to a problem that has occurred. Such collaboration can therefore be seen as preventative and proactive.

Knowledge of the curriculum content
It is understood that the teacher will have a sound awareness of the content of the curriculum which the child needs to know. Anticipating those areas for the different aspects of the curriculum that may present a difficulty for dyslexic children may however be a bit more tricky. Yet it is important that the teacher can do so.

Such areas can include information that contains lists or dates, for example in history. Learning the sequence of dates can be as difficult as remembering the dates. It is crucial therefore that such information is presented in a dyslexia-friendly manner.

Current level of literacy acquisition
An accurate and full assessment of the child's current level of attainments is necessary in order to plan effectively a programme of learning. The assessment should include

listening comprehension as well as reading accuracy and fluency. Listening comprehension can often be a more accurate guide to the abilities and understanding of dyslexic children than reading and spelling accuracy. Indeed, it is often the discrepancy between listening comprehension and reading accuracy that can be a key factor in identifying dyslexia. Information on the level of attainments is an instrumental factor in planning for differentiation.

Cultural factors
Background knowledge, particularly of cultural factors, is important, as this can influence the selection of books and whether some of the concepts in the text need to be singled out for additional and differentiated explanation. Cultural values are an important factor. It has been suggested that the 'big dip' in performance noted in some bilingual children in later primary school may be explained by a failure of professionals to understand and appreciate the cultural values, and the actual level of competence, of the bilingual child, particularly in relation to conceptual development and competence in thinking skills. It is possible for teachers to misinterpret bilingual children's development of good phonic skills in the early stages of literacy development in English and to fail to note the difficulties that these children might be having with comprehension. When the difficulties later emerge, these children can be grouped inappropriately with native speakers of English who have the more conventional problems with phonic awareness, or else their difficulties are assumed to derive from specific perceptual problems rather than from the cultural unfamiliarity of the text.

In order for a teaching approach with bilingual students to be fully effective it has to be comprehensive, which means that it needs to incorporate the views of parents and the community. This requires considerable preparation and pre-planning, as well as consultation with the parents and community organizations.

Knowledge of the child is crucial when planning for learning. This should take a holistic perspective looking at social, emotional, cultural as well as cognitive factors.

Presentation

Small steps

It is important, especially since children with dyslexia may have short-term memory difficulties, to present tasks in small steps. In fact, one task at a time is probably sufficient. If multiple tasks are specified then a checklist might be a useful way for the child to note and self-monitor his or her progress (Green and Reid 2007).

Group work

It is important to plan for group work. The dynamic of the group is crucial, and dyslexic children need to be in a group where at least one person in the group is able to impose some form of structure on the group tasks. This can act as a modelling experience for dyslexic children. It is also important that those in the group do not overpower the dyslexic child, so someone with the ability to facilitate the dyslexic child's contribution to the group is also important. This will make the dyslexic child feel he or she is contributing to the group. Even though dyslexic children may not have the reading ability of the others in the group, they will almost certainly have the comprehension ability, so will be able to contribute if provided with opportunities.

Learning styles

This is one of the key aspects in understanding the importance of presentation of materials and how the learning situation can be manipulated to promote more effective learning. It is important to recognize that different children have their own preferred learning style, and this includes dyslexic children. This means that there may be a great many similarities in how children with dyslexia learn and process information, but there will also be individual differences and these need to be taken into account in the planning and presentation of learning.

As suggested earlier, multisensory strategies are used widely in the teaching of dyslexic children. The evidence suggests that the effectiveness of these strategies is based largely on the provision of at least one mode of learning with which the learner feels comfortable. Thus if the learner has a difficulty dealing with information by way of the auditory channel, this could perhaps be compensated for through the use of the visual mode. The use of such compensatory strategies is well documented in the literature and is a feature of teaching programmes for dyslexic children. It is logical therefore that consideration of the learner as an individual should be extended to a holistic appreciation of the learner's individual style. Factors such as affective (emotional) and physiological characteristics will have some bearing on how the dyslexic child responds to the learning situation, and a holistic perspective should therefore be applied in both the assessment and the teaching of dyslexic children.

One of the most useful learning styles models is that developed by Dunn, Dunn and Price (1975–89). This model identifies five principal domains and 21 elements, all of which affect student learning. It is suggested that all these elements have to be considered during the assessment process and in subsequent planning of teaching. The domains and the elements across those domains are:

♦ environmental (sound, light, temperature, design)

♦ emotional (motivation, persistence, responsibility, structure)

♦ sociological (learning by self, pairs, peers, team, with an adult)

♦ physiological (perceptual preference, food and drink intake, time of day, mobility)

♦ psychological (global or analytic preferences, impulsive, reflective).

On examining this learning styles model, one can recognize how the elements identified can influence the performances of dyslexic learners. It must be appreciated that dyslexic learners are first and foremost learners, and like any other learners will be influenced by different learning conditions. Some dyslexic students therefore will prefer a 'silent' environment for concentration, while others may need some auditory stimuli, perhaps even music, in order to maximize concentration and performance. Similarly, as regards light, individual preferences such as dim light or bright light should be recognized.

In relation to emotional variables, two of the elements, responsibility and structure, should certainly be addressed. It has been well documented that dyslexic learners benefit from imposed structure. Most of the teaching programmes recognize this and follow a highly structured formula. At the same time, however, taking responsibility for one's own learning can be highly motivating and generate success. Dyslexic learners therefore should not be deprived of the opportunity to take responsibility, as some may possess a natural preference for responsibility and structure.

It is possible to obtain some idea of the child's learning style from observation, and knowledge of how the child tackles tasks in the classroom.

Learning styles: some tips

♦ Every effort should be made to organize the classroom environment in a manner that can be adapted to suit a range of styles.

♦ In classrooms where there are a number of dyslexic learners the environment should be global, which means lighting, design and indeed the whole learning atmosphere need to be considered.

♦ It is also important that the teacher has an awareness of what is meant by learning styles and how to identify different styles in children.

♦ Although there are many different instruments that can be used, teacher observations and discussion with students while they are engaged on a task can be extremely beneficial.

♦ The different stages of the information-processing cycle – input, cognition and output – should be considered in relation to how children learn and how this can be used within a learning styles structure.

♦ The experience of learning may be more important to children with dyslexia than the actual finished product.

♦ It is important that children with dyslexia become aware of their own learning styles. This is the first and most important step to achieving a degree of self-sufficiency in learning. Acknowledging learning styles can help to promote skills that extend beyond school.

♦ Knowledge of learning styles can equip students, and particularly students with dyslexia, for lifelong learning.

Information-processing

Learning depends on how efficiently and effectively children process information. It is important therefore to recognize the key stages of information-processing (input, cognition and output) and how these may present potential difficulties for learners with dyslexia. Some of these difficulties are discussed in Chapter 1, but it is important to recognize how these potential difficulties can be overcome with forward planning and recognition of these in teaching. Some suggestions for this are as follows:

Input

♦ Identify the student's preferred learning style, particularly visual, auditory, kinesthetic or tactile preferences, as these can be crucial in how information is presented. It is important to present new information to the learner's preferred modality.

♦ Present new information in small steps. This will ensure that the short-term memory does not become overloaded with information before it is fully consolidated.

♦ New material will need to be repeatedly presented through over-learning. This does not mean that the repetition should be in the same form – rather, it is important that it should be varied using as wide a range of materials and strategies as possible.

♦ It is a good idea to present the key points at the initial stage of learning new material. This helps to provide a framework for the new material and can help to relate new information to previous knowledge.

Cognition

♦ Information should be related to previous knowledge. This ensures that concepts are developed and the information can be placed into a learning framework, or schema, by the learner. Successful learning is often the result of efficient organization of information. It is important therefore to group information together and to show the connections between related information. For example, if the topic to be covered was the Harry Potter series of books, then concepts such as witchcraft and magic, and the words associated with these, would need to be explained and some of the related ideas discussed. This should be done before reading the text.

♦ Some specific memory strategies, such as Mind Mapping and mnemonics, can be used to help the learner remember some of the key words or more challenging ideas.

Output

♦ Often children with dyslexia have difficulty identifying the key points in new learning or in a text. This can be overcome by providing the child with these key points or words at the beginning stage of learning the new material. Additionally, the learner can acquire skills in this by practising using summaries: each period of new learning should be summarized by the learner – this in itself helps to identify the key points.

♦ It may also be beneficial to measure progress orally rather than through writing, particularly in-class continuous assessment. It is not unusual for children with dyslexia to be much more proficient orally than in written form. Oral presentation of information can therefore help to instil confidence. By contrast, often a written exercise can be damaging in terms of confidence, unless considerable preparation and planning have helped to ensure that some of the points indicated above are put in to place.

Some Tips for Supporting Learning

Materials

♦ *Use coloured paper* – there is evidence that different colours for background and font can enhance some children's reading and attention.

♦ *Layout* – the page layout is very important, and should be visual but not overcrowded. Coloured background is usually preferable. Font size can also be a key factor, and should not be too small. In relation to the actual font itself, it has been suggested that Sassoon, Comic Sans and Times New Roman are the most dyslexia-friendly fonts.

Tasks

◆ *Provide a tick list* – this can help to keep the child with dyslexia on track. It will also help him or her to monitor progress.

◆ *Break tasks into manageable chunks* – this can provide an opportunity for the learner to achieve. Children with dyslexia can have low self-esteem, because they are in a position of potential failure at school, as most learning is based on print. It is crucial therefore that they achieve and can realize that they have achieved with some tasks. It is this achievement that provides the success needed to raise their self-esteem.

◆ *Oral feedback* – it is often a good idea to get dyslexic children to provide oral feedback on the task they have to do. This ensures they have understood the task. At the same time, it is important that the teacher provides oral feedback to dyslexic children on how they have managed the task. Oral feedback can be more effective than written comments.

> Do not use red ink when writing on pupils' workbooks!

Planning

◆ *Provide a sequence to help with planning* – dyslexic children often have difficulties in developing and following an appropriate sequence. It can be useful to provide a structure that helps to sequence learning of new material. For instance, in the example that follows, the task is for the child to provide a summary of the key points in the passage. This however can be too demanding a task for the dyslexic learner. It is important therefore that the task is broken down into manageable chunks but that there is a clear sequence for the learner to follow. For example:

♦ First underline the important words in the passage.

♦ Next write them out on a separate page.

♦ Then write the meaning of each word next to it.

♦ Take one word at a time and indicate why it is important for the passage.

♦ Once you have completed this, decide which word is the most important and say why.

♦ Lastly, give a summary of the key points in the passage.

♦ *Help the learner to prioritize his or her work* – often, dyslexic students have difficulty in prioritizing their work. This can lead to them spending a lot of time on unimportant areas of the task. It can be a good idea to indicate what aspects of the task are 'very important', 'quite important' and 'less important.'

Writing

Writing frames and key words – children with dyslexia need a structure to help them write more fully when undertaking written expression. The use of writing frames can help with this. An example is shown below:

Argument

I think that _____ because _____.

The reasons for my thinking this are, firstly _____.

Another reason is _____.

Moreover _____ because _____.

These (facts/arguments/ideas) show that _____.

Some people think that _____ because

they argue that _____.

Discussion

Another group who agree with this point of view are

_____.

They say that _____.

On the other hand _____ disagree

with the idea that _____.

They claim that _____.

They also say _____.

My opinion is _____ because

_____.

(Adapted from David Wray's website,
www.warwick.ac.uk/staff/D.J.Wray/Ideas/frames.html)

Writing frames can help in comprehension of the question. This can be seen in the following common types of tasks:

♦ argument

♦ contrast

♦ comparison

♦ discussion

♦ persuasion

♦ sequence.

Dyslexia

In many situations these types of tasks can be demanding for students with dyslexia because often they do not know how to begin. Writing frames can provide the type of structure that gives a framework for their responses.

Other supports for writing include:

♦ providing key words

♦ giving paragraph headings and sub-headings

♦ providing clauses that can be used for sentence expansion, such as 'On my way to the baseball game .... and ....'

Computers and technology

Materials for learners with dyslexia can be enriched through the use of computer programs. There are a number of companies that specialize in software for learners with dyslexia. One such company is iANSYST Ltd (www.dyslexic. com). They provide a full range of text-to-speech software using the more advanced RealSpeak® voices, which are a significant improvement on previous versions and have a much more human-sounding voice. Such software can be very helpful for proofreading, as it is easier to hear mistakes than to see them and it can help to identify if any words are in the wrong place. iANSYST recommend software such as Wordsmith 2, as it can scan and edit paper-based text and images, listen to text being read back, and help the learner explore creative writing with speech support.

The TextHelp® range is also highly recommended. TextHelp Type and Touch 4.0 has integrated speech output for PC or Mac, and includes the TextHelp spellchecker, which has been specifically developed for use by learners with dyslexia.

Other computer support includes the Quicktionary Reading Pen, which transfers words from the page to the LCD display when scanned by the pen. The package can be upgraded in order to convert it into a translator, with over 20 different languages available. The reading pen also speaks the words and can define the word when requested.

There are also a number of typing tuition programs that can assist with the development of touch typing. These include the KAZ typing tutor, which has an age range of 7 to adults, and First Keys to Literacy, which has a recommended age range of 5 to 9 years. Some of the keyboarding activities include word lists, individual letter recognition, digraphs and rhymes, and picture, letter and word prompts. There is also a program called Magictype, which is a fun interactive program for the 6 to 11 age range.

There is also a wide range of software on study skills and memory training. Two such programs developed by Jane Mitchell include Mastering Memory and Time 2 Revise/Timely Reminders (www.calsc.co.uk/). Mastering Memory helps to improve short-term memory, enhances the learner's capacity to transfer new information to other areas of learning, and improves long-term retention. Time 2 Revise/Timely Reminders are packages that can help to structure the revision process, and utilize mind maps, index cards and revision notes. The emphasis is on encouraging the student to use the facts rather than to learn them by rote. This active learning has been shown to be significantly more successful for retention and recall, as well as in enhancing understanding.

There are also other popular programs that help to organize information, such as Kidspiration for the 5 to 11 age range, and Inspiration, which is also suitable for adults. These help to develop ideas and concepts with examples of concept maps and templates that incorporate a range of subject areas such as languages, arts, science and social studies.

R-E-M software also produce computer materials aimed at those with dyslexia, and have produced a specific catalogue (www.r-e-m.co.uk). A considerable range can also be found in the Educators Publishing Service website (www.epsbooks.com).

Dyslexia

Dimitriadi (2000) suggests that computer technology can facilitate access to the curriculum for bilingual children. She suggests that equipment and programs can support simultaneous input from different languages in oral, written or visual format and provide bilingual learners with the opportunity to enrich the curriculum with their diverse cultural experiences. Dimitriadi suggests that technology can help to reinforce alphabet skills by establishing correspondence between phonemes and graphemes in one language, and making the necessary connections between the way in which apparently similar graphemes have different sounds in other languages. A talking word processor provides the learners with immediate aural feedback through typing of individual graphemes.

She also puts forward the idea that a voice recognition system programmed to understand regional accents and problematic utterance will encourage the input of speech and translate it into script. This can help with spelling, and allow the opportunity to self-check and to construct simple sentences. Spellcheckers with phonically constructed wordbanks facilitate the writing process by generating lists of possible alternatives. It is possible therefore according to Dimitriadi to include simultaneously an oral and a written translation of the word rule into another language. Talking word-processors with pre-recorded word banks can provide immediate aural feedback to the users by repeating each word or sentence typed, and the learner is prompted to self-correct the sentence they typed by seeing their spelling mistakes in the form of highlighted words.

Dimitriadi suggests that computers can help with some of the difficulties related to the directional flow of the learner's written language structure, such as in Cantonese Chinese or in Arabic scripts, where the characters follow a different course to that of European languages. She suggests a multimedia computer allows learners to record their voices instead of typing the information, and temporarily they overcome the burden a new script might pose.

Technology and other resources can be very useful but there is no substitute for teaching skills and teacher–student interaction.

Key points for supporting learning

♦ Identify the strengths and take the opportunity to discuss these strengths with the child.

♦ Ensure it is possible for the child to achieve some success.

♦ Get the environment right – try out different types of learning environments.

♦ Provide short tasks.

♦ Use colour-coding and encourage the child to use his or her own strategies using colour for remembering information and for separating different pieces of information.

Often dyslexic children think visually – help them to use this as a strength!

♦ Acknowledge that over-learning is necessary – this means that instructions may have to be repeated and that the answer should be reinforced through other tasks or through oral discussion.

♦ Minimize the need for the child with dyslexia to read aloud.

♦ Help children to develop strategies to identify the key words. This can be through the use of colour coding or by underlining the main words.

♦ It is worthwhile taking time to ensure that the child has understood the task. This might mean going over some basic information. The child may have the higher-order thinking skills but not a basic understanding of the task, because his or her schema of the nature and demands of the task could be different from yours. Nevertheless, it is important that the task taps into higher-order thinking skills. This ensures that the child's thinking ability is being stretched.

♦ Do not limit the demands of the task because of the child with dyslexia's low level of literacy. Look for means of overcoming this such as the use of taped books, technology such as voice-activated software, or through working in groups.

♦ Children with dyslexia need over-learning but they also need to time to complete tasks. They may need more time than other children.

Allow more time for all tasks – do not set unnecessary time restrictions.

♦ Discuss dyslexia with the children so they have an understanding of the differences in how they learn.

♦ Try to encourage independent learning – give the children the scope to make decisions and help them to have some control over their learning.

♦ Encourage the child to have high expectations. This is important in relation to career and subject choice.

Using examples of famous and successful dyslexics can help children with dyslexia to believe in their abilities, but take time to discuss their hopes and concerns with them.

♦ Help children to monitor their own progress. This also allows them to provide a degree of control over their own learning.

♦ Give an overview of new learning first before asking them to tackle the individual aspects of it.

> Learners with dyslexia think globally – they need an overview first before embarking on further learning.

♦ Do not hand back marked work without going over it with the child first.

♦ In the class situation, do not obviously single children out because of their dyslexia.

♦ Acknowledge that performances may have an element of inconsistency and vary from day to day. Also remember that children with dyslexia will take longer to achieve automaticity. This means that they may have competence in a particular skill one day but not the next. This can be part of the process of acquiring competence in a skill, and means that they may not have automaticity in that skill. It is important therefore to provide opportunities for over-learning.

♦ Try to make the learning experience as stress-free as possible for the child with dyslexia.

♦ Above all, learning should be fun! It is important that the child with dyslexia is self-motivated to learn. This can only come about through understanding of his or her difficulties, and through success.

> Success is the key to success.

5

Planning for Learning in the Secondary School

Provision and Practice

One of the key issues in relation to successful outcomes in secondary or high school concerns the notion of responsibility. It is important to ensure that the needs of dyslexic children are met and that all members of staff become fully involved.

School management need to ensure that the following factors are in place:

♦ The ethos of the school is supportive. The philosophy of the school together with attitudes and actions must be known to all staff, including part-time support and other staff.

♦ All staff should be encouraged to acknowledge that with effective differentiation the curriculum can be accessed by dyslexic students.

♦ All teaching staff need to be supported in order to utilize some of the suggestions made in previous chapters in relation to planning, presentation and the development of materials.

♦ Parents need to be considered. Parents are a very rich support of information and support and it is important that collaboration between home and school is ongoing.

Accessing Subject Content

It can be suggested that if the subject materials and teaching plans are developed and implemented in a manner that is compatible with the dyslexic child's abilities, the student should be able to perform on the same terms as his or her peers. Although most of the subject content is determined by examination considerations and prescribed curricula, much can still be done to identify the potential areas of the curriculum that may present difficulties for dyslexic students.

There is therefore no reason why the content of all subjects cannot be developed in a dyslexia-friendly manner. It can be argued that the principles for making information dyslexia-friendly are the same for every subject: forward planning, together with an awareness of dyslexia. This also implies an awareness of differentiation, learning styles and dyslexia-friendly assessment procedures.

> The difficulties experienced by students with dyslexia can be anticipated. Forward planning therefore is necessary to prevent these difficulties becoming obstacles.

Some examples of this are shown below, for different subject areas of the curriculum.

English

In English it is important to use a range of sources, for example in literature, so that the dyslexic student can access a novel or play. It is often best to begin with discussion so that the overall story and plot can be understood before any reading begins. This also fits in with the learning style of many dyslexic children, which appears to favour holistic as opposed to analytical processing. This means that the child would need to understand the ideas and the background to the novel before reading it, which also helps to build concepts and a schema (schema essentially refers to the student's own understanding of a situation or an event). It is important therefore that the child with dyslexia has an appropriate schema before commencing to read. Having a schema or framework will help the reader use context and understanding to read difficult words and indeed understand the novel without actually reading every word.

There are many aspects relating to English that can be challenging for students with dyslexia – expressive writing, spelling and grammar as well as reading accuracy and fluency. It is important to acknowledge the different types of reading activities and the different strategies that can be used for each. Reading for examination questions and reading instructions requires a detailed and accurate form of reading. For the child with dyslexia this will mean that additional time is necessary, and the child can produce a checklist to ensure that he or she has understood the instructions. Such a list can include: what is actually being said/asked? What is required of me? How will I know if I am right? In other words, the teacher is encouraging the child to think about the implications of the question/instructions and to consider the information gleaned in different ways. By doing this it should become apparent to the student if the question has been misread.

Similarly, in reading for facts the reader can make a checklist of different types of information under different headings. It may also be helpful if the teacher actually provides the headings for the student. The child with dyslexia needs to obtain practice in scanning and reading to obtain a general overview or impression of the text. One way to help the child practise scanning is to give the child a passage to read but not give him or her sufficient time to read it. This means the child will be forced to read only the key words.

These factors emphasize the importance of forward planning and breaking challenging areas down into smaller components so that the teacher can identify which of these presents the most challenge, and then work through the range of strategies that can be used for these areas. Some of the strategies include those that can be used for good teaching in general – teaching in a multisensory manner, helping to boost the student's memory through the use of mnemonics, personal spelling notebooks, the use of ICT to help with reading, and the use of the Internet to investigate topics, for example. It can sometimes be useful if the child with dyslexia can work in groups, as he or she can share skills with others in the group: the reading part can be done by someone else in the group while the dyslexic child can deal with some of the other aspects of the task.

Geography

Geography is a subject that can be accessed by dyslexic children. It has the potential to be highly visual and the subject content relates to the study of people and activities in the community and world around us. In other words, it is a subject that has direct relevance to living in today's world. This means that information in geography can be accessed in a variety of ways – through field trips, visually, or through visits, interviews and observation, quite apart from reading materials.

Additionally, the geography curriculum lays emphasis on the enquiry approach in developing geographical knowledge and understanding, through knowledge of environments throughout the world, an understanding of maps, and using a range of investigative and problem-solving skills. These activities can take place both inside and outside the classroom.

In geography, as in many of the other subject areas, alternatives to the written answer can be used to a great extent. Students with dyslexia usually have skills in the visual/kinesthetic areas as opposed to the auditory area. This means that they will learn more effectively by active learning through projects, field trips and interviews. They may also work well in groups.

It is important to ensure that students with dyslexia can present their work in a variety of ways using multi-media, including tapes, videos and ICT.

It is important that geography is underpinned by under-standing, and this is why active participatory learning is essential for dyslexic learners. It is crucial that the skills and abilities of dyslexic students in the areas of visual processing and understanding are not restricted because of lack of access to print materials.

History

History is a subject that can be stimulating and engaging for the dyslexic student. It essentially demands investi-gation and skills in problem-solving, but too often the actual demands placed on the student relate to memory demands and the learning of massive amount of facts. This of course need not be the case, and it is necessary to consider ways in which the student might acquire the necessary infor-mation without resorting to rote memorization.

Dargie (2001) suggests that discussion is the key to this. Talking about an issue, he suggests, can help students rehearse the separate components of a topic and develop an argument that they can then use in written work.

Contributing to a discussion exercise or a group presen-tation can have positive consequences for the dyslexic learner's self-esteem. Working in groups can also provide the child with practice at experimenting and becoming more familiar with his or her own learning style. It is important, according to Dargie, that students with dyslexia gain experience in the range of specific skills needed for history, such as the ability to question, infer, deduce, propose, estimate, guess, judge and think.

Learning to talk about history can provide a launch pad for reading and writing about history. Similarly, paired homework, with an emphasis upon pupils having to check that their partner can readily explain topic vocabulary, can also provide the confidence to write.

It is important to plan and anticipate the type of difficulties the student with dyslexia may experience in history. One example of this can be listening skills. These can be enhanced by providing dyslexic children with topic content in audio cassette form for individual use in Walkman-type players. According to Dargie (2001), it is also important that history departments plan a reading strategy that seeks to create more self-aware readers, who understand the purpose of their reading and appreciate how and why the text in front of them is shaped in the way that it is.

An effective reading strategy in history might include features such as (taken from Dargie 2001):

♦ Consistent teacher pre-checking of text material and calculation of reading age to ensure students encounter historical text in a planned, progressive way.

♦ A focus upon concept vocabulary and upon discursive connectives that develop historical argument.

♦ The selective use of word-processing functions, such as emboldening and/or increasing point size, to highlight the way historical text works.

♦ The planned reading of material as homework to increase pupil familiarity with the demands of the text by using scissors and highlighter pens to analyse how different kinds of historical text are constructed.

♦ Highlighting photocopied text to given criteria, for example in search of key phrases.

♦ Persistent teacher questioning to accompany pupil reading in order to check comprehension. This is particularly important when working with dyslexic readers who may only have partially automatized the decoding of print, and who may not yet be self-generating questions as they read.

♦ Teacher awareness of the different preferred reading styles of pupils, and of the interactive nature of effective reading.

♦ Teacher awareness of the difficulties posed by 'weasel words' in history such as class, state, party and church, which have an abstract historical usage in addition to their more familiar concrete meaning.

♦ Teacher alertness to the difficulties posed by subject-specific conventions such as 'c.' for circa, 'IV' for fourth, 'C.' for century, etc.

♦ Teacher awareness of the need to structure the teacher's own text to meet the needs of different learners, e.g. by avoiding long, multi-clausal sentences, avoiding over-use of passive-voice constructions, planning ways of explaining unfamiliar vocabulary and ideas (e.g. word boxes and marginal scaffolding), keeping text concrete where appropriate rather than abstract, minimizing the use of metaphorical language, being alert to the range of tenses used in history to describe actions in the past.

Examinations can cause considerable anxiety for students with dyslexia, and this can be dealt with by the department through recognition of the type of exam anxiety and perhaps by providing specific study skills aimed at examination revision and by ensuring that the student revises effectively and uses the time available efficiently. It is often the case that children with dyslexia spend a considerable length of time revising but often to no avail – it is important then that the effort made by the student is rewarded. Guidance and support in study and study techniques is therefore as crucial as the student's knowledge and understanding of the actual content of the subject.

Physics

Physics is a subject that can present some difficulties to dyslexic students, but it is also one in which they can do well because it may involve less reading and a high degree of scientific understanding. Holmes (2001) suggests a top-down approach, first providing a whole school awareness of dyslexia and allowing subject teachers to reflect on the implications of providing for dyslexic students in their own subject.

Other factors that Holmes considers include:

♦ building a bank of support materials that can become a whole school resource

♦ recognizing the implications of secondary difficulties that can affect a student's performance in a particular subject – for example, the relationship between mathematics and physics can mean that the student's difficulties in physics are a consequence of mathematics difficulties. This emphasizes the need for a whole school approach on dealing with dyslexia.

Drama

Drama is a subject that should be enjoyable and easily accessed by students with dyslexia – often however it is not. There is much more to drama than reading plays and it is important that the dyslexic person becomes actively involved in all aspects of drama. This can include planning the sets and designing costumes. Eadon (2005) suggests that many ideas can come from the students themselves, and it is important to allow students to take some initiative, especially since children with dyslexia can have some very innovative ideas. This of course can also help to boost self-esteem.

It can be very useful to present scripts in a larger-than-normal font size. It is also helpful to use a dyslexia-friendly typeface, such as Comic Sans, Times New Roman or Sassoon. The script should also be spaced out to allow to make it easier to read – in fact each sentence can be on a new line.

One of the important aspects about drama is that it has cross-curricular implications. Drama can have a positive spin-off effect in English, art and indeed other subjects, since it has the potential to boost a student's self-concept, and this will have a transferable effect to other subject areas.

Most of the content in all subjects can be made dyslexia-friendly. Often these approaches will benefit all students, and not only those who are dyslexic.

Differentiation

Differentiation can be described as the action necessary to respond to the individual's specific requirements for curriculum access. Essentially, therefore, the differentiation required for dyslexic students should be seen not as a 'special case', but as an essential component of preparation that should be carried out for all pupils. Williams and Lewis (2001), in relation to geography, recognize that differentiation can take place

♦ by task, i.e. providing the student with a range of tasks from which to select

♦ by outcome, which means using a range of assessment strategies so that the dyslexic student can demonstrate his or her knowledge and understanding of the subject

♦ by support – this can include support staff but also parents, school management and collaboration.

It is suggested that differentiation does not mean writing worksheets with reduced content. The following factors can be useful:

♦ knowledge of the 'readability' levels of text and sources of information

♦ paying attention to the design of resources, including the layout and the use of diagrams (which need to be clearly labelled)

♦ provision of printed materials such as notes and maps, to prevent tracing and arduous note-taking

♦ provision of key words – this is important as it can help to provide the student with a framework of the topic and prevent any difficulties with word retrieval he or she may display

♦ specialized vocabulary spelling lists – this is important as in some science subjects there may be a specialized technical vocabulary

♦ tape recordings of key passages, as they can obviously be replayed by the student. It needs to be remembered, however, that there can be time implications with this, so it should be adopted prudently.

Key Issues

Some of the key issues relating to dyslexia in the secondary school therefore include:

♦ subject content – ensuring it is accessible

♦ subject delivery – ensuring that the presentation of the curriculum acknowledges the learning style and the strengths of students with dyslexia and that the planning takes into account the potential difficulties they may experience with the subject

♦ assessment – as far as possible, a wide range of assessment strategies should be used

♦ cross-curricular aspects – it is important that opportunities for collaboration with other subject teachers are provided as this can promote cross-curricular transfer of knowledge and of any particular concepts that can apply across different subject areas

♦ learning styles – it is important to acknowledge that new learning needs to be presented in a manner that suits the student's learning style

♦ training for staff in the area of dyslexia, as all staff should have at least an awareness of dyslexia.

It is important that these issues are fully addressed so that the student with dyslexic difficulties can achieve some success in different subject areas.

Teaching and learning should be planned together. This implies that knowledge of teaching strategies and of the learner's individual strengths and difficulties and learning style are all necessary in order for planning and presentation of learning to be effective.

Hunter (2001), in referring to the layout of the science classroom, highlights potential pitfalls, particularly relating to organization of group work, that can result in the dyslexic student missing vital information if, for example, the student is seated out of view of demonstrations or even the board. There are organizational implications here, particularly if there are booklets and materials to refer to, which need to be readily accessible and identifiable. The laboratory setting can however be very compatible with the learning style of a dyslexic student as it provides scope and space for group work, and flexibility in approaches to learning.

Other subjects, such as modern foreign languages, English, art and drama, which can prove challenging in terms of the amount of reading, can lend themselves quite easily to kinesthetic approaches by focusing on experiential learning activities. For example, in modern languages, often seen to be a source of considerable difficulty for the dyslexic student and consequently of frustration for the teacher, Crombie and McColl (2001) show how by use of appropriate strategies and consideration of the mode of presentation dyslexic students can achieve success. They suggest the following:

♦ the use of charts and diagrams to highlight the bigger picture

♦ adding mime and gesture to words

♦ adding pictures to text

♦ using colour to highlight gender or accents

♦ labelling diagrams and charts

♦ using games to consolidate vocabulary

♦ making packs of pocket-size cards

♦ using different colours for different purposes

♦ combining listening and reading by providing text and tape

♦ using mind maps or spidergrams

♦ allowing students to produce their own tapes

♦ presenting information in small amounts, using a variety of means, with frequent opportunities for repetition and revision

♦ providing an interest in the country, through showing films, and highlighting literature and culture.

Generally it is important in most subjects for instructions to be short and clear, preferably using bullet points. It is also worth considering the use of labels and key terms to highlight various points; the dyslexic student often has a word-finding difficulty and may need some of the terms used in some subject areas to be reinforced.

Other Considerations

Thinking skills

It is important to consider the development of higher-order thinking skills when teaching children with dyslexia. There may be a tendency to overlook these types of programmes in preference for a more direct decoding/literacy acquisition type of intervention. Some forms of assessment, such as dynamic assessment (discussed in Chapter 1), which involves providing the learner with assistance during the assessment process, offer an opportunity to utilize thinking skills. This form of assessment encourages the learner to articulate the thinking process, for example why he or she thinks a certain response is correct. This approach essentially links assessment and teaching, and highlights the child's learning process.

Multilingualism

Usmani (1999) suggests the bilingual, bicultural child may have a broad range of thinking skills that may go undetected if the professional is unaware of the cultural values, or fails to understand them in relation to the assessment and teaching programme.

Bilingualism or multilingualism is an area that can present a challenge to those involved in assessment and teaching of learners with dyslexia. Although considerable progress has been made in the development of teacher-friendly assessment and teaching materials for dyslexia, it has been assumed that these materials would be suitable for all children with dyslexic difficulties, irrespective of their cultural and social background. This may not be the case.

The British Psychological Working Party Report (BPS 1999) emphasizes the importance of culturally relevant materials for children with dyslexia, and particularly of culture-fair assessment. Dyslexia, the report suggests, may be 'masked by limited mastery of the language of tuition' (p. 60). It is acknowledged in the report that dyslexia can occur across languages, cultures, socio-economic statuses, races and genders. Yet the report notes that the tools needed to uncover the masking of dyslexic difficulties are not readily available. Furthermore, the message that this gives to teachers is that the key reason why a child is not acquiring literacy skills in the language being taught relates to the bilingual dimension, and not due to any other factor – such as dyslexia.

Many of the teaching approaches suggested for bilingual children are essentially an adaptation of those suggested in Chapter 3, which are aimed mainly at monolingual dyslexic learners. It is important that this adaptation occurs following consultation with school staff, support staff and specialist teachers, and is contextualized for the bilingual child. However, as Deponio, Landon and Reid (2000) indicate, care should be taken to note that some bilingual learners may have difficulty articulating some sounds, especially English vowels and final consonantal morphemes, and speakers of syllable-timed languages such as Cantonese may have difficulty in hearing unstressed syllables in stress-timed English utterances. Previous experience of reading logographic, as opposed to alphabetic, script may also cause difficulties with analogical reading for a literate Chinese pupil. Therefore, more practice in recognizing rhyme and syllable may be necessary for learners from certain language backgrounds.

Awareness raising

The key to successful planning and presentation of the curriculum and differentiation for dyslexic children is for all staff to have an understanding of the characteristics of dyslexia and the processing style of the individual dyslexic children in their class. This can be done through awareness-raising staff training that can be directed to all staff, and not just to a few specialists (as has been the case in many schools). This is a list of the potential topics that can be included in awareness-raising staff development:

Dyslexia

- what is dyslexia?
- identification and assessment of dyslexia in the classroom
- teaching programmes
- teaching strategies
- learning skills and learning styles
- differentiation
- using a reading scheme effectively with dyslexic children
- planning and presenting curricular materials
- thinking skills and the implications of these for dyslexic children
- role of parents
- whole school programmes
- study skills
- role of computers.

> Awareness-raising training should be more than a one-off snapshot, but rather a carefully constructed and contextualized course over a period of time. This can pay dividends as it is very likely that every teacher in every country will have at least one child with dyslexia in his or her class.

Summary

This chapter has suggested that there is no 'off-the-shelf' answer to dealing with dyslexia. Ideally a curriculum perspective should be adopted, and this implies that the onus is not on the learner but on the teacher to ensure that the curriculum and the tasks are suitably planned, presented and differentiated for children with dyslexia. Part of this involves knowledge of the child and his or her individual learning and processing style. A comprehensive and curriculum-contextualized assessment is therefore necessary before planning commences. It is suggested throughout this book that contextualized assessment can be conducted by the class teacher, with support from specialists, if available. The class teacher will acquire knowledge of the child in the normal course of teaching the class, and this knowledge is essential to the planning and presentation of the curriculum for children with dyslexia.

6

Dyslexia, Learning and Study Skills

Effective learning involves a number of interactive cognitive processes. The learner can control these processes to make learning efficient and effective. To enable this to happen, the skills associated with learning need to be developed from an early age, yet surprisingly these skills are not given the attention they warrant within the school curriculum. Study skills, for example, which can provide the learner with an opportunity to practise and experiment with learning to find the most efficient methods, are often not given full prominence in the curriculum; yet they can help to develop not only retention of information, but also comprehension and language concepts. It is vitally important therefore that learning skills are addressed at an early stage in education.

Study skills should be taught at an early age.

Learning Skills and Dyslexia

It is very important that children with dyslexia develop learning skills. One of the difficulties associated with dyslexia is in identifying key points and using efficient learning strategies. People with dyslexia may use many different steps to get an answer to a question, compared to someone who can achieve the answer using a more direct process. In some mathematical problems children with dyslexia may take twice the number of steps to get to the correct response as compared with other children (Chinn 2002). This means that they may lose track of the actual problem, and certainly the additional time needed to solve problems in this tangential manner can be to their disadvantage. This emphasizes the importance of developing effective learning skills and strategies at an early age. This can be achieved through:

♦ the use of study skills

♦ discussion of how the child is learning

♦ using strategies such as scaffolding that can help to develop concepts and schemata

♦ comprehension-building exercises

♦ the use of learning styles.

The Process of Learning

The model of social constructivism proposed by Vygotsky (1986) has been applied to many areas of assessment and learning. It essentially states that one needs to look at how the child's understanding of language and learning is mediated by the learning context and the classroom environment. Burden (2002) suggests that the cultural and social context within which learning takes place is crucial in mediating how a child learns. This implies that learning involves more than just presentation of information: it embraces factors relating to the whole child, and particularly the child's previous cultural and learning experiences. Previous experiences and learning can make new learning meaningful. It is important to establish this before or when new learning is being presented. This process has been temed 'reciprocal teaching' (Palincsar and Brown 1984). This is where the interaction between learner and teacher can establish a scaffold to help the child bridge his or her existing knowledge and experiences with the new material.

Essentially this is achieved through effective question-and-answer interaction between teacher and child. This interaction should build on the child's responses in order to extend his or her thinking.

Reciprocal teaching and scaffolding

Reciprocal teaching refers to a procedure that both monitors and enhances comprehension by focusing on processes relating to questioning, clarifying, summarizing and predicting (Palincsar and Brown, 1984). This is an interactive process:

♦ the teacher leads the discussion by asking questions

♦ this generates additional questions from participants

♦ the questions are then clarified by the teacher and participants together

♦ the discussion is then summarized by the teacher or participants

♦ then a new 'teacher' is selected by the participants to lead the discussion on the next section of the text.

Zone of Proximal Development

Reciprocal teaching stems from what Vygotsky describes as the 'Zone of Proximal Development'. This refers to the interaction between the teacher and the child, and how much of the learning can be independently accessed by the child and how much requires the teacher to mediate in order for the child to access full understanding and develop further additional related concepts.

Burden (2002) describes the Zone of Proximal Development as the zone where learning can be scaffolded by others: then, when independent cognitive activity takes place, the scaffolding is gradually removed at appropriate moments. This can be seen as active rather than passive learning as it is a dynamic process and the child can actually determine the nature and extent of the learning experience. This has considerable implications for children and adults with dyslexia as they benefit from active learning, and the scaffolding experience can also help to clarify and establish concepts before the child moves on to further learning. An example is shown below.

Skill to be acquired
Learning to ride a bicycle

Zone of Proximal Development (skills already achieved)
Able to balance
Able to pedal
Has control over the handlebars
Knows how to use the brakes

Scaffolds (supports needed to acquire the skill)
Stabilizers on the bicycle – then removed
Someone holding the seat of the bicycle – then removed

The scaffolds are therefore the link that can help to take the learner out of his or her comfort zone and into a new learning zone and skill.

Scaffolds for reading

Poor readers can find it difficult to make the transfer from book language to their own writing. As a result of this, their writing quite often lacks the precise vocabulary that was perhaps evident during reading. To overcome this difficulty,

Dyslexia

Cudd and Roberts (1994) introduced a scaffolding technique to develop both sentence sense and vocabulary. They focused on sentence expansion by using vocabulary from the children's readers, and used these as sentence stems to encourage sentence expansion. Thus the procedure used involved:

♦ selecting vocabulary from the basal reader

♦ embedding this vocabulary into sentence stems

♦ selecting particular syntactic structures to introduce the stem

♦ embedding the targeted vocabulary into sentence stems to produce complex sentences

♦ discussing the sentence stems, including the concepts involved

♦ completing a sentence using the stems

♦ repeating the completed sentence, providing oral reinforcement of both the vocabulary and the sentence structure

♦ encouraging the illustration of some of their sentences, helping to give the sentence a specific meaning.

Cudd and Roberts found that this sentence expansion technique provided a 'scaffold' for children to help develop their sentence structure and vocabulary. The children, including those with reading and writing difficulties, were seen to achieve better control over the writing process and gained confidence from using their own ideas and personal experiences.

It is important that people with dyslexia gain some control over their own learning process.

118

Transfer of skills

Transfer of skills can best be achieved when emphasis is firmly placed on the *process* of learning, and not on the product. This encourages children to reflect on learning, and to interact with other learners and with the teacher. In this way effective study skills can help to activate learning and provide the child with a structured framework for effective learning.

This involves preparation, planning and reflection:

♦ *Preparation* looks at the goals of the current work and how these goals relate to previous work.

♦ *Planning* looks at the skills and information necessary in order to achieve these goals.

♦ *Reflection* assesses the quality of the final piece of work, asking such questions as 'What did the children learn from the exercise?' and 'To what extent could the skills gained be transferred to other areas?'

This example displays a structure from which it is possible to plan and implement a study skills programme and at the same time evaluate its effectiveness in relation to the extent of transfer of knowledge and skills to other curricular areas.

> It is important that children with dyslexia are able to reflect on how they learn, and discuss this.

Metacognitive strategies

'Metacognition' means thinking about thinking, and this has an important role in how children learn. It can also be vital in helping dyslexic children clarify concepts and ideas, and can make reading and learning more meaningful.

It can help the child to consider:

- *text* – i.e. the material to be learnt
- *task* – the purpose of reading or the exercise
- *strategies* – how he or she understands and remembers information
- *characteristics of the learner* – his or her prior experience, background knowledge, interests and motivation.

It is important for children to be aware of how they learn and for teachers to get some insights into this. This can be achieved by:

- encouraging children to obtain some knowledge of their own metacognitive activities (this can be achieved through thinking aloud as they perform particular tasks)
- encouraging conscious awareness of cognitive activity such as self-questioning, e.g. 'Have I done this before? How did I do it? Is this the best way to tackle this problem?'
- encouraging control over learning in order to develop particular strategies for dealing with a task, whether it be reading, spelling or creative writing
- helping learners to generate questions as they read
- helping them to transfer what they read into mental images
- helping them have a clear purpose regarding the 'what' and 'why' of the reading material
- assisting in the development of concepts through strategies such as mind maps and self-questioning, and through the use of cue cards that contain ideas for thinking aloud.

> Try to get children to think about how they are learning or have learnt something. Get them to think aloud.

Assessing metacognitive awareness
This can be achieved by asking yourself if, when tackling a new task, the child demonstrates self-assessment by asking questions such as:

◆ Have I done this before?

◆ How did I tackle it?

◆ What did I find easy?

◆ What was difficult?

◆ Why did I find it easy or difficult?

◆ What did I learn?

◆ What do I have to do to accomplish this task?

◆ How should I tackle it?

◆ Should I tackle it the same way as before?

This information can inform both the teacher and the child on how the child learns – that is, the processes involved in learning. Using metacognitive strategies is important, because they can help the learner to develop reading comprehension and expressive writing skills. Metacognitive strategies include:

◆ visual imagery – discussing and sketching images from text

◆ summary sentences – identifying the main ideas in text

◆ webbing – the use of concept maps of the ideas from a text

♦ self-interrogation – asking questions about what learners already know about a topic and what they may be expected to learn from the new passage.

Healy Eames and Hannafin (2005) have acknowledged many of the points above in their study skills text *Switching on for Learning* (www.fheLearning.com). They emphasize that the learner needs to take responsibility to find out what his or her preferred learning conditions are. This encourages learners to reflect on the learning environment and the optimum environment for them. Healy Eames and Hannafin suggest that learners should reflect on their attitude to learning, as well as the social aspects of learning and the psychology of learning. This ensures that they are ready for the task and have self-knowledge on the best way to tackle it.

> Try to enable learners to monitor their own perform-ances throughout the learning process.

Assessment through retelling

Ulmer and Timothy (2001) developed an alternative assessment framework based on retelling as an instruc-tional and assessment tool. This indicated that informative assessment of a child's comprehension could take place by using criteria relating to how the child retells a story. Ulmer and Timothy suggested the following criteria:

♦ textual – what the child remembered

♦ cognitive – how the child processed the information

♦ affective – how the child felt about the text.

Their two-year study indicated that of the teachers in the study assessed for textual information, only 31 per cent looked for cognitive indicators, and 25 per cent for affective.

Yet the teachers who did go beyond the textual found rich information. Some examples of information provided by the teachers indicated that assessing beyond the textual level in relation to the use of the retelling method of assessment could provide evidence of the child's 'creative side', and they discovered that children could go 'beyond the expectations when given the opportunity'. This is a good example of how looking for alternative means of assessing can link with the child's understandings of text and promote and develop thinking.

It can be suggested that assessment instruments are often based on restrictive criteria, often examining at a textual level what the child may be expected to know but ignoring other rich sources of information that can inform about the child's thinking, both cognitive and affective, and therefore provide suggestions for teaching. Metacognitive assessment strategies go beyond the basic textual level and look at how the child actually relates to the information to be learnt. This is important for children with dyslexia as often they may not grasp the basic point but are able to consider more elaborate and higher-order thoughts. Tom West (1997), in his book *In the Mind's Eye*, highlights this well when he said that for learners with dyslexia, 'the easy is hard and the hard is easy'.

Assessment – dynamic and metacognitive

Traditional forms of assessment such as standardized assessment can provide information on the child's level of attainments, but usually they do not provide information about the process of thinking utilized by the child. Metacognitive aspects that focus on this process can be extremely valuable and can identify the strategies being used by the child, and also be a useful teaching tool, through the development of concepts and ideas through teacher–student interaction.

> Assessment should identify the learning strategies used by the student.

Reflective exercise

How did you learn to ride a bike ?

How did you learn to swim?

How did you learn the times tables?

How do you make sure you have added a column of figures correctly with a calculator?

How do you revise for exams?

How do you remember birthdays?

How do you remember telephone numbers?

How do you remember people's names?

The exercise above can help people work out the most effective way of learning for them. Some will have well-established strategies and be able to recollect these easily. For others, it might be the first time they have actually thought about how they did something. It is important to reflect on learning, as it can help to identify the most effective way for the individual to learn.

Multiple intelligences

Since Howard Gardner wrote *Frames of Mind* (Gardner 1983), the concept of intelligence and its applicability to education has been re-examined. Before then there was a commonly held view of intelligence as a unitary concept, although that was constantly being re-examined during the second half of the twentieth century. Gardner suggests that when Binet attempted to measure intelligence in the early part of the twentieth century there was indeed an assumption that intelligence was a single entity, and that this could be measured by a single paper-and-pencil instrument (Gardner 1999). This of course had considerable implications for how children were assessed and taught during the mid-twentieth century, and was particularly influential in streaming and in deciding the most appropriate education provision for children. Gardner acknowledges however that there has been considerable movement away from this view and application of intelligence, and attempts to highlight the need to 'pluralize the notion of intelligence and to demonstrate that intelligences cannot be adequately measured by short answer paper and pencil tests' (1999, p. vii).

Gardner also acknowledges that his conceptualization of intelligence is part of a larger effort to examine and define the concept and pluralization of intelligence. At present the multiple intelligence concept developed originally by Gardner involves eight intelligences (see p. 131).

Gardner himself therefore has developed his concept of multiple intelligence since the publication of *Frames of Mind*, and accepts that now he does not see intelligence as a set of human potentials but sees it rather 'in terms of the particular social and cultural context in which the individual lives'. According to Gardner, this means that a significant part of an individual's intelligence exists outside his or her head, and this therefore broadens the notion of assessing intelligence to involve many different aspects of a person's skills, thoughts and preferences. The notion of multiple intelligence therefore sits well with this contextualization view of intelligence, and because of this can be more comfortably applied to educational settings. Gardner accepts that intelligences do not work in isolation but usually interact and combine with other intelligences, and where one differs from another is in that combination and how that combination works for the learner. Gardner suggests that all of us possess these eight intelligences in some combination and all have the potential to use them productively. This has clear implications for the classroom and indeed for children with dyslexia, as they will possess these intelligences, perhaps in a different combination from some others, but with the same potential to develop

Logical/Mathematical
Albert Einstein

Visual/Spatial
Walt Disney
Lord Richard Rogers (architect)

Intrapersonal
John Irving
Agatha Christie

Interpersonal
Richard Branson
Peter Stringfellow

Naturalistic
Jack Homer (inspiration for Jurassic Park)

Musical/Rhythmic
Cher
Noel Gallagher

Verbal/Linguistic
Sir Winston Churchill
W.B.Yeats

Bodily/Kinesthetic
Sir Jackie Stewart
Sir Steve Redgrave

Figure 7 Famous dyslexics within the multiple
intelligence framework

these in classroom activities. It is important therefore that the notion of multiple intelligence is incorporated not only into assessment but also into the teaching and learning process in schools.

Lazear (1999) has made considerable efforts to incorporate Gardner's model of intelligence into both assessment and teaching. Each of the eight intelligences can be incorporated, and if this is achieved within one's teaching and in curriculum development, then children who may have weakness in some aspects of language or other processing (such as dyslexic children) will benefit. This essentially turns the concept of deficits on its head, and as Gardner points out, every child has the potential for effective learning but their learning preferences and strengths need to be accessed. The eight intelligences can be summarized as follows:

♦ *verbal/linguistic* involves language-processing

♦ *logical/mathematical ability*, which is associated with scientific and deductive reasoning

♦ *visual/spatial* deals with visual stimuli and visual planning

♦ *bodily/kinesthetic* involves the ability to express emotions and ideas in action (such as drama and dancing)

♦ *musical/rhythmic* is the ability to recognize rhythmic and tonal patterns

♦ *interpersonal* involves social skills and working in groups

♦ *intrapersonal* involves metacognitive-type activities and reflection

♦ *naturalist* relates to one's appreciation of the natural world around us, the ability to enjoy nature and to classify (for example) different species of flora, and how we incorporate and react emotionally to natural environmental factors such as flowers, plants and animals.

Each of these intelligences can be incorporated into teaching and learning and into curriculum development. It is important therefore that the skills and preferences of, for example, children with dyslexia are utilized within a multiple intelligences curriculum. Lazear (1999) has made considerable effort to highlight the potential of multiple intelligences within daily classroom activities.

♦ *verbal linguistic* – creative writing, poetry and storytelling

♦ *logical/mathematical* – logic and pattern games, problem-solving

♦ *visual/spatial* – guided imagery, drawing and design

♦ *bodily/kinesthetic* – drama, role-play and sports

♦ *musical/rhythmic* – classroom activities relating to tonal patterns, music performance

♦ *intrapersonal* – thinking strategies, metacognition and independent projects

♦ *naturalist* – fieldwork projects on conservation, evolution and the observation of nature.

Multiple intelligences as a guide to classroom practice can be very helpful in ensuring that the curriculum and the learning and teaching provide the opportunity for the child to display and extend his or her natural abilities in many areas. Historically, there has been considerable preoccupation with the verbal/linguistic aspects of intelligence, and this has resulted in a curriculum and examination system that appears to give a preferential status to these areas. This can be disadvantageous to children with dyslexia. It is interesting to note the comment by Pringle-Morgan made as long ago as 1896 (Pringle-Morgan 1896) that there is a group of otherwise intelligent people who have difficulty in expressing their understanding of a situation in writing, and if this group were provided with the opportunity to present their knowledge in some other form (such as orally) they would score considerably higher in examinations. Over 100 years later this message is beginning to get through, but there have been many casualties along the road, and children with dyslexia can account for some of these.

> It is important that people with dyslexia are able to demonstrate their skills in some way. They should not be restricted by the examination system.

Study Skills

Study skills should be considered when developing a programme for dyslexic children. There is evidence that dyslexic children require help in this area principally due to their organizational and memory difficulties. A well-constructed study skills programme is essential and can do much to enhance concept development, metacognitive awareness, transfer of learning and success in the classroom.

Programmes will vary according to the age and stage of the learner. A study skills programme for primary children, for instance, would be different from one to help students cope with examinations at secondary level. Well-developed study skills habits at the primary stage can provide a sound foundation for tackling new material in secondary school and help equip the student for examinations. Some of the principal factors in a study skills programme include:

♦ organization of information

♦ sequencing of events, arranging text into logical sequence

♦ the use of context – memory strategies, using familiar items, thinking about the purpose of learning

♦ the development of schemata: this provides a framework for learning and suggests that the meaning and the understanding of the material to be learnt is important

♦ the development of self-confidence and motivation – this is also crucial. Learners will be more successful if they have intrinsic motivation: that means they want to do something for themselves and not to please others. There is also a great deal of evidence to suggest that self-confidence is one of the most important determinants in successful learning.

Organization

Children with dyslexia require help with organization. A structure should therefore be developed to help encourage this. This involves not just physical organization, but also how they organize their thinking, learning and retention.

Children may need help with the organization of responses (output), and this can in turn help to organize learning through comprehension (input). The teacher can develop a framework to help develop this type of organization. For example, when discussing a book that has recently been read, a possible framework will include the following questions:

♦ What was the title?

♦ Who were the main characters?

♦ Can you describe the main characters?

♦ What did the main characters try to do?

♦ Who were the other characters in the story?

♦ What was the story about?

- What was the main part of the story?
- How did the story end?

In this way a structure is provided for the learner to retell the story. Moreover, the learner will be organizing the information into a number of components such as 'characters', 'story' and 'conclusion'. This not only will make it easier for the learner to retell the story orally, but will help to give him or her an organizational framework that will facilitate the retention of detail. The learner will also be using a strategy that can be used in other contexts. This will help with the new learning and the retention of new material.

> Children with dyslexia will need a structure and a framework to guide their responses to a task.

Sequencing

Dyslexic children may have some difficulty in retelling a story or giving information orally in the correct sequence. It is important that sequencing of information should be encouraged, and exercises that help to facilitate this skill should be developed. For example, in the retelling of a story, children should be provided with a framework that can take account of the sequence of events. Such a framework could include:

- How did the story start?
- What happened after that?
- What was the main part?
- How did it end?

Various exercises, such as the use of games, can be developed to help facilitate sequencing skills.

The use of context

Contextual aspects are also important elements in acquiring study skills. Context can be used to help the learner in both the sequencing and organization of materials, as well as providing an aid to comprehension.

Context can be in the form of syntactic and semantic context. In study skills, semantic context can be particularly valuable as a learning and memory aid. If the learner is using or relying on semantic context, this provides some indication that the material is being read and learnt with some understanding. The context can therefore help to:

♦ retain information and aid recall

♦ enhance comprehension

♦ transfer learning to other situations.

The development of schemata

The development of schemata helps the learner organize and categorize information. It also ensures the utilization of background knowledge. This can aid comprehension and recall.

When children read a story or a passage, they need to relate this to their existing framework of knowledge – i.e. to their own schema. So when coming across new knowledge, learners try to fit it into their existing framework of knowledge based on previous learning, which is the schema they possess for that topic or piece of information. It is important for the teacher to find out how developed a child's schema is on a particular topic, before providing more and new information. This helps the teacher to ensure that the child develops appropriate understanding of the new information. Thus some key points about the passage could help the reader understand the information more readily and provide a framework into which the reader can slot ideas and meaning from the passage. A schema can help the learner:

♦ attend to the incoming information

♦ provide a scaffolding for memory

♦ make inferences from the passage which also aid comprehension and recall

♦ utilize his or her previous knowledge.

There are a number of strategies which can help in the development of schemata. An example of this can be seen in an examination of a framework for a story. In such a framework two principal aspects can be discerned:

♦ the structure of the story

♦ the details related to the components of the structure.

The *structure* of a story can be seen in the following components:

♦ background

♦ context

♦ characters

♦ beginning

♦ main part

♦ events

♦ conclusion.

The *details* relating to these components can be recalled by asking appropriate questions. Taking the background as an example, one can see how appropriate questioning can help the learner build up a schema to facilitate understanding of the rest of the story:

♦ What was the weather like?

♦ Where did the story take place?

♦ Can you describe the scene?

♦ What were the main colours?

Background knowledge is an important aid to comprehension, although it is postulated that background knowledge in itself is insufficient to facilitate new learning; it must be skilfully interwoven with the new material being learnt. It is important that the learner is able to use the new information in different and unfamiliar situations. Hence, the connections between the reader's background knowledge and the new information must be highlighted in order for the learner to incorporate the new knowledge in a meaningful manner.

The ideas contained in a text therefore must be linked in some way to the reader's background knowledge, and the ideas need to be presented in a coherent and sequential manner. Such coherence and sequencing of ideas at the learning stage not only allows the material to be retained and recalled, but also facilitates effective comprehension. Being aware of the learner's prior knowledge of a lesson is therefore of fundamental importance. Before the learner embarks on new material, prior knowledge can be linked with the new ideas, in order to pave the way for effective study techniques and for strategies to enhance comprehension and recall (Green and Reid 2007).

Self-confidence and motivation

One of the most important ingredients in any intervention programme for children with dyslexia is self-esteem:

without a positive self-concept, children with dyslexia will soon opt out of learning. It is important therefore that all teaching should be directed at enhancing self-esteem. There are several ways of achieving this.

There are some programmes that have been specifically developed to boost self-esteem, and others that can indirectly boost self-esteem through the students' achievements. Of the first type, some of the best-known are the circle time programmes (Mosley 1996). There have been many variations on these programmes but essentially they involve a degree of positive feedback, and place a high focus on the individual person. They also promote group work, peer support and conflict resolution (Lannen 1990). These can be particularly suitable for children with dyslexia because they are whole-class activities, and so while they can be beneficial in boosting the self-esteem of children with dyslexia, they have the added benefit that the dyslexic child is not being given different activities.

Self-esteem can also be boosted through achievements in literacy or any other area of the curriculum. Some of the programmes based on behavioural principles with targets and goals to achieve can be extremely useful in this respect. One such programme is Phonic Codecracker (Russell 1992). This programme provides opportunities for students to monitor their own learning and their progress. Indeed, they may get some tangible reward (such as a certificate) for completing a particular objective. It is important that children with dyslexia can see that they are making some progress – however small that progress may seem. A programme operating in this manner is usually developed through a step-by-step approach, and is based on mastery learning. One of the benefits of this for children with dyslexia is that it can also promote over-learning and therefore help to achieve automaticity. It is important for children with dyslexia to attain a degree of automaticity because there is a tendency to forget, for example, spelling rules if these are not used. Automaticity can be achieved by using these rules, or indeed any skill, in different learning contexts. So, for example, if a new word is being learnt it should be introduced into different subject areas and in different ways. Using the new word in this way will help with automaticity as well as in the development of comprehension skills. Programmes based on mastery principles or behavioural objectives can therefore help to achieve this as they can be quite readily be adapted to develop automaticity.

Programmes which boost self-esteem have a beneficial effect on confidence and motivation. Such programmes:

♦ Enable the student to succeed. This is important, as the learner needs to have some initial success when beginning a new topic. Success builds on success, and early and significant success is an important factor when new material is being learnt.

♦ Encourage independent thinking. This is also important, as it encourages independent decision-making and helps the student to come to conclusions without too much direction from the teacher. These abilities can also develop confidence in a learner, and help to motivate the learner to tackle new material.

Some of the above study skills can be achieved through the use of thinking skills programmes such as the CORT programme devised by Edward De Bono (De Bono 1986). These can not only help to enhance thinking skills, but also help students to use these skills by helping them to structure their own studying. This can aid the development of appropriate study habits and maximize retention and transfer of information.

Transfer of Knowledge and Skills

A key aspect of effective study skills training is the transfer of skills to other curriculum areas. A number of studies support the view that to achieve this, great importance must be given to the context in which learning takes place. Study skills should be integrated into day-to-day teaching in a meaningful way, and not as a separate area of the curriculum.

Visual skills

Children and adults with dyslexia may have orientation problems, which may be evident in directional confusion. This aspect, even though it may not directly affect every aspect of the curriculum, can lead to a loss of confidence that may permeate work in other areas. To what extent can the teacher help to promote and enhance visual and orientation skills in children with specific difficulties?

According to the principles of skill transfer, it is important that such enhancement takes place within the curriculum and is contextualized within a meaningful task. Games or specific exercises in mapping and orientation can help to build up confidence in the learner, but there is some uncertainty as to whether such exercises, in isolation, would have a significant skill enhancement effect, and so it is important to use directional and visual cues as much as possible within the context of the curriculum. It may be advantageous to develop specific exercises from materials the learner is using.

Lazear (1999) suggests that visual/spatial skills can be developed through multiple intelligence training that is integrated into the everyday class work. This can be done through exercises involving active imagination; creating patterns with colour pencils and paper; forming mental images and describing these; developing graphic representations; and using perceptual puzzles in games involving spotting similarities and differences.

Lazear (1999) suggests that our education system, which has an emphasis on reasoning, can diminish the importance of imagination. Often the imagination is very fertile in young children but that quality can be lost in the shift to the importance of logic and reason as they progress through school. Lazear emphasizes the importance of awakening the visual/spatial intelligence and suggests that this can be developed in everyone. This is particularly important for children and adults with dyslexia, as they can have significant abilities in the visual area (West 1997) and need to have the opportunity to develop this strength.

Memory skills

Children with dyslexia may have difficulties in remembering, retaining and recalling information. This may be due to working memory and short-term memory problems, or naming difficulty, particularly at speed (i.e. difficulty in recalling the name or description of something without cues). It is important therefore to encourage the use of strategies that may facilitate remembering and recall. Such strategies can include repetition and over-learning, the use of mnemonics and Mind Mapping©.

Repetition and over-learning

Short-term memory difficulties can be overcome by repetition and rehearsal of materials. This form of over-learning can be achieved in a variety of ways, and not necessarily through conventional, and often tedious, rote learning.

In order to maximize the effect of repetition of learning, it is important that a multisensory mode of learning is utilized. Repetition of the material to be learnt can be accomplished through oral, visual, auditory and kinesthetic modes. The learner should be able to see, hear, say and touch the materials to be learnt. This reinforces the input stimuli and helps to consolidate the information for use, meaning and transfer to other areas. There are implications here for multi-mode teaching, including the use of movement, perhaps drama, to enhance the kinesthetic mode of learning.

Mnemonics

Mnemonics can be auditory, visual or both. Auditory mnemonics may take the form of rhyming or alliteration, while visual mnemonics can be used by relating the material to be remembered to a familiar scene, such as the classroom.

Mind Mapping©

Mind Mapping© was developed by Buzan to help children and adults develop their learning skills and utilize their abilities to the greatest extent possible. The procedure is now widely used and can extend one's memory capacity and develop lateral thinking (Buzan, 1993). It can be a simple or a sophisticated strategy, depending on how it is developed and used by the individual. It is used to help the learner to remember a considerable amount of information and encourages students to think of, and develop, the main ideas of a passage or material to be learned.

Essentially, mind maps are *individual* learning tools, and someone else's mind map may not be meaningful to you. It is important, therefore, that children create their own, in order to help both with understanding of key concepts and with the retention and recall of associated facts.

Mind Mapping can help children not only to remember information, but also to organize that information, and this exercise in itself can aid understanding. Elaborate versions of mind maps can be constructed using pictorial images, symbols and different colours.

Metacognitive strategies and study skills are important for children with dyslexia. It is therefore essential that the development of these skills in children with dyslexia is given a high priority in the curriculum.

Summary

A study skills programme should include the following:

- communication skills
- organization
- sequencing
- context
- schemata
- confidence and motivation
- the transfer of these skills to other areas of the curriculum
- mapping and visual skills
- strategies in remembering and retention.

These aspects can be developed with and by the learner. Although the teacher can help to facilitate these strategies and skills, it is still important that they are personalized by the learner. This means that different learners will adopt different ways of learning and remembering materials, but the responsibility to allow the learner to do this and to understand the principles associated with study skills rests with the teacher.

7

Specific Learning Difficulties

Overlap, Continuum and Intervention

A frequently asked question is, what is the difference between specific learning difficulties and dyslexia? What do we mean by the term 'specific learning difficulties'? Specific learning difficulties refers to a specific processing difficulty which is significantly discrepant in relation to that individual's other processing abilities. Some of these discrepancies can provide a profile with a label such as dyspraxia, dysgraphia and dyscalculia. Weedon and Reid (2002) identified 15 specific learning difficulties during the development work for a screening procedure for specific learning difficulties called SNAP (Special Needs Assessment Profile). It was indicated during the piloting of the instrument that at least seven of these had strong correlations (Weedon and Reid 2003, 2005).

The range of the specific learning difficulties in SNAP (Weedon and Reid 2003, 2005) was as follows:

♦ coordination difficulties

♦ hyperlexia (low comprehension but good decoding skills)

♦ language and communication difficulties

♦ dyslexia

♦ auditory processing difficulties

♦ hyperactivity

141

- attention difficulties
- dyscalculia
- working memory difficulties
- information-processing difficulties
- non-verbal difficulties
- literacy difficulties
- phonological processing difficulties
- visual difficulties
- social awareness difficulties.

Generally, however, the broad range of specific learning difficulties can be grouped into

- language-related difficulties
- attention difficulties
- motor difficulties
- social difficulties.

Like dyslexia, many of the other specific learning difficulties can be seen within a continuum. The term 'co-morbidity' is now used to describe the overlap between the different specific learning difficulties. It is not unusual for dyslexia, dyspraxia and to a certain extent attention deficit hyperactivity disorder (ADHD) to share some common factors. Perhaps the syndrome which has attracted the most interest in terms of co-morbidity is ADHD, yet this syndrome itself is subject to controversy and debate about whether it has a distinct aetiology. Some of the specific learning difficulties that can overlap with dyslexia are described in what follows.

Dyspraxia or Developmental Coordination Disorder

Dyspraxia and Development Coordination Disorder (DCD) are motor/coordination difficulties. These can be seen within a continuum from mild to severe and can affect fine motor activities such as pencil grip and scissors control, and gross motor activities such as movement and balance. Portwood (2001) describes dyspraxia as 'motor difficulties caused by perceptual problems, especially visual-motor and kinesthetic motor difficulties'. According to the classification in DSM-IV (American Psychiatric Association 2000), DCD is recognized by a marked impairment in the development of motor coordination, particularly if this impairment significantly interferes with academic achievement or activities of daily life.

These children may, however, have a range of other difficulties that can be associated with other types of specific learning difficulties. It may therefore be more useful for the teacher to be aware of the specific characteristics of an individual child's profile, rather than labelling them. This also highlights the view that children can have different profiles for the same difficulty. For example, some children with characteristics of DCD may also have significant difficulties in working memory, while other children may not.

Characteristics for a number of specific learning difficulties can include, to a greater or lesser extent, aspects relating to

♦ working memory

♦ auditory processing

♦ fine motor skills

♦ phonological skills

♦ non-verbal skills

♦ literacy skills.

143

These processing difficulties relate to skills that are necessary for a range of learning tasks and that affect attention, memory and reading. It is not surprising therefore that some overlap exists between them. One common element shared by all the special learning difficulties is the resulting low level of self-esteem often experienced by children. This can be addressed without recourse to a label, as a self-esteem programme can have a beneficial effect on all children. Jones (2005) suggests that even low-level intervention significantly increases self-esteem and has the secondary effect of improving classroom performance. This point is reinforced by Kirby (2003), particularly in relation to adolescents. Kirby suggests that adolescence is a difficult period for most children, but for an individual with DCD it can be twice as hard. Amanda Kirby, the Medical Director of the Dyscovery Centre in the UK and the mother of a DCD child herself, suggests that it is important that the child with DCD obtains support and practice in building relationships and coping with secondary or high school.

Irrespective of the approach adopted in the conceptual understanding of, the identification of and the intervention for DCD (and the other specific learning difficulties), it is important to see the bigger picture and view the child and the learning environment in a holistic and global manner.

Attention Deficit and Hyperactivity Disorder (ADHD)

There has been considerable debate regarding the concept of attention disorders, covering the medical, educational and social perspectives. It is however interesting to note that in the American Psychiatric Association's *Diagnostic and Statistical Manual of Mental Disorders* (2000), ADHD is noted as the most prevalent neuro-developmental disorder of childhood. The manual provides criteria for diagnosis which include factors relating to inattentiveness, hyperactivity and impulsivity such as 'often has difficulty in sustaining attention in tasks or play activities', 'often runs about or climbs excessively' and 'often interrupts or intrudes on others'. These factors need to have persisted for at least six months, and to a degree that is maladaptive and inconsistent with developmental level.

Although there has been a considerable amount of literature on ADHD, there is still controversy regarding its unitary model as a discrete syndrome. There is also some debate on the nature of the syndrome, and particularly on its primary causes and the intervention needed (Reid 2006). For example, Barkley (1997) suggests that it is a unitary condition and that the primary impairment relates to behaviour inhibition, with this having a cascading effect on other cognitive functions. This view is countered by Rutter (1995), who suggests that a cognitive deficit specific to ADHD has still to be determined, and even if the majority have cognitive impairments, the trait is not common to all children with ADHD. It is perhaps useful at this point to attempt to place the symptoms and characteristics of ADHD into some form of framework to help understand the different strands and various characteristics that can contribute to ADHD.

Framework for attention difficulties

The framework used to describe dyslexia in Chapter 1, the causal modelling framework (Morton and Frith 1995), can also be applied to ADHD. Levine (1997), although he does not relate ADHD to a framework such as the causal modelling framework, makes many of the comments shown below.

Neurological level
At the neurological level, the following factors may be relevant to attention difficulties:

♦ hemispheric preferences – usually a child with ADHD is a right hemisphere processor

♦ saliency determination – that is, recognizing what is relevant: often a child with ADHD would having difficulty in recognizing the relevant features of conversation or written work

♦ auditory distractibility – this would imply that the child is easily distracted by noise of some sort

♦ tactile distractibility – similarly, touch could be distracting, and often the child with ADHD may want to touch in order to be distracted

♦ motor inhibition – often, children with ADHD have difficulty in inhibiting a response and may react impulsively in some situations.

Cognitive level
In relation to the cognitive dimensions, the following factors may be significant:

♦ Depth of processing – if the child is not attending to a stimulus then it is likely that the processing will be at a shallow as opposed to a deep level. Clearly, if this is the case then the child will not gain much from the learning experience, either in understanding or in pleasure – therefore the learning experience will not be automatically reinforced.

♦ Information processing – just as in the case of dyslexia, the information processing cycle of input, cognition and output can be influential in identifying the type of difficulties that may be experienced by children with attention difficulties. This therefore has implications for teaching.

♦ Metacognitive factors – these are important for reinforcing learning, transferring learning and developing concepts. It is likely the child with attention difficulties will have poor metacognitive skills, and this will make learning less meaningful and have a negative effect on attention span.

Classroom level
In relation to educational or classroom factors, the following can be considered:

♦ Factors associated with free flight – this means that the child will have little control over the thinking process (essentially what may be described as a right hemisphere processing style). This means that the individual requires some structure to help to direct their thinking processes.

♦ Unpredictability, inconsistency and impulsivity – these again indicate that there is little control over learning and that many actions are impulsive.

♦ Pacing skills and on-task factors – lack of pacing skills again indicates a lack of control over learning, and indicates that students with attention difficulties have a problem with pacing the progress of work and therefore may tire easily or finish prematurely.

Identifying and defining attention difficulties

Examining the factors described above would lead one to believe that attention difficulties and ADHD can be confused easily, and the syndrome would be difficult to identify as a discrete syndrome.

It is not surprising therefore that a number of definitions of ADHD are currently used, and a considerable amount of literature on the subject has expounded different views and a variety of interventions. Essentially, however, identification seems to be through the use of diagnostic checklists or observations such as the Brown Rating Scale (Brown 1996) and the Conners scale (Conners 1996). These are widely used but they do demand an element of clinical judgement on the part of the assessor. The important aspect about these is not so much whether they give a diagnosis or not, but rather that they provide a list of definable and observable characteristics that can inform a teaching programme, irrespective of the diagnosis.

It is therefore feasible to identify attention difficulties within an education setting, although in practice much of this type of diagnosis appears to be undertaken by medical professionals – even though the actual 'presenting' difficulties are usually more obvious in school. If a child is said to have attention difficulties then these should be obvious in every subject and in all activities. In practice this is rarely the case, and this must cast some doubt on the validity of the diagnosis.

Intervention

Intervention can be medical, in the form of drugs such as Ritalin; educational, in relation to classroom adaptations, task analysis and investigation of the students' learning preferences; or even dietary, in relation to examining children's reactions to certain foods. There is also a view (Lloyd and Norris 1999) that ADHD is a social construction. There is certainly a strong commercial basis to ADHD and this may have fuelled the impetus for acceptance of it as a discrete specific difficulty.

Indeed, there is a view that 'special educational needs', whatever the particular need might be, can be approached from a situation-centred perspective (Frederickson and Cline 2002). Frederickson and Cline (p. 40) quote Deno (1989), who argues that proponents of this view believe that special educational needs 'can only be defined in terms of the relationship between what a person can do and what a person must do to succeed in a given environment'. This view indicates that learning difficulties are in fact environmental and a construction of the education system. This would imply that teaching and curriculum approaches hold the key to minimizing the effect on the child of what may be termed a 'special educational need'. Along the same continuum of the environmentally focused approach, one can also view the interactional approach to SEN. Frederickson and Cline suggest that this is the 'complex interaction between the child's strengths and weaknesses, the level of support available and the appropriateness of the education being provided' (p. 420).

Co-morbidity and ADHD

It is not surprising that there is a strong view that an overlap exists between ADHD and dyslexia. Many of the cognitive attention-processing mechanisms that children with ADHD seem to have difficulty with, such as short-term memory, sustained attention, processing speed and accuracy in copying, can also be noted in children with dyslexia. Willcutt and Pennington (2000) noted in a large-scale study that individuals with reading disabilities were more likely than individuals without reading disabilities to meet the criteria for ADHD, and that the association was stronger for inattention than for hyperactivity.

However, this notion of co-morbidity has been criticized, and the value of the term questioned, by Kaplan *et al.* (2001). They suggest that the term 'co-morbidity' assumes that the aetiologies of the different specific difficulties are independent. Yet in practice, according to Kaplan *et al.*, it is very rare to see discrete conditions existing in isolation. In a research study involving 179 children, in order to investigate the notion of co-morbidity the researchers used criteria to assess for seven disorders – reading disability, ADHD, DCD, oppositional defiant disorder, conduct disorder, depression and anxiety. It was found that at least 50 per cent of the sample tested met the criteria for at least two diagnoses, and the children with ADHD were at the highest risk of having a second disorder. The question presented by Kaplan *et al.* is whether children are actually displaying several co-morbid disorders, or are displaying manifestations of one underlying disorder. This of course raises questions regarding the assessment procedures, and was the rationale behind the special needs assessment procedures (SNAP, see below) (Weedon and Reid 2003). The thinking is that it is likely that children will show indicators of other conditions, and the accumulation of descriptive information on the presenting difficulties can be useful for the class teacher. It is important however that information is not based solely on clinical assessment or clinical judgement, but also gathered from the evidence of professionals and parents about how the child performs in different situations.

It is important to obtain descriptive data from observations, interviews and assessments conducted on the child. The usefulness of these data does not lie in the provision of a label, but lies in the description of the presenting characteristics (which may or may not lead to a label): these should be informative and beneficial in terms of intervention.

Identifying Specific Learning Difficulties

The overlap between the different specific learning difficulties can cause some confusion. For that reason Weedon and Reid (2003, 2005) developed the instrument known as SNAP (special needs assessment profile). This instrument profiles 17 specific learning difficulties. From this, clusters and patterns of weaknesses and strengths help to identify the core features of a child's difficulties: visual, dyslexic, dyspraxic, phonological, attentional or any other of the 17 key deficits (see earlier in this chapter). This can suggest a diagnosis that points the way forward for a teaching programme for that individual child.

SNAP involves four steps:

- Step 1 (*Pupil Assessment Pack*): structured question-naire checklists for completion by teachers and parents give an initial 'outline map' of the child's difficulties.

- Step 2 (*CD-ROM*): the learning support staff chart the child's difficulties, using the CD-ROM to identify patterns and target any further diagnostic follow-up assessments to be carried out at Step 3.

- Step 3 (*User's Kit*): focused assessments from a photo-copiable resource bank of quick diagnostic 'probes' yield a detailed and textured understanding of the child's difficulties.

- Step 4 (*CD-ROM*): the computer-generated profile yields specific guidance on support (including person-alized information sheets for parents) and practical follow-up.

The kit helps to facilitate the collaboration between different groups of professionals, and between professionals and parents, which is extremely important in order to obtain a full picture of the student's abilities and difficulties. There is a dedicated website that can be accessed by anyone and contains a number of ideas on teaching to cover difficulties associated with 17 different specific learning difficulties: www.SNAPassessment.com.

Specific Learning Difficulties and Alternative Therapies

One area that may have far-reaching consequences and potential is that of the interventions which can be classed as 'alternative therapies'. These tend to be popular, new and often have media appeal. That is not to say they are not helpful – some of the evidence in fact seems to support the use of some of these alternative forms of interventions.

Dietary interventions

There has been considerable popular coverage of the use of food additives, and much anecdotal evidence to support the view that these may have an adverse affect on learning, particularly for children with ADHD. Richardson (2001) suggests that there is a wide spectrum of conditions in which deficiencies of highly unsaturated fatty acids appear to have some influence. Further, she argues that fatty acids can have an extremely important influence on dyslexia, dyspraxia and ADHD. Richardson argues that it is not too controversial to suggest that there is a high incidence of overlap between these three syndromes – in fact, she suggests that overlap between dyslexia and ADHD can be around 30 to 50 per cent, and even higher in the case of dyspraxia. She argues that the essential fatty acids (EFAs), which cannot be synthesized by the body, must be provided in the diet – these are linoleic acid (omega 6 series) and alpha-linoleic acid (omega 3 series). She suggests that the longer-chain highly unsaturated fatty acids (HUFA) that the brain needs can normally be synthesized from the EPAs: but this conversion process can be severely affected and limited by dietary and lifestyle factors. Some of the dietary factors which can block the conversion of EFA to HUFA include excess saturated fats, hydrogenated fats found in processed foods, and deficiencies in vitamins and minerals, as well as excessive consumption of coffee and alcohol, and smoking.

Richardson says that the claims connecting hyperactivity and lack of EFA are not new. Studies on dyspraxia have also highlighted the possibility of the links with EFA and suggested that fatty acid supplements can be beneficial (Stordy 1995, 1997). In relation to dyslexia and ADHD, Richardson suggests that fatty acid supplements have been shown to be successful and supplementation has been associated with improvements in reading. Richardson also reports on school-based trials indicating that this intervention can be realistically applied in schools (Richardson 2001; Portwood 2002).

Exercise and movement

There has been a longstanding interest in exercise and therapies based on movement for children with specific learning difficulties. Fitts and Posner (1967) provided an account of the learning stages in motor skill development and particularly the development of automaticity. Denckla and Rudel (1976) found that children with dyslexia had a deficit in rapid automatized naming, and suggested that they are characterized by a 'non-specific developmental awkwardness' which is irrespective of athletic ability. In terms of intervention, the work of Ayres (1979) has been developed considerably by Blythe (1992, 2001), Blythe and Goddard (2000) and McPhillips, Hepper and Mulhern (2000). See the website for the Institute for Neuro-Physiological Psychology (INPP), www.inpp.com. The work of Dennison and Dennison (1989, 2001) in relation to Brain Gym©, and that of Hannaford (1995, 1997) on the importance of dominance and laterality and, particularly, the influence of dominance patterns on learning, have also been influential in classrooms and in particular with children with specific learning difficulties.

The inhibition of primitive reflexes

Blythe (1992) found that 85 per cent of children with specific learning difficulties that do not respond to various classroom intervention strategies have a cluster of aberrant reflexes. He argues that as long as these reflexes remain undetected and uncorrected, the educational problems will persist. These reflexes should only be present in a very young baby, and then become redundant after about six months of life. But if they continue to be present, Blythe argued, the development of the mature postural reflexes is restricted, and this will adversely affect writing, reading, spelling, copying, mathematics, attention and concentration.

Blythe (1992) and Goddard-Blythe (1996) have developed the Developmental Exercise Programme, an assessment and intervention programme for assessing the presence of these reflexes, and a series of exercises designed to control the primitive reflexes and release the postural reflexes. A study in Western Australia (Taylor 2002) examined the effects of retention of primitive reflexes in children diagnosed as having ADHD. The results supported the evidence of the importance of this area for cognitive development and learning, and also suggested 'cumulative associations between high stresses, atypical brain lateralization and uninhibited reflexes on scholastic competency' (pp. 216–17).

Educational kinesiology

Educational kinesiology is a combination of applied kinesiology and traditional learning theory, although some aspects of yoga and acupressure are also evident in the recommended programme.

Kinesiology is the study of muscles and their functions, and particular attention is paid to the patterns of reflex activity that link effective integration between sensory and motor responses. Children can develop inappropriate patterns of responses to particular situations, and these can lock the child into inappropriate habits.

Dennison and Hargrove (1985) have produced a series of exercises (Brain Gym©) from which an individual programme can be devised for the child relating to the assessment. Many of these exercises include activities that involve crossing the mid-line, such as writing a figure eight in the air, or cross-crawling and skip-a-cross, in which hands and legs sway from side to side. The aim is to achieve some form of body balance so that information can flow freely and be processed readily. Brain Gym© has been widely and successfully implemented in the school settings.

Dennison and Dennison (1989, revised 2000) developed a system called Brain Organization Profile (BOP) to visually represent their theory. Taylor (2002) examined the basis and application of this profile with children with ADHD, and was able to develop a useful brain organization profile for each child in the research sample, which found that children with ADHD did show more evidence of mixed laterality processing than the control group.

Dyslexia, Dyspraxia, Attention Disorder Treatment (DDAT)

DDAT (now called the Dore Programme) is the name given to the exercise-based treatment (Dore and Rutherford 2001) based on the cerebellar deficit theory (Fawcett and Nicolson 1994; Nicolson and Fawcett 1999; Nicolson, Fawcett and Dean 2001), which implies that the cerebellum has an important function in relation to dyslexia and other learning difficulties. Their hypothesis is supported by earlier work on automaticity (Nicolson and Fawcett 1990) and more recent work on the role of the cerebellum in language (Fawcett and Nicolson 2004). The treatment programme also implicates other aspects of neurological/biological development, such as the functioning of the magnocellular system, the inhibition of primitive reflexes and fatty acid deficiencies. Dore and Rutherford suggest that the cerebellum maintains its plasticity throughout childhood and therefore it is theoretically possible to retrain the cerebellum to function more efficiently. The resultant Balance Remediation Exercise Training Programme assesses the vestibular and cerebellar functioning and implements a series of exercises directly related to the individual profile of each child, following a series of sophisticated tests.

Other alternative treatments

There are many other alternative treatments that have not been discussed here, but that are popular with parents, such as the Davis Dyslexia Correction methods, which involve orientation and symbol mastery (Davis and Braun 1997), and Sound Therapy (Johanson 1997), which is based on frequency-specific left hemisphere auditory stimulation with music and sounds (Auditory Discrimination Training), and many others, often too many for the parent or teacher to handle or understand. This further underlines the need for collaboration between parents and professionals – the approach that always works is called 'effective communication'.

8

Role of Parents

Parents have an important role to play in supporting their child with dyslexia. Parents have had an impact on policy and practice in the UK, Europe, New Zealand, Australia, Canada and the USA. But by far the most accessible and potentially rewarding means of influencing practice is through direct communication with the school. This, without doubt, is the parents' first port of call, as communication at this level has the potential to quell anxieties and maximize use of both the potential support of parents and the skills of teachers. Yet in practice this may be difficult. Some parents, rightly or wrongly, are still reluctant to approach the school and may therefore find it difficult to openly consult about any difficulties their child may be experiencing.

It is essential that schools develop proactive working policies to promote home–school partnerships, particularly in relation to parents of children with dyslexia. This will help not only to utilize the skills of parents, but also to avoid the potential legal wrangles and tribunals that have been evident in the last ten years.

Constructive home–school links are vital to ensure the success of any intervention for children with dyslexia.

Parental Concerns

The concerns experienced by parents are usually due to the lack of a diagnosis or a feeling that their child's educational needs are not being recognized or met. Understandably there is strong belief among parents that a label is necessary in order to get their child appropriate help. This may be the case in some instances, particularly if the child is significantly lagging in attainments, and additional resources, examination support or a review of provision is needed. In many cases however a label is not the most essential factor. The most essential factor is for the school to be aware of the child's progress in all aspects of the curriculum, to communicate this to parents and to discuss together how the school (and parents) plan to deal with any lack of progress.

A comment often made by parents is that 'the school does not accept dyslexia'. While this may unfortunately be the case, it is not the end of the world. All schools accept responsibility for the child's progress and will investigate this by whatever means, and seek to find an explanation for any lack of progress. All this will be done without any recourse to a label. A label of course is helpful and in some situations, such as examination support, essential. Parents often feel considerable relief when the label 'dyslexia' is provided. Often parents remark, 'I was so relieved to know that it had a name', or 'People had begun to hint he might be mentally retarded because he was illiterate', or 'The diagnosis helped me to understand exactly why he had difficulties.'

It is important to consider that a label can often be accompanied by acceptance, and this can pave the way for constructive collaboration between home and school.

Anxieties often arise from the potential conflict between the views of individuals and interest groups who may have different agendas. This potential conflict can be noted between parents and teachers, and indeed may force them into opposition. It is important that this is avoided, as anxieties and stresses can usually be felt by the child. It is vital therefore to ensure that the aims of the school in relation to any particular child are made clear to the parents, and that both parents and teachers share a common agenda in relation to the child's progress and level of work.

Cooperation and collaboration between school and parents should be at the heart of any policy on dyslexia. Good communication with parents, and an understanding of dyslexia, will enable teachers to discuss openly with the parents any anxieties they may have relating the child's progress.

Effective communication between schools and parents can have a positive impact on the child's development. It is important to establish this collaboration at an early stage so that effective partnership with parents can result.

An interesting and innovative example of parent–teacher partnership can be seen in the development of a baseline assessment procedure in Australia: the 'parent screening inventory for learning, and behaviour, difficulties' (PSILD) (Reddington and Wheeldon 2002). The instrument was developed to cover the potential areas that might predict learning and behaviour problems. Following a number of years of clinical research and revision, the usability with parents in school, the construct and content validity and the predictive validity of the PSILD were established. In addition to providing a parent–teacher collaborative baseline assessment tool, the PSILD was also seen to have a role in early identification by providing school-entry data, as well as helping teachers implement individual strategies and structure parent–teacher interviews. Reddington and Wheeldon point out that this combination of parent screening and teacher evaluation has actually expanded the utility of baseline assessments, as well as providing illuminative insights into the needs of individual children, and appears to fulfil a function similar to that of the early screening procedures developed and reported by Crombie (2002). The key point about both the Crombie and the Australian initiative is that both value the input of the parents, and see it as an integral component of the development of the procedures.

Parental Support

It has been outlined that:

♦ effective communication can provide a strong platform for parental support

♦ diagnosis and a label can be welcome and can provide reassurance and relief to parents

♦ a label can in fact make a difference to the child.

One of the questions most frequently asked by parents is how much homework the child with dyslexia should undertake. This anxiety can stem from the fact that it may take the child much longer than others in the class to complete the same exercise. It is important to maintain the motivation of children with dyslexia, and excessive nightly homework may not be the most effective way to achieve this. Parents however should not spend too much time focusing on their child's difficulties, as this can become counter-productive.

There are a number of activities which parents can use to help their child. Without exception however, whatever the parent is doing should be communicated to the school and vice versa. Some programmes can be used in conjunction with parents, particularly some reading programmes. Paired Reading is one example of this: this involves the parent and the child reading aloud at the same time (see Chapter 3).

It is important however in this procedure for the parents to sit back slightly when the child is beginning to master the text. Parents usually know when to do this (Figure 8).

Reid (2004) points out there are many teaching programmes, many of which will be useful for children with dyslexia. It may be misguided for parents or for teachers to pin their hopes on any one programme.

> Programmes and teaching approaches should be considered in the light of the individual child's learning profile.

The school should have a good knowledge of both the child and specific teaching approaches. Again, because there is such a wealth of materials on the market, it is important to monitor and evaluate the approach and the progress

Figure 8 Paired reading: the child masters the text.

periodically. It is also important that parents share in this monitoring.

It is also vital to recognize that support should not be measured in terms of 'hours' or 'days'. It is difficult to quantify the optimum length of support for any individual young person with dyslexia. Consistency is important, and frequent periodic reviews should provide guidance on the effectiveness of the approaches being used, and if particular approaches should be continued. It is also important to recognize that such monitoring need not be in terms of reading and spelling ages. These are important of course, but it is also necessary to obtain information and assess performances on particular aspects of curriculum work, such as comprehension, problem-solving and other curriculum activities that embrace much more than reading and spelling accuracy.

> Support should not be measured in terms of 'hours' or 'days'. Consistent intervention is very important and this should incorporate periodic reviews on the child's progress.

Parental Responses

Reid (2003) interviewed a number of parents on the issues they had to deal with on discovering their child was dyslexic. The main challenges in parenting a child with dyslexia included:

♦ helping to maintain the child's self-esteem

♦ helping the child start new work when he or she had not consolidated previous work

♦ protecting the dignity of the child when dealing with professionals/therapists

- personal organization of the child
- peer insensitivity
- misconceptions of dyslexia
- homework.

These responses are quite interesting because they touch on some of the key areas, particularly the emotional aspect of dyslexia. They also include the misunderstandings and misconceptions that many can have of dyslexia.

Emotional aspects

It can be too easy to ignore the emotional aspects of dyslexia. Often the child's main difficulty will relate more directly to learning and to literacy, and this can be the main area of concern. If a child however is failing in literacy and finds school work challenging, then it is likely that he or she will suffer emotionally. It is important that this feeling is addressed and, preferably, prevented.

Children can be very sensitive, particularly if they feel they are, in any way, different from others. Children with dyslexia usually have to visit psychologists and other specialists. For some children this can indicate that they are different, and they may feel stigmatized as a consequence. Even young adults at college and university can experience these feelings. Assessments and support for students with dyslexia are very often carried out at the 'disability office' within the college or university, and many do not want, or in fact need, the 'disability label' and so may be reluctant to enter an office which is called this.

This highlights the importance of full, frank and informative feedback following an assessment with the child or young adult, as well as with the parents. In fact this initial feedback is as important as the eventual follow-up and intervention.

Dyslexia

There are a number of ways of helping to maintain and to boost children's self-esteem, but one of the most obvious and effective ways is to ensure that they achieve some success and are given genuine praise. In order for praise to be effective the child has to be convinced that the praise is worthy of his or her achievements. When children feel a failure it is difficult to reverse these feelings, and often they need to change their perceptions of themselves. This can be a lengthy process, and ongoing support, praise and sensitive handling are necessary.

It is important that the term 'dyslexia' is explained to the child following an assessment and that he or she has a good understanding of what it means. This can become a positive tool for the young person if it is explained in terms of differences rather than in terms of deficits. It is often good for the person to receive an explanation of why he or she is finding some tasks challenging.

What Parents Find Useful

The research conducted by Reid (2004) showed that parents found the following useful:

♦ training in positive thinking

♦ Paired Reading

♦ Mind Mapping, including software mapping

♦ memory games

♦ using learning styles

♦ opportunities for the child to use verbal ability and discussion

♦ focusing on areas of success.

One parent suggested that

Self-esteem is a huge issue and one that is not helped by dyslexia being seen as a deficit! The continued emphasis on academic achievement and the issues of labelling are problematic for me. A major difficulty with the teaching profession is attitudinal – a lack of knowledge of dyslexia is apparent (although I have found there are also some exceptional teachers), but it is always difficult for a parent to know what advice to take. By the time they are in a position to decide it can be too late, or less effective than it could have been.

The balance between home and school is a key issue and although I have had little advice on this I have still had to argue a case for the need for school to understand the fatigue element in a long day. I feel like my child is a square peg in a round hole.

Some of the key issues to emerge from Reid's study include the following:

Frustration

Parents can experience considerable frustration with the education system. This may not necessarily be because of a problem with the system, but rather a problem stemming from a breakdown in communication, and from different priorities and agendas.

Without question, all schools and all teachers want to do their best for all children. Schools however have to meet the needs of individuals as well as the common needs of all learners. Teachers have also to meet the demands placed on them by the management and the education system. These demands are usually set by politicians and are often based on principles relating to accountability and results. These principles can present a difficulty in relation to dyslexia, because progress made by children with dyslexia may not always be easily measured, and certainly not by conventional means. For example, for some children with dyslexia merely attending school can be a measure of success, but schools may not record this as progress and would rather focus on progress on attainments such as reading, spelling and writing. This is perfectly reasonable but children with dyslexia may not make significant progress in this area, at least in the short term. This can lead to some frustration on the part of parents and highlight very clearly the different agendas between home and school. This underlines the importance of effective and shared communication.

Trust

Different perspectives can lead to a degree of mistrust. This is obviously a negative emotion and one that can seriously damage the relationship between home and school. It can sometimes be difficult for parents to place their trust in a system that may not even seem to recognize dyslexia, but this is exactly what they have to do! Some parents who responded to the questionnaire in fact suggested that they, the parents, are a source of information on dyslexia for the school. It is a question of balance: of placing some trust in the education system, but also ensuring that parents are aware of exactly what is going on in school regarding their child's education. There may be differences of opinions between home and school but these should not break down any trust between the two. Parents are permitted to question and to seek explanations from school on how their child is being educated, but it is best to use this right in a constructive manner.

Balance

Parents often ask how they balance the stress their child can experience in school work with life at home. This can be a difficult point, as often the stress that can be experienced at school can spill over into home life, especially since potential stresses, such as homework, can take up an unduly large amount of time at home. One parent indicated very strongly in the questionnaire that work at home should be fun. This may be difficult to achieve without making light of the work that the child has to do, but what this parent meant was that the family should try to provide a fun environment and one that will be free from stress. She suggested the family should try to provide activities or games that can provide learning strategies for the child. This could be the use of mnemonics or even board games, both of which can be useful for developing memory skills. One parent suggested that games were extremely important in ensuring that her son did not take the stress at school into the home. She suggested the following:

'Kitchen cupboards' is a favourite: you have to identify all the products in the kitchen, play around with the products using part of the name, adding it on to part of another product's name. For example, we may take flour, marmalade, milk, washing powder and work our way through the different combinations of sounds from each of the products. From this we make up silly products like 'marwashder'. My son remembers the sounds and combinations much more easily when I relate it to some fun activity.

Understanding

Another of the issues relates to understanding. Many parents indicated that schools, or some teachers in schools, did not have much knowledge of dyslexia. This clearly varies from country to country, and indeed even within countries from area to area. Additionally, the level of knowledge of dyslexia within a school will be different. Parents need to realize this and may have to take it upon themselves to inform the school of some of the current interventions and thinking in dyslexia. At the same time however there does appear to be a considerable thrust in schools, and within education authorities, to increase teacher training and whole school awareness of dyslexia (Reid 2001, 2003; Reid, Green and Zylstra 2005). Having spoken on dyslexia to parents' associations in many different countries, I can confirm that this trend is becoming very apparent, and almost without exception a scheduled and advertised talk to a parents' association will include many teachers in the audience. It is important that parents understand what dyslexia is, and this should be explained to them as soon as their child is assessed, and so it is equally important that teachers also know the different aspects relating to dyslexia.

Emotions

As indicated above, the emotional impact having dyslexia has on their child is an important consideration for parents and can be a real concern to children and to adults with dyslexia. Indeed, due to the anxieties they experience and the frustrations they can encounter, many parents can themselves become emotionally affected. As a parent myself of a young man with autism, I know only too well the long-lasting emotional impact of supporting him and living through crisis and trauma. Parents do become affected if they do not seek out the best form of support (usually other parents), and if they continually see their child's education in terms of a 'struggle'. One parent in fact remarked at the end of the questionnaire: 'I am very cynical.' This is unfortunate, and this type of emotion can be destructive, but it can also be appreciated why in some situations parents feel like this. Low self-esteem is often accompanied by negative emotions.

Careers

Many people with dyslexia have succeeded to a high level and have become confident and well-adjusted adults in highly successful careers. This is the hope of course of every parent of a child with dyslexia, and, to be fair, the quest of every teacher. There are however many influences along the way that can prevent this from happening. Yet there is more support available for dyslexia than ever before, and there is no reason why parents should not be optimistic regarding the career opportunities available to young people with dyslexia. It is important to seek advice from a careers professional at an early stage.

While there are some anxieties experienced by parents over the child's educational provision, there is considerable scope for optimism. Teachers and policy-makers in most countries have now accepted the need to make special and specialized provision for dyslexia, and in general there has been some evidence of teacher training and staff development to ensure that both the acceptance and the recognition of dyslexia are a reality at all stages of education.

9

Suggestions for Follow-Up

Staff Development

One of the most effective means of ensuring that dyslexia is understood by professionals is through staff development. This is an important area and one that is increasing in importance. For example, the International Dyslexia Association (IDA) regularly has over 3,000 attendees at its annual conference. This conference is recognized by many schools for staff development credits. Similarly, in the UK the British Dyslexia Association (BDA) has now accredited over 30 certificated courses with university validation on dyslexia. Additionally, many schools and associations in different countries are requesting training in dyslexia. I myself have conducted such training in over 35 countries, including The Gambia, Norway, the Netherlands, Hungary, Austria, Australia, New Zealand, the USA, the UK, Slovenia, Poland, Slovakia, the Czech Republic, South Africa, Kuwait, Dubai, Italy, Germany, Canada, Singapore and Hong Kong in recent years. This illustrates the awareness and the need for training in this area.

The international awareness of dyslexia is further highlighted by the range of contributors to the *International Book on Dyslexia* (Smythe, Everatt and Salter 2004). Fifty-three countries are represented in this volume, including countries in Europe, Asia, North America, South America and Australasia.

It is important therefore that teachers and other professionals have an awareness of dyslexia and that there is someone on the staff who can develop and implement training programmes on dyslexia.

Guidance on training

An example of aims, objectives and content for a course on dyslexia is shown below.

Aims

◆ To raise the standard of all school students' achievements through improved individual literacy development.

◆ To raise teachers' awareness of the barriers to learning faced by some students as a result of their difficulties in literacy and dyslexia.

◆ To support teachers in exploring and reflecting on appropriate curriculum responses to the needs of students who are dyslexic.

◆ To embrace the concept of an inclusive school, through literacy attainment and parental and pupil participation.

◆ To embrace the notion of dyslexia-friendly practices and provision.

Objectives

◆ To develop an understanding of terminology and controversies evident in the field of specific learning difficulties/dyslexia.

◆ To discuss the different perspectives held by professionals and parents/carers in the field of specific learning difficulties.

◆ To develop competence in using a range of strategies used to assess students' strengths and difficulties.

◆ To develop an awareness of the assessment process in educational settings.

171

Dyslexia

◆ To develop awareness of a range of teaching approaches to overcome the difficulties associated with dyslexia.

◆ To encourage critical reflection on policy, practice and provision in the area of specific learning difficulties and dyslexia.

◆ To develop understanding of the importance of emotional factors for students with dyslexia.

◆ To recognize individual and whole school approaches to the needs of students with dyslexia.

Content
The assessment process
This part of the course will examine a range of assessment strategies for students with dyslexia. The emphasis will be on the course member's need to contextualize these for his or her own educational setting and stage. There will also be an emphasis on critical reflection and evaluation of assessment. The focus will be on identifying the barriers to learning, and the assessment of barriers to learning at the following three levels will be referred to:

1. the curriculum

2. the learner

3. the learning environment.

Unit 1 – Overview of assessment

◆ Criteria

◆ Aims and rationale

◆ Purpose of assessment – what, why, how, effect

◆ Considerations – parents', students' perspectives

◆ Inclusion

◆ Multilingualism

◆ Linking assessment with intervention

◆ Coexistence with other difficulties

Unit 2 – Range of tests and strategies

◆ Standardized

◆ Diagnostic

◆ Diagnostic spelling

◆ Numeracy

◆ Screening

◆ Phonological

◆ Components approach

◆ Observational

◆ Metacognitive

Unit 3 – Standardized/psychometric (understanding psychologists' tests)

◆ Wechsler tests, Wechsler dimensions

◆ ACID profile

◆ BAS

◆ Interpretation of reports

Unit 4 – Diagnostic/standardized (teacher tests)

◆ Reading and spelling tests

◆ Miscue analysis/diagnostic assessment of reading and spelling

◆ Other tests as appropriate to the country/context

Dyslexia

Unit 5 – Phonological assessment

♦ Aims and rationale

♦ Examples of tests that show the principles and practice of phonological assessment

Unit 6 – Screening

♦ Issues around screening

♦ Proactive screening

♦ Dyslexia screening tests

♦ Interview/observation techniques

♦ Visual/motor screening

♦ Checklists

Unit 7 –Tests of attainments – principles and practice

♦ Some examples of tests

♦ Identifying key principles

♦ Using these in practice

Unit 8 – Curriculum assessment

♦ Task differentiation

♦ Different subject area of the curriculum

♦ Barriers to literacy – the classroom and the curriculum

Unit 9 – Examinations

♦ Dyslexia-friendly assessments

♦ Alternative assessments

Unit 10 – Metacognitive assessment

♦ Assisted assessment/dynamic tests

♦ Self-report

♦ Role of multiple intelligences

Unit 11 – Components approach

♦ Decoding

♦ Listening comprehension

Unit 12 – Observational assessment

♦ Criteria/framework

♦ Learning context

♦ Learning styles

Unit 13 – Early identification

♦ Pre-school

♦ Multi-professional collaboration

♦ Role of parents

♦ Examples of practice

Unit 14 – Models of Identification

♦ Expert/intervention model/attainment discrepancy model

♦ Stage/process model

♦ Models and policy

♦ Curriculum-focused models

♦ Monitoring and review

Unit 15 – A framework for assessment

♦ The development of a contextualized framework for assessment, to be carried out by course members in their own setting

Dyslexia

Unit 16 – Issues in assessment

♦ Linking assessment to intervention

♦ Roles of professionals

♦ Provision

♦ Coexistence with other specific learning difficulties

♦ Post-school issues

♦ Whole school approaches/parents' partnerships

♦ Issues raised by course members

Example of slide presentation introduction to a course or presentation on dyslexia

Framework for a presentation on dyslexia, 'Dyslexia in the Classroom: Five signposts for success'

Five signposts:

♦ acknowledge differences

♦ understanding dyslexia

♦ understanding learning

♦ planning for practice

♦ attainable outcomes.

Signpost 1: Acknowledge the differences
Highlight the learning styles of children with dyslexia.

Signpost 2: Understanding dyslexia
The degree of dyslexia and the degree of its impact on the child can vary according to the:

♦ nature of the task

♦ and the nature of the learning context.

- Children with dyslexia can show different characteristics and therefore their needs should be addressed on an individual basis.

- Principal difficulties relate to literacy – but children with dyslexia can also show other difficulties relating to

  - memory

  - coordination

  - organization

  - processing speed.

- There is a need for recognition that the learning process is important in intervention.

- There is a need to understand the task

- There is a need to consider the role of the curriculum.

- There is a need to consider differentiation and learning styles.

- It is important to recognize the need to boost the self-esteem of children.

- It is important to identify and recognize the strengths shown by children and adults with dyslexia.

Dyslexia definition:
Dyslexia is a processing difference experienced by people of all ages, often characterized by difficulties in literacy. It can affect other cognitive areas such as memory, speed of processing, time management, coordination and directional aspects. There may be visual and phonological difficulties and there is usually some discrepancy in performances in different areas of learning. It is important that the individual differences and learning styles are acknowledged since these will affect outcomes of learning and assessment. It is also important to consider the learning and work context as the

nature of the difficulties associated with dyslexia may well be more pronounced in some learning situations. (Reid 2003)

Key points in a definition:

♦ processing difference

♦ can affect cognitive areas

♦ may be visual and phonological difficulties

♦ discrepancy in performances in different areas of learning

♦ important that individual differences and learning styles are considered

♦ important to recognize the importance of the learning and work context.

(Reid 2003)

Assessment criteria difficulties:

♦ decoding

♦ speed of processing

♦ short-long-term memory

♦ reading fluency

♦ automaticity

♦ metacognition

♦ syntax

♦ organization.

Discrepancies:

♦ decoding and listening comprehension

♦ different subject areas of the curriculum

Differences:

- ♦ learning style
- ♦ environmental preferences for learning.

Differences:

- ♦ methods of processing information
- ♦ speed of processing information
- ♦ strategies
- ♦ learning styles.

Observational framework:

- ♦ interaction
    - ♦ pupil–teacher
    - ♦ peers.
- ♦ attention/concentration
    - ♦ focus on tasks
    - ♦ major sources of distraction
    - ♦ concentration span on different tasks
- ♦ organizational aspects
    - ♦ sequence of activities
    - ♦ organizational strategies
    - ♦ materials and desk in order
    - ♦ teacher direction
    - ♦ reliance on concrete aids
- ♦ memory strategies
    - ♦ listening/auditory skills

Dyslexia

- ◆ oral skills
- ◆ visual approaches
- ◆ learning sequentially
- ◆ learning Globally
- ◆ self-esteem
- ◆ confidence
- ◆ motivation
- ◆ signs of tension.

Framework for an assessment:

- ◆ sensory assessment
- ◆ word recognition test
- ◆ non-word recognition test
- ◆ spelling test
- ◆ phonological assessment
- ◆ miscue analysis
- ◆ reading/listening comprehension test
- ◆ free writing
- ◆ curriculum information
- ◆ observational assessment
- ◆ additional relevant information

Factors to consider:

- ◆ what is the context for the assessment?
- ◆ why is the assessment being carried out?
- ◆ obtain information on the child's strengths and weaknesses, attainment profile/cognitive profile

- how is learning carried out?
- level of attainment, learning behaviours.

Issues in assessment:

- whose responsibility?
- at what age can dyslexia be identified?
- how reliable is screening?
- role of class teacher in assessment?
- role of parents?
- differences between dyslexia and other learning difficulties

Signpost 3
Understanding learning:

- the learning process
- learning environment
- learning styles.

Learning needs

- achievable outcomes
- structure
- responsibility
- curriculum access/subject choice
- transfer of learning
- success.

Signpost 4
Planning for practice/achievable outcomes:

- curriculum approaches

Dyslexia

- individualizing learning
- learning styles

Environmental factors:

- light
- sound
- design
- general
- ambience
- furniture
- layout.

Parents' perspective – issues:

- communication
- support
- home intervention
- alternative treatments
- child's perspective
- self-esteem
- beyond school.

Some topics for staff development

- understanding dyslexia
- identifying dyslexia
- intervention programmes
- differentiation
- learning styles

♦ getting the classroom environment right

♦ research in dyslexia

♦ overlap with other specific learning difficulties

♦ working with parents

♦ multisensory learning

♦ different subject areas of the secondary school

♦ study skills

♦ thinking skills

♦ metacognition

♦ policy and practice

♦ reading, writing and spelling.

This list could be made longer. Staff development should arise from staff needs. It is important therefore to take a whole school perspective in order to obtain an understanding of staff's concerns and needs in relation to dyslexia.

Support at Home

School can be quite an exhausting experience for children with dyslexia. They have to participate in some challenging activities, and these can easily deplete their energies and their motivation. Home should not be a 'second school', but rather a supportive environment. There are activities that can be undertaken at home to reinforce school work.

♦ *Reading programmes*: some reading programmes can be carried out at home, as the programme may not require any specialist training. The school will be able to advise on this.

- *Reading schemes*: these usually have follow-up readers that can be used at home.

- *Paired Reading*: this is discussed in Chapter 3. It can be carried out very successfully at home as it is based on the parent and the child reading together. It is intended only for use with individually chosen, highly motivating, non-fiction or fiction books that are *above* the independent readability level of the tutee. One of the important aspects of Paired Reading is praise – the parent should look pleased when the child succeeds when using this technique.

- *Discussion*: this is also a good reinforcing vehicle. It is important for parents to find out what their child is doing in history or geography and other subjects, as the content of many topics can be incorporated into family outings or discussions. For example, a family trip in the car can be used to reinforce some historical landmarks or the names of crops grown in the area. Similarly, a visit to a castle, museum or art gallery can reinforce names, events and experiences the child may have encountered in some of his or her school subjects.

- *Reinforcement*: At best, any input at home can re-inforce what the child is learning at school. This is particularly important for dyslexic children because they have a difficulty with automaticity. This means that even when they have learnt a new word or skill it may not be fully automatized. The implication of this is that they may forget the word or skill after a short while, for example during a school holiday, if it is not being used. Automaticity is achieved through practice and actually using the new word in as many different settings and ways as possible. The research indicates that dyslexic children take longer than others to achieve automaticity and therefore require over-learning in order to consolidate the new learning. Parents can reinforce the use of a word or skill at home or on family outings without necessarily referring to school work.

♦ *Motivation*: it is important to ensure that children with dyslexia are motivated to read. This can be challenging, since it may be difficult to find age-appropriate reading material that is at the child's reading level. Books that emphasize high interest and lower levels of vocabulary can be extremely useful, as these can help with reading fluency, reading comprehension and processing speed.

Information for Parents and Teachers

There is a great deal of information available for parents and teachers. Voluntary groups can offer advice and support to parents. It is important however that parents recognize that the school should be the first 'port of call', as often at least one member of staff will have some knowledge of dyslexia, and the school may also have suitable resources for parents.

Some contact organizations in different countries are shown in Appendix 1.

This book is intended as a reference for both parents and teachers. Although some of it can be seen as quite specialized and more for teachers than parents, it is important that the two groups are linked. Each has an important role to play and it is important that this is carried out in a collaborative and constructive manner. I suggested earlier that the most effective approach in dealing with dyslexia is effective communication between home and school. This helps to ensure that the holistic needs of the child and the family are taken into account. This is crucial as it will ensure that the resources, expertise and strategies described in this book are used in the most effective way. Dealing with dyslexia is not the responsibility of one person, whether teacher or parent, but a whole school/community concern, and one that is of national and international importance, with implications for the successful inclusion of all in today's society.

Appendix 1

Contacts

North and South America and Canada

USA
International Dyslexia Association (IDA): www.interdys.org
Learning Disabilities Association of America: www.ldaamerica.org

Argentina
APHDA: aphda@hotmail.com

Brazil
Associação Brasileira de Dislexia: www.dislexia.org.br

Canada
e-mail: info@dyslexiaassociation.ca
International Dyslexia Association British Columbia Branch: www.idabc.com
International Dyslexia Association Ontario Branch: www.idaontario.com/dyslexia_ONBIDA_resources.html
Canadian Academy of Therapeutic Tutors: www.ogtutors.com
Reach O-G Learning Center, Vancouver: www.reachlearningcenter.com

Caribbean
Caribbean Dyslexia Association: Haggart Hall, St Michael, Barbados

Australia and New Zealand

Australia
SPELD Victoria: www.vicnet.net.au/~speld
SPELD South Australia: www.speld-sa.org.au/index.html
SPELD New South Wales: www.speldnsw.org.au
SPELD (Tasmania): speldtasmania@bigpond.com
SPELD Western Australia: speld@opera.iinet.net.au; www.dyslexia-speld.com
SPELD Queensland: www.speld.org.au

New Zealand
SPELD New Zealand: www.speld.org.nz/contact.html
Learning and Behaviour Charitable Trust: www.lbctnz.com

Europe

DITT
www.ditt-online.org/About.htm
Dyslexia International – Tools and Technologies (DITT) aims to bring full awareness of the problems associated with specific learning difficulties into the education systems of all EU member states.

European Dyslexia Association (EDA)
www.dyslexia.eu.com

Croatia
Croatian Dyslexia Association: lencek@antun.erf.hr

Cyprus
Cyprus Dyslexia Association: dyslexiacy@cytanent.com.cy

North Cyprus
dyslexia_ncda@hotmail.com

Appendix 1

Czech Republic
Czech Dyslexia Association: zelinkova@mymail.cz

Denmark
Danish Dyslexia Association: www.ordblind.com

Greece
www.dyslexia.gr

Hungary
www.diszlexia.hu
Start dyslexia: Tan Studio, 1118, Hegyalja, UT. 70, Budapest

Republic of Ireland
www.dyslexia.ie

Italy
Associazione Italiana Dislessia: www.dislessia.it

Luxembourg
Dyspel asbl: www.dyspel.org/

Poland
Polskie Towarzystwo Dysleksji: psymbg@univ.gda.pl

Scotland
www.dyslexiascotland.org.uk

Sweden
Swedish Dyslexia Association: www.ki.se/dyslexi

UK
www.bda-dyslexia.org.uk

Wales
www.welshdyslexia.info

Russia

Russia
olgainsh@land.ru

Middle East

Israel
www.orton-ida.org.il

Kuwait
www.kuwaitdyslexia.com

Asia

Hong Kong
Dyslexia Association (Hong Kong): www.dyslexia.org.hk/
Hong Kong Association for Specific Learning Difficulties:
www.asld.org.hk

Japan
Japan Dyslexia Society – info@npo-edge.jp

Singapore
Dyslexia Association of Singapore: www.das.org.sg

Taiwan
Learning Disability Association in Taiwan: www.dale.nhctc.
edu.tw/ald

Africa

Egypt
www.elda-egypt.org/
Egyptian Dyslexia Centre: www.dyslexia-egypt.com/eng/
about.html

Appendix 1

Gambia
Madonna Jarret Thorpe Trust: PO Box 4232, The Gambia, West Africa. Tel: 00220 9902099. Email: mjtt@airtip.gm

Ghana
Crossroads Dyslexic Centre at U2KAN: PO Box KD525 Kanda, Accra, Ghana, West Africa
Tel. 00233-21-230391/020 811 6198
Email: joybanad@yahoo.com

South Africa
SAALED, PO Box 2404, Cape Town 7740, South Africa
The Remedial Foundation, PO Box 32207, Braamfontein 2017, Johannesburg, SA

Uganda
Rise and Shine Dyslexia Organization: PO Box 2882 Kampala, Uganda

Other Websites

Dr Gavin Reid
www.gavinreid.co.uk

Red Rose School
Provides for the educational, emotional and social needs of up to 48 boys and girls, aged between 7 and 16 years, of average and above average intelligence who experience specific learning difficulties and/or experiences which cause them to become delicate and vunerable in a mainstream setting.
www.redroseschool.co.uk

REACH Learning Center, Vancouver, BC, Canada
www.reachlearningcenter.com
REACH Orton–Gillingham Learning Center is an academic remediation centre that was formed to assist individuals who are struggling to learn to read or spell.

Fun Track Learning
www.funtrack.com.au/

Arts Dyslexia Trust
www.sniffout.net/home/adt

Learning Works Int.
www.learning-works.org.uk
Focus on learning and motivating learners whatever their shape, size or ability! Specialize in designing professional development courses, team challenges and learning resources to meet the needs of staff, pupils and parents.

Creative Learning Company New Zealand
www.creativelearningcentre.com

Dyslexia Association of Ireland
www.acld-dyslexia.com

Dyslexia Action (formerly Dyslexia Institute)
www.dyslexiaaction.org.uk

Dyslexia Online Magazine
http://www.dyslexia-parent.com/magazine.html

Articles and reviews about dyslexia

Dyslexia Online Journal
www.dyslexia-adults.com/journal.html
Articles and research for professionals working in the field of dyslexia.

Dyslexia Parents Resource
www.dyslexia-parent.com/
Information and resources about dyslexia for parents of children who are, or may be, dyslexic.

European Dyslexia Academy for Research and Training (E-DART)
www.psyk.uu.se/edart

Family Onwards
www.familyonwards.com

Helen Arkell Dyslexia Centre
www.arkellcentre.org.uk

I am dyslexic
A site put together by an 11-year-old dyslexic boy.
www.iamdyslexic.com

Institute for Neuro-Physiological Psychology (INPP)
www.inpp.org.uk

Dr Loretta Giorcelli
A well-known international consultant.
www.doctorg.org/

Mindroom
A charity dedicated to spreading much greater awareness and understanding of learning difficulties. Goal is that by 2020 all children with learning difficulties in the UK are identified and helped.
www.mind-room.org

School Daily
New Zealand up-to-date educational news and debate.
www.schooldaily.com

SNAP assessment
www.SNAPassessment.com

World Dyslexia Network Foundation
A series of advice and help sheets have been written by leading experts in their fields.
http://web.ukonline.co.uk/wdnf/advice.html

World of Dyslexia
www.worldofdyslexia.com
www.dyslexia-parent.com/world_of_dyslexia

Literacy

Buzan Centres Ltd
www.Mind-Map.com

Centre for Early Literacy
Links to Reading Recovery project and literacy for primary children.
www.ume.maine.edu/~cel/

Crossbow Education
Games for learning.
www.crossboweducation.com

Iansyst Ltd
www.dyslexic.com

International Reading Organization
Bulletin boards, information on associations and links etc.
www.reading.org/about/

The National Literacy Strategy
www.standards.dfes.gov.uk/literacy/

Appendix 1

Paired Reading, writing and thinking
www.dundee.ac.uk/psychology/TRW

PRO-ED Inc.
www.proedinc.com/index.html

SEN Marketing
www.sen.uk.com

THRASS
www.thrass.co.uk

United Kingdom Reading Association
Newsletter, publications, links worth looking at.
www.ukra.org

Appendix 2

Tests Used for Dyslexia

Selection of internationally used tests

Bangor Dyslexia Test

This is a commercially available short screening test developed from work conducted at Bangor University (Miles 1983). The test is divided into the following sections:

♦ left–right (body parts)

♦ repeating polysyllabic words

♦ subtraction

♦ tables

♦ months forward/reversed

♦ digits forward/reversed

♦ b–d confusion

♦ familiar incidence.

www.LDAlearning.com

Cognitive Profiling System

Lucid Creative Ltd, Beverley, Yorkshire, UK

This is a computerized screening programme and constitutes a user-friendly package complete with facilities for student registration, graphic report and print-out of results. It is used in over 3,500 primary schools in the UK and elsewhere in the world.

Comprehensive Test of Phonological Processing (CTOPP)
Richard Wagner, Joseph Torgesen and Carol Rashotte
The Comprehensive Test of Phonological Processing (CTOPP) assesses phonological awareness, phonological memory and rapid naming. Persons with deficits in one or more of these kinds of phonological processing abilities may have more difficulty learning to read than those who do not.

DIBELS
http://dibels.uoregon.edu/
The Dynamic Indicators of Basic Early Literacy Skills (DIBELS) is a set of standardized, individually administered measures of early literacy development. They are designed to be short (one-minute) fluency measures used to regularly monitor the development of pre-reading and early reading skills.

Dyslexia Screening Test (DST) (Fawcett and Nicolson 1996)
The screening instrument can be used for children between 6.6 and 16.5 years of age, although there is also an alternative version developed by the same authors for younger children, *Dyslexia Early Screening Test*, and an adult version (Nicolson and Fawcett 1996). The test consists of the following attainment tests:

♦ one-minute reading

♦ two-minute spelling

♦ one-minute writing.

Additionally, there are the following diagnostic tests:

♦ rapid naming

♦ bead threading

♦ postural stability

♦ phonemic segmentation

♦ backwards digit span

♦ nonsense passage reading

♦ verbal and semantic fluency.

The dyslexia screening tests can be accessed by all teachers and are available from the Psychological Corporation, 24–28 Oval Road, London NW1 1YA. Email cservice@harcourt-brace.com

GORT-4: Gray Oral Reading Tests, Fourth Edition
J. Lee Weiderholt and Brian R. Bryant
The Gray Oral Reading Tests, Fourth Edition (GORT-4), provides an efficient and objective measure of growth in oral reading and an aid in the diagnosis of oral reading difficulties. Five scores give you information on a student's oral reading skills in terms of:

♦ Rate – the amount of time taken by a student to read a story

♦ Accuracy – the student's ability to pronounce each word in the story correctly

♦ Fluency – the student's Rate and Accuracy Scores combined

♦ Comprehension – the appropriateness of the student's responses to questions about the content of each story read

♦ Overall Reading Ability – a combination of a student's Fluency (i.e. Rate and Accuracy) and Comprehension scores.

Appendix 2

Launch Into Reading Success – Test of Phonological Awareness

Lorna Bennett and Pamela Ottley

Phonological awareness programme designed just for young children. Can prevent reading failure at an early stage if it is identified and intervention with the right programme is used. *Launch Into Reading Success* is a phonological skills training programme designed for use by teachers and other professionals in schools and for parents at home. Can provide an effective first step for a child to take in the pursuit of literacy.

Listening and Literacy Index (LLI) (Weedon and Reid 2001)

The Listening and Literacy Index comprises group tests for profiling literacy development and identifying specific learning difficulties. It contains linked standardized tests of listening, reading and spelling and is designed for use by the classroom teacher with whole class groups. The tests have been standardized with a large UK sample and the handbook contains norms, guidelines for scoring and teaching follow-up. There are four sub-tests:

◆ listening, which assesses the child's ability to understand spoken language about everyday situations

◆ regular spelling, which assesses phonological processing and memory

◆ sight word spelling, which assesses visual processing and memory

◆ reading comprehension, which assesses the ability to read silently, for meaning.

The results of this test can display comparisons between these factors and this may provide an early indicator of the presence or at least the risk of dyslexia or any other specific learning difficulty. For example, in the comparison between listening and the other scores it may be noted that a child can listen well and with understanding, but has poor spelling and finds silent reading laborious, and this may may mean he or she has a specific difficulty of a dyslexic type. If sight word spelling is better than regular spelling there may be an auditory difficulty. Where the two tasks that need sustained attention (listening and reading comprehension) are relatively weak, there may be an attention difficulty.

PRO-ED Inc.
A leading publisher of nationally standardized tests.
www.proedinc.com/index.html

Special Needs Assessment Profile (Weedon and Reid 2003) version 2, 2005
The Special Needs Assessment Profile (SNAP) is a computer-aided diagnostic assessment and profiling package that makes it possible to 'map' each student's own mix of problems onto an overall matrix of learning, behavioural and other difficulties. From this, clusters and patterns of weaknesses and strengths help to identify the core features of a student's difficulties – visual, dyslexic, dyspraxic, phonological, attentional or any other of the 17 key deficits targeted – and suggests a diagnosis that points the way forward for that individual student. It provides a structured profile which yields an overview at the early stages of 'School Action' in the Code of Practice – and also informs the process of external referral, at 'School Action Plus'.
     SNAP involves four steps:

♦ Step 1 *(Pupil Assessment Pack)*: structured questionnaire checklists for completion by class teachers and parents give an initial 'outline map' of the child's difficulties.

♦ Step 2 *(CD-ROM)*: the SENCO or Learning Support staff charts the child's difficulties, using the CD-ROM to identify patterns and target any further diagnostic follow-up assessments to be carried out at Step 3.

♦ Step 3 *(User's Kit)*: focused assessments from a photo-copiable resource bank of quick diagnostic 'probes' yield a detailed and textured understanding of the child's difficulties.

♦ Step 4 *(CD-ROM)*: the computer-generated profile yields specific guidance on support (including personalized information sheets for parents) and practical follow-up.

The kit helps to facilitate the collaboration between different groups of professionals and between professionals and parents – a collaboration which is vital in order to obtain a full picture of the student's abilities and difficulties. There is a dedicated website (accessible to anyone) that contains a number of ideas on teaching to cover difficulties associated with the 17 different specific learning difficulties.
www.SNAPassessment.com

Step Into Phonics
Lois Lindsay and Corey Zylstra
A structured guide for sequential phonics based on the Orton–Gillingham approach for multisensory teaching. Developed by Orton–Gillingham Tutor Trainers, *Step Into Phonics* is an easy-to-use manual that aids in the speed of lesson preparation while offering a wealth of information about phonograms, spelling rules, syllables and nonphonentic words.
www.stepintophonics.com

Test of Phonological Awareness – Second Edition: PLUS (TOPA-2+)
Joseph K. Torgensen and Brian R. Bryant
This is a group-administered, norm-referenced measure of phonological awareness for children between the ages of five and eight. The scale, which can also be administered

individually, has demonstrated reliability and the test yields valid results that are reported in terms of percentile ranks and a variety of standard scores.

TOWRE – Test of Word Reading Efficiency
Joseph Torgesen, Richard Wagner and Carol Rashotte
The *Test of Word Reading Efficiency* (TOWRE) is a nationally normed measure of word reading accuracy and fluency.

WIST (Word Identification and Spelling Test
Barbara Wilson
Many teachers who are Orton–Gillingham trained use this test. Can pinpoint whether Orton–Gillingham would help the student (can also be done in a group).

References

American Psychiatric Association (2000) *Diagnostic and Statistical Manual of Mental Disorders* (fourth edition). Washington, DC: American Psychiatric Association.

Augur, J. and Briggs, S. (1992) *The Hickey Multisensory Language Course*. London: Whurr.

Ayres, A.J. (1979) *Sensory Integration and the Child*. Los Angeles: Western Psychological Services.

Barkley, R.A. (1997) *ADHD and the Nature of Self-Control*. New York: Guilford Press.

Bell, N. (1991a) 'Gestalt imagery: A critical factor in language comprehension.' Reprint from *Annals of Dyslexia*, vol. 41. Baltimore: Orton Dyslexia Society.

Bell, N. (1991b) *Visualizing and Verbalizing for Language Comprehension and Thinking*. Paso Robles, CA: Academy of Reading Publications.

Bell, N. (2005) 'The role of imagery and verbal processing in comprehension'. Paper presented at the 56th Annual Conference IDA, Denver, 9–12 November 2005.

Blythe, P. (1992) *A Physical Approach to Resolving Specific Learning Difficulties*. Chester: Institute for Neuro-Physiological Psychology.

Blythe, P. (2001) personal communication.

Blythe, P. and Goddard, S. (2000) *Neuro-Physiological Assessment Test Battery*. Chester: Institute for Neuro-Physiological Psychology.

Bradley, L. (1989) 'Specific learning disability: Prediction–intervention–progress'. Paper presented to the Rodin Remediation Academy International Conference on Dyslexia, University College of North Wales.

Bradley, L. (1990) 'Rhyming connections in learning to read and spell', in P.D. Pumfrey and C.D. Elliott (eds), *Children's Difficulties in Reading, Spelling and Writing*. London: Falmer Press.

Bradley, L. and Bryant, P. (1991) 'Phonological skills before and after learning to read', in S.A. Brady and D.P. Shankweiler (eds), *Phonological Processes in Literacy*. London: Lawrence Erlbaum.

Bradley, L. and Huxford, L.M. (1994) 'Organising sound and letter patterns for spelling', in G.D. Brown and N.C. Ellis, (eds), *Handbook of Normal and Disturbed Spelling Development: Theory, Processes and Interventions*. Chichester: Wiley.

British Psychological Society (BPS) (1999) *Dyslexia, Literacy and Psychological Assessment*. Leicester: British Psychological Society.

Brown, T.E. (1996) *Brown Attention-Deficit Disorder Scales*. London: Psychological Corporation.

References

Burden, B. (2002) 'A cognitive approach to dyslexia: Learning styles and thinking skills', in G. Reid and J. Wearmouth (eds), *Dyslexia and Literacy: Theory and Practice*. Chichester: Wiley.

Buzan, T. (1993) *The Mind Map Book: Radiant Thinking*. London: BBC Books.

Chinn, S. (2002) '"Count me in". A comparison of the demands of numeracy and the problems dyslexic learners have with maths'. Paper presented at North Kent Dyslexia Association, Conference for Teachers, Greenwich, London (5 October 2002).

Clay, M. (1985) *The Early Detection of Reading Difficulties: A Diagnostic Survey with Recovery Procedures*. Auckland: Heinemann Educational.

Clay, M. (1992) *Reading: The Patterning of Complex Behaviour*. London: Heinemann.

Clay, M. (1993) *An Observational Survey of Early Literacy Achievement*. Auckland: Heinemann Educational.

Conner, M. (1994) 'Specific learning difficulties (dyslexia) and interventions', *Support for Learning* (9)3, 114–19.

Conners, C.K. (1996) *Conners' Rating Scale (Revised)*. London: Psychological Corporation.

Cox, A.R. (1985) 'Alphabetic phonics. An organization and expansion of Orton, Gillingham' – *Annals of Dyslexia*, 35, 187–98.

Crombie, M. (2002) 'Dyslexia: A new dawn'. Unpublished Ph.D. thesis, University of Strathclyde, Glasgow.

Crombie, M. and McColl, H. (2001) 'Dyslexia and the teaching of modern foreign languages', in L. Peer and G. Reid (eds), *Dyslexia: Successful Inclusion in the Secondary School*. London: David Fulton.

Cudd, E.T. and Roberts, L.L. (1994) 'A scaffolding technique to develop sentence sense and vocabulary', *The Reading Teacher*, 47(4), 346–9.

Dargie, R. (2001) 'Dyslexia and history', in L. Peer and G. Reid (eds), *Dyslexia: Successful Inclusion in the Secondary School*. London: David Fulton.

Davis, R.D. and Braun, E.M. (1997) *The Gift of Dyslexia: Why Some of the Smartest People Can't Read and How They Can Learn*. London: Souvenir Press.

De Bono, E. (1986) *CORT Thinking*. Oxford: Pergamon Press.

Denckla, M.B. and Rudel, R.G. (1976) 'Rapid "automatised" naming (RAN): Dyslexia differentiated from other learning disabilities', *Neuropsychologia*, 14, 471–9.

Dennison, G.E. and Dennison, P.E. (1989) *Educational Kinesiology Brain Organisation Profiles*. Glendale, CA: Edu-Kinesthetics.

Dennison, G.E. and Dennison, P.E. (2000) *Educational Kinesiology Brain Organisation Profiles*. Teachers' training manual third edition. Glendale, CA: Edu-Kinesthetics.

Dennison, P.E. and Hargrove, G. (1985) *Personalized Whole Brain Integration*. Glendale, CA: Educational Kinesthetics.

Deno, S.L. (1989) 'Curriculum-based measurement and special education services: A fundamental and direct relationship', in M.R. Shinn (ed.) *Curriculum-based Measurement: Assessing Special Children*. New York: Guilford Press.

Deponio, P., Landon, J. and Reid, G. (2000) 'Dyslexia and bilingualism – Implications for assessment, teaching and learning', in L. Peer and G. Reid

References

(eds), *Multilingualism, Literacy and Dyslexia. A Challenge for Educators.* London: David Fulton.

DfES (2005) *Rose Report on the Teaching of Reading.* London: DfES.

Dimitriadi, Y. (2000) 'Using ICT to Support Bilingual Dyslexic Learners', in L. Peer and G. Reid (eds), *Multilingualism, Literacy and Dyslexia: A Challenge for Educators.* London: David Fulton.

Dore, W. and Rutherford, R. (2001) 'Closing the gap'. Paper presented at the BDA International Conference on Dyslexia, York.

Dunn, R., Dunn, K. and Price, G.E. (1975, 1979, 1985, 1987, 1989) *Learning Styles Inventory.* Lawrence, KS: Price Systems.

Eadon, H. (2005) *Dyslexia and Drama.* London: David Fulton.

Fawcett, A.J. and Nicolson, R.I. (1992) 'Automatisation deficits in balance for dyslexic children', *Perceptual and Motor Skills,* 75, 507–29.

Fawcett, A.J. and Nicolson, R.I. (1996) *The Dyslexia Screening Test.* London: Psychological Corporation.

Fawcett, A.J. and Nicolson, R.I. (2001) 'Dyslexia: the role of the cereballum', in A.J. Fawcett (ed.), *Dyslexia: Theory and Good Practice.* London: Whurr.

Fawcett, A.J. and Nicolson, R.I. (2004) 'Dyslexia: the role of the cereballum', in G. Reid and A.J. Fawcett (eds), *Dyslexia in Context: Research, Policy and Practice.* London: Whurr.

Fitts, P.M. and Posner, M.I. (1967) *Human Performance.* Belmont, CA: Brooks Cole.

Frederickson, N. and Cline, T. (2002) *Special Educational Needs, Inclusion and Diversity.* Buckingham: Open University Press.

Frederickson, N., Frith, V. and Reason, R. (1997) *Phonological Assessment Battery.* London: nferNelson.

Frith, U. (2002) 'Resolving the paradoxes of dyslexia', in G. Reid and J. Wearmouth (eds), *Dyslexia and Literacy: Theory and Practice.* Chichester: Wiley.

Gardner, H. (1983) *Frames of Mind: The Theory of Multiple Intelligences.* New York: Harper and Row.

Gardner, H. (1999) 'Foreword', in D. Lazear (1999) *Eight Ways of Knowing: Teaching for Multiple Intelligences* (third edition). Arlington Heights, IL: SkyLight Professional Development.

Given, B.K. and Reid, G. (1999). *Learning Styles: A Guide for Teachers and Parents.* St Anne's-on-Sea: Red Rose Publications.

Goddard-Blythe, S. (1996) *Developmental Exercise Programme.* Chester: Institute for Neuro-Physiological Psychology.

Green, S. (2006) 'Reading comprehension and the OG approach'. Presentation at the conference 'From Inclusion to Belonging', SAALD, Johannesburg, 15–17 May 2006.

Green, S. and G. Reid. (2007) *100 Ideas for Supporting Children with Dyslexia.* Continuum Publications: London.

Hales, G. (2001) 'Self-esteem and counselling', in L. Peer and G. Reid (eds), *Dyslexia: Successful Inclusion in the Secondary School.* London: David Fulton.

Hannaford, C. (1995) *Smart Moves: Why Learning Is Not All in Your Head.* Arlington, VA: Great Ocean Publishers.

Hannaford, C. (1997) *The Dominance Factor: How Knowing Your Dominant Eye, Ear, Brain, Hand and Foot Can Improve Your Learning.* Arlington, VA: Great Ocean Publishers.

References

Hatcher, P. (1994, 2004) *Sound Linkage: An Integrated Programme for Overcoming Reading Difficulties.* London: Whurr.

Healy Eames, F. and Hannafin, M.J. (2005) *Switching on for Learning: A Student Guide to Exam and Career Success.* Oranmore, Co. Galway: FHE Learning.

Henry, M. (1996) 'The Orton–Gillingham approach', in G. Reid (ed.), *Dimensions of Dyslexia.* Vol. 1: *Assessment, Teaching and the Curriculum.* Edinburgh: Moray House Publications.

Henry, M.K. (2003) *Unlocking Literacy: Effective Decoding and Spelling Instruction.* Baltimore: Paul Brookes Publishing Co.

Holmes, P. (2001) *Dyslexia and Physics* in L. Peer and G. Reid (eds) *Dyslexia: Successful Inclusion in the Secondary School.* London: David Fulton.

Hunter, V. (2001) 'Dyslexia and general science', in L. Peer and G. Reid (eds) *Dyslexia: Successful Inclusion in the Secondary School.* London: David Fulton.

Johanson, K. (1997) 'Left hemisphere stimulation with music and sounds in dyslexia remediation'. Paper presented at the 48th annual conference of the International Dyslexia Association (formerly the Orton Dyslexia Association), Baltimore.

Johnston, R., Connelly, V.D. and Watson, J. (1995) 'Some effects of phonics teaching on early reading development', in P. Owen and P. Pumfrey (eds), *Emergent and Developing Reading: Messages for Teachers.* London: Falmer Press.

Jones, N. (2005) 'Children with developmental coordination disorder: Setting the scene', in N. Jones (ed.), *Developing School Provision for Children with Dyspraxia.* London: Paul Chapman.

Kaplan, B.J., Dewey, D.M., Crawford, S.G. and Wilson, B.N. (2001) 'The term comorbidity is of questionable value in reference to developmental disorders: Data and theory', *Journal of Learning Disabilities,* 34(6), 555–65.

Kirby, A. (2003) *The Adolescent with Developmental Co-ordination Disorder.* London: Jessica Kingsley.

Kirby, A. and Drew, S. (2002) *Guide to Dyspraxia and Developmental Coordination Disorders.* London: David Fulton.

Lannen, S. (1990) Personal correspondence based on Ph.D. study on conflict resolution.

Lazear, D. (1999) *Eight Ways of Knowing: Teaching for Multiple Intelligences* (third edition). Arlington Heights, IL: SkyLight Professional Development.

Levine, M.D. (1997) *All Kinds of Minds.* New York: Educators Publications.

Liberman, I.Y. and Shankweiler, D.P. (1985) 'Phonology and the problems of learning to read and write,' *Remedial and Special Education,* 6(6), 8–17.

Lidz, C.S. (1991) *Practitioner's Guide to Dynamic Assessment.* New York: Guilford Press.

Lindsay, L. and C. Zylstra, (2005) 'Step into phonics.' www.stepintophonics.com.

Lloyd, G. and Norris, C. (1999) 'Including ADHD?', *Disability and Society,* 14(4), 505–17.

McPhillips, M., Hepper, P.G. and Mulhern, G. (2000) 'Effects of replicating primary-reflex movements on specific reading difficulties in children: A randomised, double-blind, controlled trial.' *The Lancet,* 355, 537–41.

Miles, T.R. (1983) *Dyslexia: The Pattern of Difficulties.* London: Collins Educational.

References

Morton, J. and Frith, U. (1995) 'Causal modelling: A structural approach to developmental psychopathology', in D. Cicchetti and D.J. Cohen (eds), *Manual of Developmental Psychopathology*. Chichester: Wiley.

Mosley, J. (1996) *Quality Circle Time*. Cambridge: LDA.

Nicolson, R.I. and Fawcett, A.J. (1990) 'Automaticity: A new framework for dyslexia research?', *Cognition*, 35, 159–82.

Nicolson, R.I. and Fawcett, A.J. (1996) *The Dyslexia Early Screening Test*. London: Psychological Corporation.

Nicolson, R.I. and Fawcett, A.J. (1999) 'Developmental dyslexia: The role of the cerebellum', *Dyslexia: An International Journal of Research and Practice*, 5, 155–77.

Nicolson, R.I. and Fawcett, A.J. (2000) 'Long-term learning in dyslexic children', *European Journal of Cognitive Psychology*, 12, 357–93.

Nicolson, R.I., Fawcett, A.J. and Dean, P. (2001) 'Developmental dyslexia. The cerebellar deficit hypothesis', *Trends in Neurosciences*, 24(9), 508–11.

Norwich, B. and Lewis, A. (2001) 'Mapping a pedagogy for special educational needs', *British Educational Research Journal*, 27(3), 313–31.

Palincsar, A. and Brown, A. (1984) 'Reciprocal teaching of comprehension-fostering and comprehension-monitoring activities', *Cognition and Instruction*, 1(2), 117–75.

Portwood, M. (2001) *Developmental Dyspraxia: A Practical Manual for Parents and Professionals*. London: David Fulton.

Portwood, M. (2002) 'School based trials of fatty acid supplements'. Paper presented at Durham County Council Education Conference, June 2002.

Pringle-Morgan, W.P. (1896) 'A case of congenital word-blindness', *British Medical Journal*, 2, 1378.

Reason, R., Brown, P., Cole, M. and Gregory, M. (1988) 'Does the "specific" in specific learning difficulties make a difference to the way we teach?', *Support for Learning*, 3(4), 230–6.

Reddington, R.M. and Wheeldon, A. (2002) 'Involving parents in baseline assessment: Employing developmental psychopathology in the early identification process', *Dyslexia*, 8(2), 119–22.

Reid, G. (2001) 'Specialist teacher training in the UK: Issues, considerations and future directions', in M. Hunter-Carsch (ed.), *Dyslexia: A Psychosocial Perspective*. London: Whurr.

Reid, G. (2003) *Dyslexia: A Practitioner's Handbook* (third edition). Chichester: Wiley.

Reid, G. (2004) *Dyslexia: A Complete Guide for Parents*. Chichester: Wiley.

Reid, G. (2005) 'Dyslexia and learning styles'. Presentation at the European Independent Schools Council, The Hague, the Netherlands, 20 November.

Reid, G. (2005a) 'Specific Learning Difficulties – the Spectrum' in N. Jones (ed.) *Developing School Provision for Children with Dyspraxia*. London: Paul Chapman.

Reid, G. (2006) 'Managing attention difficulties in the classroom: A learning styles perspective', in G. Lloyd and J. Stead (eds), *Critical New Perspectives on AD/HD*. London: Routledge.

Reid, G., Green, S. and Zylstra, C. (2005) 'Parents and dyslexia: Issues, concerns and successes, Experiences from both sides of the Atlantic'. Presentation at the IDA 56th Annual Conference, Denver, 9–12 November 2005.

References

Richardson, A.J. (2001) 'Dyslexia, dyspraxia and ADHD – Can nutrition help?' Paper presented at fourth Cambridge Conference, Helen Arkell Dyslexia Association.

Robertson, J. and Bakker, D.J. (2002) 'The balance model of reading and dyslexia', in G. Reid and J. Wearmouth (eds), *Dyslexia and Literacy: Theory and Practice.* Chichester: Wiley.

Rohl, M. and Tunmer, W. (1988) 'Phonemic segmentation skills and spelling acquisition', *Applied Psycholinguistics,* 9, 335–50.

Russell, S. (1992) *Phonic Code Cracker.* Glasgow: Jordanhill College Publications.

Rutter, M. (1995) 'Relationships between mental disorders in childhood and adulthood', *Acta Psychiatrica Scandinavica,* 91, 73–85.

Silverman, L. (2005) personal correspondence.

Slingerland, B.H. (1993) *Specific Language Disability Children.* Cambridge: Educators Publishing Service.

Smythe, I., Everatt, J. and Salter, R. (eds) (2004) *International Book of Dyslexia.* Chichester: Wiley.

Snowling, M.J. (2000). *Dyslexia* (second edition). Oxford: Blackwell.

Snowling, M.J. (2005) 'Language skills and learning to read: Risk and protective factors'. Presentation at the 56th Annual Conference IDA, Denver, 9–12 November 2005.

Stordy, B.J. (1995) 'Benefit of docosahexaenoic acid supplements to dark adaptation in dyslexia', *The Lancet,* 346: 385.

Stordy, B.J. (1997) 'Dyslexia, attention deficit hyperactivity disorder, dyspraxia – do fatty acids help?', *Dyslexia Review,* 9 (2).

Stanovich, K.E. (1991) 'Discrepancy definitions of reading disability: Has intelligence led us astray?', *Reading Research Quarterly,* 26(1), 7–29.

Taylor, M.F. (2002) 'Stress-induced atypical brain lateralization in boys with attention-deficit/hyperactivity disorder. Implications for scholastic performance.' Unpublished Ph.D. thesis. University of Western Australia.

Ulmer, C., and Timothy, M. (2001) 'How does alternative assessment affect teachers' practice? Two years later'. Paper presented at the 12th European Conference on Reading, Dublin, 1–4 July 2001.

Usmani, K. (1999) 'The influence of racism and cultural bias in the assessment of bilingual children', *Educational and Child Psychology,* 16 (3), 44–54.

Vygotsky, L.S. (1986). *Mind in Society: The Development of Higher Psychological Processes.* Cambridge, MA: Harvard University Press.

Weedon, C. and Reid, G. (2001) *Listening and Literacy Index.* London: Hodder and Stoughton.

Weedon, C. and Reid, G. (2002) *Special Needs Assessment Profile Pilot Version.* Edinburgh: George Watson's College.

Weedon, C. and Reid, G. (2003, 2005) *Special Needs Assessment Profile (SNAP).* London: Hodder Murray.

West, T.G. (1997) *In the Mind's Eye: Visual Thinkers, Gifted People with Learning Difficulties, Computer Images and the Ironies of Creativity* (second edition). Buffalo, NY: Prometheus Books.

Willcutt, E.G. and Pennington, B.F. (2000) 'Comorbidity of reading disabilty and attention-deficit/hyperactivity disorder: Differences by gender and subtype,' *Journal of Learning Disabilities,* 33(2), 179–91.

References

Williams, F. and Lewis, J. (2001) 'Dyslexia and geography', in L. Peer and G. Reid (eds), *Dyslexia: Successful Inclusion in the Secondary School*. London: David Fulton.

Wolf, M. and O'Brien, B. (2001) 'On issues of time, fluency and intervention', in A. Fawcett (ed.) *Dyslexia, Theory and Good Practice*. London: Whurr.

Yoshimoto, R. (2005) 'Gifted dyslexic children: characteristics and curriculum implications'. Presentation at the 56th Annual Conference IDA, Denver, 9–12 November 2005.

Zylstra, C. (2005) 'Fun and games in an OG lesson'. Paper presented at the 56th Annual Conference IDA, Denver, 9–12 November 2005.